Our bunker shuddered under the numbing explosion. Dirt, rocks, and dust poured through the firing slits. We lifted our heads in time to see another rocket sizzling toward us.

"They're inside the wire!" Red pointed as he yelled over the clamor of the screaming NVAs. Silhouettes moved across the road to our right. "Shoot anything that moves!"

I knew the positions to our right were being overrun; self-torturing thoughts of hand-to-hand combat darted through my mind. I thought, God, I hate knives! A fleeing Vietnamese ran by our door. Red turned and fired a burst through the opening, dropping two ARVNs five feet from the bunker. I couldn't believe what was happening. I stared at the dead ARVNs for a couple of seconds until Red started firing again. I watched the tracers of the M60 ripping into the sappers on the bridge. Only three still stood. Others tried to crawl forward. . . .

By Johnnie M. Clark
Published by Ballantine Books:

GUNS UP!
SEMPER FIDELIS
THE OLD CORPS
NO BETTER WAY TO DIE

GUNS UP!

Johnnie M. Clark

BALLANTINE BOOKS • NEW YORK

A Ballantine Book
Published by The Ballantine Publishing Group
Copyright © 1984 by Johnnie M. Clark
New epilogue copyright © 2001 by Johnnie M. Clark

www.ballantinebooks.com

ISBN 0-345-45026-4

Manufactured in the United States of America

Revised Edition: January 2002

10 9 8 7 6 5 4 3 2 1

To the Corps, "Semper fidelis."

My lifelong thanks to my wife, Nancy, for believing in me, to Fred Wright and Marvette Carter for teaching me, to Pamela Strickler for the break of my life, and to all my friends who prayed for me.

I dedicate this book to Jesus Christ for loving me in spite of me.

CONTENTS

I CORPS, VIETNAM, 1968

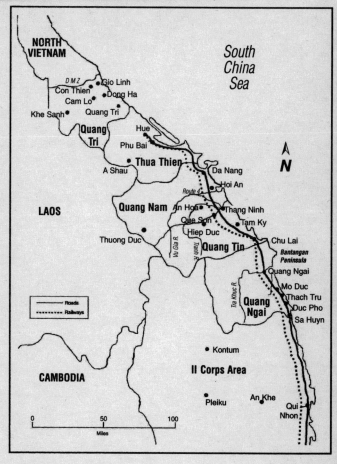

NORTH VIETNAM

South China Sea

DMZ
Gio Linh
Con Thien
Dong Ha
Cam Lo
Khe Sanh
Quang Tri

Quang Tri

Hue
Phu Bai
Thua Thien
A Shau

N

Da Nang
Hoi An

LAOS

Route 4

Quang Nam
An Hoa
Que Son
Hiep Duc
Thuong Duc
Thang Ninh
Tam Ky

Vu Gia R.
Tranh R.

Quang Tin

Chu Lai
Bantangan Peninsula
Quang Ngai
Mo Duc
Thach Tru
Duc Pho
Sa Huyn

Tra Khuc R.

Quang Ngai

Kontum

II Corps Area

CAMBODIA

Pleiku
An Khe
Qui Nhon

Roads
Railways

0   50   100
Miles

PROLOGUE

This insanity really happened. It may sound like fiction—it does to me, and I lived it—but it's true the way you'll read it. I didn't rely on memory alone. Recently declassified secret information from the United States Marine Corps History and Museums Division, Washington, D.C., helped me in documenting some of the stories. I also had the benefit of checking the facts as I remembered them with two of the men who lived through Vietnam with me.

I was seventeen when I joined the Marine Corps, extremely naive, and dangerously close to competence in several fields of endeavor that served absolutely no purpose: football, baseball, and basketball. Obviously I was in no danger of being classified a genius. I remember sincerely fearing that the war would be over before I got there. Like I said, in no danger of being a genius.

My first twelve years were spent in the West Virginia mountains and in poverty, one being synonymous with the other, I suppose. Don't get me wrong. I don't knock West Virginia. Poor or not, mountain people have character, guts, and down-home honesty.

My mom's first husband was a census taker out in the mountains of Lincoln County, right up the holler from the famous Hatfields. He first found my mom plowing a field on the McClellan farm. She was a raving beauty in those days, and he grabbed her right up. Later he got killed in the Battle of the Bulge and left her with two kids, an eighth-grade education, and a job in a bomb factory. She married my dad, who promptly lost his job and everything else right after they had my sister. They gave the kids to the grandparents because the grandparents had food. I was the last one out of the shute. Mom couldn't part with another kid, so she decided I'd starve with them before she gave me up.

Dad got in a car wreck and was blind and crippled for the last seven years of his life. After he died Mom and I took off for Florida on Mom's guts and no money. She married a tough man from New York, a 1935 Golden Gloves boxer and a hard worker who helped me talk Mom into signing the papers that would get me into the Corps. I was inducted in Jacksonville. They put all the inductees up at the old Florida Hotel downtown. My first night there, some wide-eyed, shirtless lunatic ran into the lobby of the hotel waving a .45-caliber pistol. I stood on the stairway not believing my eyes until he scattered four shots around the lobby. One hit the stairway right under my foot. Then he turned and ran back into the street. A minute later two Navy Shore Patrol guys burst into the lobby with pistols drawn. The desk clerk started screaming and pointing. The SPs turned and ran out. I never did find out what happened or why, but I knew a bad omen when it shot at me.

It left me with that "Oh no, what have I done?" feeling. You know, the feeling you get deep in the pit of your stomach when you step in a pile of dog crap and don't realize it until you've walked across the living room carpet. I didn't smell anything, but my stomach said "check your boots" as the big green Braniff 727 touched down in Da Nang.

WELCOME TO THE FIFTH MARINES AND THE BATTLE FOR TRUOI BRIDGE

The one comforting thought was that I wasn't alone. The plane bulged with young Marine Corps faces. Private First Class Richard Chan was the only one I knew very well. We had been together since Parris Island, the Marine Corps boot camp.

Chan had been born in Red China. His father and mother smuggled him out as an infant. He wasn't your average Marine. Besides being Chinese-American, he had his pre-med degree from the University of Tennessee with a minor in ministry. He could have been playing doctor in New York, but he joined the Corps because he felt that he owed the country a debt for taking him in. Corny as it might sound, he also wanted to be the best, a Marine, a feeling we all shared.

We couldn't get away from each other. Bunkies at Parris Island, bunkies at ITR (Infantry Training Regiment) School, bunkies at jungle warfare school in Camp Pendleton, California. Now we sat beside each other on a plane landing in Da Nang.

The blistering sun stung my eyes as I reached the first step of the drab gray departing ramp. I tried to be ready to duck. Scuttlebutt had it that one planeload of Marines had gotten hit on the runway, but I couldn't hear any gunshots, just some moronic sergeant screaming, "Move it! Move it! Move it!" By the time I reached the bottom of the ramp, my eyes adjusted enough to see a hot blue

3

sky without a single cloud. A sleek, impressive camouflaged Phantom jet whined to a stop nearby. Thundering
artillery echoed across the airstrip. The Marine in front
of me whistled. "Man! They mean business." God, I
thought, this is the real thing. I'm in a war. I mumbled a
quick prayer, something I hadn't done since I was fourteen.

A skinny-looking helicopter floated down one hundred meters to our right. Its camouflaged body bristled
with rockets and machine guns. The roar of another
camouflaged Phantom streaking down a runway snatched
my eyes as it sprang off the ground and climbed sharply
above the steep green mountains surrounding Da Nang.

We double-timed over to a processing area. It was a
couple of hundred yards away, but by the time we
stopped, I was dripping wet. The pilot of the Braniff had
said it was 119 degrees. I'd thought he'd been joking.

The Tet Offensive was in full swing, and the battle for
Hue City had covered the front page of every newspaper
back home. On TV the house-to-house fighting looked
like World War II films.

Chan stood in front of me in the alphabetical line of
Marines filing past a loud dispersing officer. Each man
handed him a set of orders which he grabbed quickly and
stamped with a big rubber stamp as he screamed, "Fifth
Marines!" I tapped Chan on the shoulder.

"Why's everybody going to the Fifth Marines? They
can't need this many replacements."

Chan looked over his shoulder with one of those "Boy
have I got news for you" looks. "Oh, I think they might
have accommodations for us. That's the regiment that's
taking Hue City."

"Thanks, buddy," I said with a hard slap on his back.
"I can always depend on you to find a bright spot in all
this."

"Move it! Move it! Move it!" shouted the sergeant.

A moment later the big rubber stamp came down on
my orders like the authority of God. "Fifth Marines!"

We marched to a large dusty tent that was surrounded by a four-foot wall of sandbags. As a darkly tanned corporal called out names, each man stepped into the tent. Inside, a corporal with a huge black mustache handed me an M16 rifle, five magazines, and two bandoliers of ammunition. One of the men got a rifle with a bullet hole through the stock. When they gave the same guy a helmet with a bullet crease on the side, he nearly came unraveled.

Twenty minutes later we were herded into a waiting C-130 for a short flight north to a place called Phu Bai. The flight would have been more comfortable with seats or windows and without rifles sticking in my ear. One guy said we were flying over the South China Sea to avoid potshots. I wanted to be mentally ready for people shooting at me, but I could tell already there was a fine line between ready and panic.

Phu Bai was the base camp for the Fifth Marines. It didn't look like a dangerous place. One part even looked fairly civilized, with groups of tin-roofed houses made of wood and screen. Sandbag bunkers dotted the camp, and everything was colored beige over green from the dust of tanks, trucks, and jeeps rolling through the dirt streets. I soon found out that the civilized part of Phu Bai belonged to the Army. The Marine area was all tents. As usual, the Army was equipped far better than the Corps— a constant source of irritation to Marines.

Phu Bai sat fifteen miles from Hue City. Just a quick truck ride north on Highway 1 would take me to Hue. Another little longer ride would take me to a place called Khe Sanh.

We were taken to a large tent where an old, crusty-looking master gunnery sergeant with a giant silver handlebar mustache screamed, "Attention!" The chattering tent went silent.

"I am Master Gunnery Sergeant O'Connel. I will help

you in your indoctrination on the Fifth Marine Regiment." The old sergeant gave his great mustache a slow proud twirl and turned to a large blackboard behind him. "This is the most decorated regiment in the United States Marine Corps." He spoke as he wrote "French Forteget" at the top of the blackboard. "Some of you may remember hearing about the Belleau Woods in boot camp. The Fifth took the woods in twenty-four hours of hand-to-hand combat. You will wear on your dress uniform the French Forteget. We are the only Marines in the Corps allowed to wear any item other than Marine Corps issue. The Fifth Marines have taken Guadalcanal; New Guinea; New Britain; Peleiu; Okinawa; Tientsin, China; Pusan; Inchon, in Seoul, Korea; and the Chosin Reservoir. Now it's Hue City." He put his hands on his hips, standing with his boots more than shoulder-width apart. He beamed with pride as he stuck out his barrel-shaped chest. "We have the highest kill ratio in Vietnam. The colonel does not intend for that to change. Unless we are given permission to invade the North we shall continue fighting under the rules now in effect. You will not kill people who are not in uniform unless you are fired upon by them. You will kill anyone in a North Vietnamese Government . . ."

As the indoctrination continued I became more confused. I wasn't sure if this guy was saying this crap because it was procedure or if we were really supposed to wait to be fired upon before returning fire.

Thoughts of all kinds scrambled through my mind like a blender. I felt scared and excited and lonely at the same instant, but mostly excited. I couldn't wait to write the first letter home and tell everyone all about it. I didn't know a bloody thing about it yet, but I knew I had to keep a few girls worried to make sure I got a lot of mail.

After the indoctrination, we were led to a small firing range where we got a chance to make sure our weapons worked, a small item I hadn't given a thought to.

A sunburned sergeant began shouting. "The first ten in column spread out facing the targets at the ready position. Feet spread! Rifles at the ready! Move it! Count off!"

"Nine!" I shouted as my turn came to jog into a position facing ten large black-and-white bull's-eyes staked to the side of a fifty-foot-long by ten-foot-tall mound of dirt. The targets looked about one hundred meters away, just inside the barbed-wire perimeter surrounding Phu Bai.

"Lock and load!" I checked my magazine and flicked my rifle off safety.

"Step two of the prone position! Drop to the knees holding rifle securely! Drop to your stomach breaking your fall with the butt of the rifle!" I dropped to my stomach and took aim at the bull's-eye straight ahead.

"Aim and fire!" shouted the sergeant, and I did. Nothing! I squeezed the trigger again. My weapon sent out a harmless klick amidst the continuous firing from the other nine rifles. My stomach churned as I looked past the targets to the unfriendly mountains beyond.

The sergeant quickly found me a rifle that worked, but the broken firing pin left me with serious doubts. "Check your boots," my stomach said.

Now that my confidence was thoroughly shaken we were led back to a row of large dusty tents. A voice shouted to get in a formation, so we did. A truckload of Marines drove by, covering us with a solid layer of dust. The men in the truck howled with laughter at us. Some shouted friendly insults about our stateside utilities. We stuck out like big green thumbs. Every person we'd seen so far was dressed in jungle utilities. The men in the truck looked hard. Their jungle clothes were tattered and torn. The men hadn't shaved in a long time, their skin was dark from the jungle sun, and they looked lean and mean like Marines are supposed to look. We looked like fat, happy kids, clean-shaven, with side-walled haircuts and spit-shined stateside boots.

A small snappy corporal began shouting our names in alphabetical order. Once we were all accounted for, we filed into the first in the long row of tents. Once inside, a tough-looking supply sergeant shouted at me, "What's your size, Marine?" Like everyone else, I received a flak jacket, cartridge belt, canteens, four grenades, one pack, jungle boots, and utilities. After that we were led to different tents according to the platoons and companies we had been assigned. Unbelievably, Chan and I were together again—same company, same platoon.

Inside our tent were two rows of cots. At the end of one row, dwarfing the small cot he slept on, rested a giant red-headed man. His arms looked as big as my legs, and he must have had on size fifteen boots, which, like his utilities, were bleached beige from the sun and rain. They looked molded to his feet as if they were moccasins he hadn't taken off for years.

I wanted to talk about this adventure with him right now. Chan must have thought the same thing. We walked to the end of the tent and sat side by side on the cot next to him. I wasn't sure what he might think, since the rest of the tent was empty. It reminded me of standing at the end of a row of twenty unoccupied urinals and having one guy walk in and take the one right next to me.

He looked like a giant Viking. A big red mustache matched his hair. He was the most handsome red-headed man I'd ever seen. A real billboard Marine. I leaned closer to tap him on the shoulder. As he rolled over, the cot creaked under the strain. I knew one thing for sure: I wanted this monster on my side when the fighting started. He opened one large blue eye, which focused in on Chan.

"What's this gook doing in here?"

Chan jumped to his feet. He rambled off a series of insults, some of which included the biological background of the big redhead's parents, his speech, his looks, his smell, and his intelligence.

The big redhead opened both eyes fully as if he couldn't believe his ears. I wanted to calm things down but couldn't find the words. A friendly smile appeared from behind the large red mustache. He laughed deep and strong, then stuck out his hand. Chan hesitated for an instant then shook it.

"My name is Red. They call me Big Red. You look like boots."

"We are," I said. "Just got in today."

"What platoon are you in?" He rolled back to a comfortable position.

"Second Platoon," Chan said. "First Battalion, Fifth Marines."

"That means you're with me. What's your MOS?"

"My military occupational specialty is 0331," Chan said dryly.

"We're both 0331s," I said.

A big smile stretched across Red's face.

"Both gunners? Oh boy, they're sure going to be glad to see you two."

"Why is that?" asked Chan.

"I'm a gunner too," he said. "I got hit on the first day of Operation Hue City, and when I left I was the last gunner with machine-gun MOS in the whole company. They were grabbing mortar men and sticking M60s in their hands, and believe me, they don't like humpin' through the bush with grunts. Do you remember that crap they told you in machine-gun school about the life expectancy of a gunner after a firefight begins?"

We nodded in unison.

"Well, they meant it. Seven to ten seconds. Don't get too worried, though," Red said. "I heard we might invade. If we do, this war will be over in a couple of weeks. Just don't panic out there. Go at it gung-ho. If you're too careful you'll just make a better target."

With those last encouraging remarks, Red rolled over and went back to sleep. I thought he meant well, but he had planted a seed of doubt in me that was quickly growing into a large tree. I tapped him on the shoulder. I felt like one of the little people waking up Gulliver. "You weren't kidding just a little were you?" I asked quietly. "I mean, we can't be the only three gunners in all of Alpha Company."

"We are unless they got some more boots while I was in the hospital." He opened his eyes again. "Look, you guys, don't worry about it, 'cause it won't help. Find a salt when you get to the unit and stick with him like glue. If you don't get killed the first couple of months you'll be okay."

"What should we do to get ready? I mean is there anything we should know?" I asked.

"You probably oughta take your dog tags off the chain. They make noise at night; it'll get you killed. If your head gets blown off they probably won't find the tags and you won't be identified. String 'em into your boot laces. The boots usually hold together, and they won't make noise. And color 'em up with something so they won't shine with the sun- or moonlight. If you got anything you want to keep dry, put it in plastic and stick it between your helmet and helmet liner." He pointed at our grenades lying on my cot. "Bend the pins on those frags right now. When you hump through the bush, sticks get caught in the ring and pull out the pin and you get blown away."

Red's advice made me realize for the first time all of the assorted ways I could get myself killed in this place. His information scared me, but I knew it was important, and I was thankful for it.

"Don't ever take your boots off unless you're in some area like Phu Bai. Put your crap-paper in plastic if you want any hope of keeping it dry—writing paper too. If you don't put Halazone tablets in each canteen of water you'll get dysentery with the first drink. When it's a hundred and twenty degrees you'll drink a lot of water. Take your malaria pills every day or you'll get malaria and it'll stay with you even when you go home. The salt tabs, too. Forget your salt tab and you'll pass out from heat exhaustion. And take your helmet off when you get the chance. I saw one boot get his brain fried 'cause he left that pot on all day when it was about a hundred and twenty degrees. Ask whoever is writing you to send some care packages with Kool-Aid and stuff that won't spoil in the heat."

"Does the M16 rifle malfunction consistently under jungle conditions as projected?" Chan asked with his usual overdose of vocabulary.

Red looked at me quizzically. "Does he always talk like that?"

I nodded the affirmative.

Red chuckled, then answered, "No, not if you keep it clean. Clean it every single day or it'll jam. The M60 too. Use lots of oil. During the monsoon season your weapon will start to rust every few hours. If you light a cigarette up at night, you can kiss your butt goodbye. If the gooks don't kill you another Marine probably will. More important for you two than anything else is this: When you hear 'Guns up!' you got to get that gun to a firing position and open up."

With the end of that list Red rolled back over to try sleeping again. Then he rolled back as if he had remembered one last thing. "I almost forgot. Don't pull off the leeches. Burn 'em off with a match, or the head of the leech will stay in your skin. Tie the strings real tight at the bottom of your trousers and you can keep some of them out."

After that Red went to sleep. I had a thousand more questions, but I didn't dare wake him again. I couldn't understand how he managed to sleep. The tent was full of flies, the heat was sweltering, and every time a truck went by, heavy clouds of dust poured into the tent like the receiving bag of a vacuum cleaner.

Chan leaned back on his cot, using his pack for a pillow. He pulled his writing paper out of his shirt pocket.

"Tell Valerie hi for me," I said.

"I'm writing my parents." I wasn't surprised. Chan seemed very close to his parents.

"How's it been going with you and Valerie?" I asked.

"She loves me, and I love her." He paused, then shook his head dejectedly. "But her mother's another story. Mrs. Gallina is doing everything she can to stop our relationship."

"Because you're Chinese?"

"That's part of it. But the main reason is because I'm not Italian and I'm not Catholic."

"But you know the Bible backwards."

"That doesn't matter to Valerie's mother. She doesn't know the Old Testament from the New. She worships a religious system and doesn't really know the Lord at all." Chan didn't sound angry. He spoke as if he pitied her, as if he was honestly worried about her. Chan often said we were best friends because we were alike in many ways. Maybe, but I would have told this meddling Gallina broad to shove it up her diddy-bag. I leaned back on my cot and stared at the roof until it was too dark to see.

A heavy rain pelted the tent all night and didn't stop until morning. I knew because I was too excited to sleep. The day started like all the other days in the Corps, with a formation. The mud was drying fast. It was six A.M., and I was already grimy with sweat. We marched to the chow hall, where I received my first clue to what the country of Vietnam was all about: dysentery.

My stomach felt like it was getting an oil change. I wanted to puke, but I was too busy putting it out the other end. Chan thought it was hilariously funny until he came down with the same thing. We spent the rest of the day and the majority of the next as close to a row of outhouses as possible.

On the third day the entire group of boots was herded into a large tent with sandbag walls. The atmosphere was serious. Fifty to seventy-five of us crowded in, and no one spoke. I felt nervous. Ten rows of benches made the tent look like a chapel. A large blackboard surrounded by two large maps stood at the front. Someone yelled, "Attention!" We jumped to our feet. I felt like I was in a movie, getting orders to bomb Germany.

A small man with prematurely gray hair and dark sunglasses strode into the tent. He hustled to a platform in front of the maps. He looked more like a stockbroker than a major in the Marine Corps. "At ease." He picked up a pointer stick and began to talk.

"You are members of the Fifth Marines. The Fifth is now completing Operation Hue City. Hue has always been treated as an open city in recognition of its place as the ancient imperial capital and cultural seat of Vietnam. This is the only reason we have not bombed the NVA into dust. Hue has never been heavily fortified like Da Nang. The First ARVN Division has its headquarters in a corner of the Citadel. There is also the Black Panther Company, an elite unit of the Vietnamese Marines. That is the substance of the Vietnamese Army strength within the city. The Fifth Marines have been given the job of retaking Hue, which was occupied by the NVA on 31 January. By February 9 the enemy death count had reached 1,053. It is estimated that two enemy battalions had been destroyed by that point. All we have left can be considered mopping up. That does not mean people won't be shooting at you. If an enemy soldier shouts 'Chieu Hoi!' he is surrendering and is not to be fired upon. The Chieu Hoi program must be respected. We have dropped hundreds of thousands of leaflets telling the NVA soldier that he can drop his weapon and shout 'Chieu Hoi' and that he will be treated well. These prisoners are changing sides. They will fight for the South Vietnamese Government. Now, I know you all have a lot of questions, but this is all you have to know: You are United States Marines, the finest fighting men in the history of the world. We have never lost a major battle. No other fighting unit on earth can make such a claim. Now, attention!"

The tent full of white sidewall haircuts snapped to attention. "Repeat after me: Yea, though I walk through the valley of the shadow of death"—the chorus of youthful voices stuttered out the words like they had never heard them before—"I shall fear no evil." We repeated the second part more clearly: "For I am the meanest mother in the valley!" I loved it! I didn't feel quite right about using the Lord's word in vain, but I felt psyched enough to go all the way to Russia and stop this crap where it started.

"Saddle up!"

My stomach jumped up to my throat. This was it, not a daydream. I was really going into battle. Half of me wanted to get into this war and get it over with. The other half wanted my mommy to wake me up for school before this dream got carried away.

Ten minutes later I found myself in the back of a deuce-and-a-half truck bouncing up Highway 1 toward Hue. I didn't even remember getting in the truck. "Are you all right?" The voice was coming out of a fog. "John, are you okay?" It was Chan.

"Yeah. I'm fine."

Red was sleeping against the tailgate. It was good to see him. I'd only known the guy for a couple of days, and I was hard-pressed to squeeze more than a sentence at a time out of him, but he radiated self-confidence, and some special quality in him, possibly his honesty, made me trust him immediately.

The ride down Highway 1 was slow and bumpy. We passed another deuce-and-a-half that had been pushed to the side of the road. Its cab stuck into the air, and the front wheels lay mangled nearby.

The ride got slower. Two huge American tanks appeared from somewhere to lead the convoy. A strange-looking vehicle pulled out from a smaller dirt road and was now bringing up the rear.

"Chan, what's that?" I pointed to the odd-looking vehicle. It had the bottom of a tank, but instead of a turret it had six big cannons, three on each side.

"That's an Ontos. A tank killer. Those are six 106s."

"That thing could knock out this whole convoy!"

Chan looked at me with a friendly look of disdain. "Brilliant, Sherlock."

I did sound a bit "gee-whiz," but emotions I had never known were bouncing around from my brain to my stomach. My body tingled. I felt overwhelmed with expectation. I felt exhilaration like never before, then paranoia, then excited again. This is crazy, I had to keep telling myself. I have to control myself or I'm going to get killed for sure.

I thought I heard artillery. A flight of Phantom fighter planes roared over our truck just above treetop level. Now the sounds of war echoed more clearly. My hands were clammy. My mouth tasted like vinegar. A skinny Marine sitting close to Red knocked on his helmet. Red peered from underneath the helmet with one groggy eye. The other eye remained closed.

"Yeah?"

The skinny guy hesitated then blurted out, "What's it like?"

"It's a job."

"How bad is Hue?" asked another Marine. "I heard we're takin' heavy casualties."

Red pulled out a cigarette, then took his helmet off and removed a pack of matches from inside the liner straps. He looked like a Marlboro poster.

"If you want to keep anything dry you better put it in your helmet right now." The men started fumbling for their wallets. Chan and I had already done that. "Don't worry about Hue. Just don't go playing John Wayne. The battle is just about over. I heard we're getting bridge duty."

"What's that?" I asked.

"We guard the bridges on Highway 1."

"Is it bad?" blurted the skinny guy.

"It's skate duty. Slack city. You don't have to hump through the bush except for a few patrols, and sometimes you get beer or Cokes off the trucks going by. Take advantage of it, man. It won't last long. You'll know what war is when you start humping thirty klicks a day in the bush with two hours' sleep a night."

"What's a klick?" a Marine beside me asked, already squinting like he was afraid of the answer.

"One klick is a thousand meters. It's for calling in artillery."

The men moved in closer to Red, hoping for that one piece of advice that might keep them alive. Everyone started asking questions at once. He held up one hand to stop the onslaught.

"Now listen up. The smartest thing each of you can do is this: When you get to your squad, find a salt, somebody who's been here awhile. Ask him what you have to know, stick with him, and do what he says. Keep that M16 clean or it'll jam on ya. If you fall asleep on line, one of your own men might kill you and you'll deserve it."

Twenty questions later we pulled off the road on the outskirts of the city. Sporadic gunfire echoed from somewhere up ahead. An old gunnery sergeant ran by our truck shouting, "Get off those trucks and spread out! Move it! Move it!"

The trucks turned around and headed for Phu Bai as soon as we were out. The gunny shouted us into two columns, one on each side of the road, with a ten-yard interval between each man. Then he spotted Red. "Red, is that you? It's good to see you. Boy, do we need a gunner." He walked over to Red, turned his head, and spit out a shot of tobacco like a major leaguer. They shook hands. The gunny lowered his voice to say something only Red was supposed to hear. I heard two words too many: ". . . got killed." The butt of a pump shotgun rested on the gunny's hip. He wore special bandoliers full of shotgun shells, and small leather pouches full of more shells on his cartridge belt. He looked like my grandpa coming back from a hunting trip in West Virginia. He even spit like Grandpa. I didn't know the Marine Corps allowed men to carry any weapon other than Marine Corps issue.

Red followed the gunny to the front of the column, then we started a slow nervous walk down the dirt road. Sweat poured down me like a sticky shower, but a cool breeze blew over my face. Twenty meters later the breeze blew a sickening, rotting odor into my nose. I had the uneasy feeling I had just smelled my first corpse.

Two hundred meters and a thousand horrible imaginings later we came to a small bamboo hootch. The hut turned out to be battalion headquarters. A quick roll call and we were sent to our respective platoons. I still couldn't see the city, but the steady pounding of heavy machine guns rang closer. Black smoke billowed above the treetops and into the gray sky, then an explosion. A Phantom whisked by.

Chan and I followed Red down a well-trodden path with heavy brush on both sides. We came to a small clearing and another hootch. A group of tired, dirty men stood near the grass and plywood huts sipping coffee out of C-ration cans. A tall, lanky character spotted Red first. His pitted face opened into a wide, ugly smile as he ran up with his hand out. He smelled worse than he looked.

"You big mother!" He shook Red's hand and slapped him on the back. "Man, you missed some real heavy crap. How was the hospital? Get any Red Cross girls?"

"It's good to see ya, Sam."

"I thought I heard you out here." A young officer who

looked as if he were just out of college stood grinning in the door of the hootch.

"How've you been, Lieutenant?" Red gave a casual salute.

"A lot better now." The lieutenant came forward with his hand out. They exchanged a quick, firm handshake.

"Who do you have with you?" the lieutenant looked at me.

"Boots," said Red. "0331s."

"Outstanding! Sam, take Red and these two down to the chief's squad."

We turned to follow the ugly Sam. I noticed something pinned to his camouflaged helmet cover. Whatever it was, it was covered with flies. I moved closer to get a better look. It was an ear. A human ear. It looked brittle and baked grayish green from the sun. I wanted to ask him about it, but I hesitated, trying to remember his name.

"Sam," I said. Before I got another word out, the lieutenant started speaking.

"And Red, send that stupid mortar man back to mortars before he kills himself with the gun. Break in the boots. They're your new gun team."

"Sam," I said again. "Is that an ear pinned to your helmet?"

"Yeah, man. I used to have more, but they drew too many flies. I saved this one to suck on. Want a lick?"

I laughed. "No thanks."

"Well, I do." He took his helmet off and unpinned the ear, then stuck it in his mouth and sucked on it like a lollipop. I don't know what my face looked like, but my mouth had no response. Even Chan was left speechless.

Sam led us down a narrow path for about two hundred meters when a driving rainstorm hit us with the monsoon fury we'd been told about. When we reached the squad, the men were relaxing in a muddy circle behind the remains of a cement wall and making no effort to stay dry. Faces seemed to light up as they recognized

Red, and the most excited one belonged to a short, rather chunky Marine with "DON'T SHOOT I'M NOT A GRUNT" printed on his helmet and flak jacket.

When Red said he was taking over the gun, the fat little man actually jumped into the air and clicked his heels. "Take this bull's-eye off my back. I'm going back to mortars, baby!" With that, he threw on his pack and disappeared without so much as a goodbye or good luck.

My stomach tightened. The situation looked worse every time somebody opened their mouth. Suddenly a machine gun opened up from the city. I hit the ground with a splash. When I opened my eyes I discovered Chan and I were the only ones ducking. The rest of the squad stood looking over the cement wall and laughing.

I stood up cautiously and peered over the wall. Running down the street directly to my front was a black Marine. He weaved back and forth, trying to present a difficult target, but that wasn't what was funny. He was pushing a small Honda motorcycle while balancing a television set on the seat. The machine gun opened up again. It sounded bigger, slower, and more powerful than the M60.

"Chief!" Red shouted. "That's a fifty! I thought the city was cleaned up?"

"You thought wrong," a deep voice answered. It belonged to a tall, dark-skinned corporal with a nose like a Roman's and a chin that looked like it had been cast from iron. Though the closest I'd ever been to a real Indian was Tonto, even I could tell that this guy was the real thing. He was the only one not laughing. "There's still a couple of fifties left. They chained 'em to walls so they couldn't run. They're too doped up to surrender." The big Indian looked bored.

The black Marine reached the cover of the cement wall, gasping for air and grinning an utterly happy grin. He hung on to the TV like it was a kid he had just rescued from a fire. He crumpled to the ground still smiling.

No one noticed the lieutenant until he slid in like he was stealing third base. He looked at the black Marine as if he'd never seen him before. His mouth opened to speak, but the words weren't forming very well.

"Jackson! Where do you think you are, Marine! This ain't no riot in Watts!"

"Spoils of war, Lieutenant." Jackson's big smile was catching. Just looking at him made me grin too.

"The guy who owned the store was dead anyway, Lieutenant. Would you mind keeping this stuff for me till we go back to Phu Bai so I can mail it home?" The lieutenant looked horrified.

"And look at this!" Jackson lifted his chin, revealing a vicious-looking green rubber snake with bloody teeth that clamped onto Jackson's shirt like a clothespin.

"Drop that garbage and saddle up. We're moving out in ten minutes."

"What?" the Indian corporal asked.

"That's right, Chief."

"Why?"

"To preserve the honor of the South Vietnamese we're pulling out so they can mop up. Saddle up! We got choppers on the way."

An hour later I jumped off a troop helicopter in Phu Bai. The base looked strangely different this time, no longer dangerous and foreign, but actually safe.

Early the next morning the whole company was bouncing down Highway 1 away from Hue City. We reached the first bridge in twenty-five minutes. The convoy stopped. The first platoon was shouted out of the last two trucks in the column.

The rest of the convoy started up again. A mile down the road we came to a stop at a large old steel bridge that was painted black. It looked like an old suspension bridge for trains, but it was strictly for road traffic. It stretched across a wide jungle river that was reddish black from decaying leaves that swirled near its surface and lay in piles on its bed. Rolls of barbed wire encircled the bridge, and thick, five-foot-high sandbag bunkers guarded each end. Another sandbag bunker sat on a huge cement piling that supported the center of the bridge.

The big Indian corporal jumped out of our truck and started shouting, "Truoi Bridge! Second Platoon, get out! Move it! Move it! Hurry up, you're makin' a great target!" We lined up in formation in front of a rusting old tank with a French emblem on the turret. Twenty yards to the right of the tank stood a three-story sandbag bunker with the barrel of a .30-caliber machine gun sticking out near the top.

Just to the left of the bridge and behind the three-story bunker sat five small white cement-block buildings with tin roofs. Directly in front of us on the other side of the road was a long cement-block building riddled with bullet holes. Vietnamese children ran around it, screaming like normal kids in a playground. Thirty meters to the right of that building was a huge camouflaged parachute spread fully open and tied to three trees. Under the parachute, sheltered from the murderous sun, sat twelve Marines. Some were playing cards; others were sleeping.

"Who are they?" I asked Red.

"That's a Civil Action Patrol unit. CAP, they're called. They work with the villagers. They try to keep 'em on our side, protect their rice, and give 'em medical aid."

On the south end of the bridge was a long village that paralleled the river for as far as I could see. ARVNs (Army of the Republic of Vietnam) walked in and out of the white block buildings. Most of them didn't carry weapons. The lieutenant stood at the door of the smallest block building talking to an ARVN major. The major first pointed to the largest of the buildings, then pointed at us. They exchanged salutes, and the lieutenant strode over to us.

"Listen up!"

Chan and I were the only two who did. The rest of the platoon kept chattering. Then the big Indian said the same thing, only different: "Shut up!" The chatter stopped. "Okay, Lieutenant."

"We're spending the night in the ARVN compound." He pointed to the nearest and largest of the tin-roofed buildings. "The ARVNs are standing lines tonight so we can get some sleep. If we're lucky, we will probably be here for a couple of weeks. Go ahead and stow your gear." He turned to the Indian corporal. "Swift Eagle, I want a guard on the gear so our ARVNs don't pick something up by mistake."

"Yes, sir."

"Dismissed!"

The building didn't impress me much, but the rest of the men acted like it was the Hilton. Chan and I dumped our gear and quickly strolled toward the village to avoid getting picked for guard duty.

As we reached the south end of the bridge, a Vietnamese boy ran up to us with two eight-ounce Cokes in each hand.

"I sell Coke. One dollar MPC."

"No thanks," Chan said.

"What you need, Marine?" The boy looked at me. "You need boom-boom. I can get."

"Chan, what's boom-boom mean?"

"I assume it's a reference to a prostitute."

The kid looked at Chan.

"Why you look like Marine? You same-same me."

Chan's face tightened. He clenched his fists, and for an instant I thought he was going to belt the kid. I grabbed his arm and patted him on the shoulder.

"Hey! What's wrong?"

Chan ignored me and glared at the kid like he still wanted to smack him.

"I'm not same-same Vietnamese." Chan shook my hand loose and grabbed the kid by the throat. "I'm

American. Chinese-American. Not Vietnamese." When Chan let go, the kid ran back a few feet and turned back to us.

"You dink-ki-dow, Marine!" he sneered as he made circles with his index finger around his right ear, then ran away.

"The kid thinks you're nuts," I said.

"He's probably right," Chan mumbled angrily.

"What's wrong?"

"I don't know." He looked me in the eyes. "It just hit me the wrong way. Sometimes I get fed up with explaining my nationality. I'm a good eight inches taller than your average Vietnamese, and they still assume that I'm one of them. You know that corporal that you think so highly of?" he said sarcastically.

"Corporal James? The stocky little jerk that acts like a general?"

"Yes. Him. He told me he didn't trust Kit Carson Scouts, and for me to watch it."

"You're kidding! What did you say?"

"I told him I didn't particularly trust Vietnamese scouts either, or corporals who weren't aware of new replacements. That seemed to stump him. He walked off with this ignorant look on his face."

I was caught off guard by Chan's reaction. Usually he drove me crazy with his forgiving Christian attitude. He'd practically become my conscience. He didn't wag fingers at me or anything like that, but if I ever made the mistake of arguing with him over something being right or wrong, sin or not sin, he would just open up his little Bible and shoot my view full of more holes than Swiss cheese. He sure wasn't anyone's angel. Sometimes he sounded arrogant, but that was usually because he knew what he was talking about. Overall he was disgustingly honest and disgustingly fair, and I was quite sure that I could depend upon him right to the end. I didn't say anything. I knew he would feel badly about the kid soon enough. He finally shook his head and smiled. "That was pretty stupid, wasn't it?" I nodded yes. "I'll have to make it up to the kid when I see him. You ready to go see downtown Truoi?"

"Let's go," I said.

As we started through the village I noticed that every hootch had its own bunker. Actually they weren't bunkers so much as small underground caves. Red had told us the people slept in these things, but I'd thought he was exaggerating. He hadn't been. It was a village of human groundhogs. They only came up in the daylight. We peeked into one hole to see how it was furnished. Two pieces of rotting plywood lined the floor. Two filthy old Army blankets and a dozen spiders. One had a body as big as a fifty-cent piece.

The primitive existence of these people fascinated me. Civilization drove right by on Highway 1, but twenty feet away women squatted together beating their clothes on rocks. The villagers looked and sounded unhealthy. Everyone coughed and hacked as if they all had TB. We decided to keep curiosity from getting the better of us. We turned back.

The night started quietly. Having off from work was a big deal, because most of the men hadn't slept a full eight hours straight in over two months. We cleaned our weapons, then Sam pulled out a deck of cards and started saying "Back-alley, bro. Back-alley," grinning with a mouth full of rotten teeth.

So far it looked like Sam would receive the platoon's vote for strangest person in the Fifth Marines. His sense of humor was as strange as the rest of his personality, and although I didn't particularly like him, I didn't particularly dislike him either. He seemed to have an almost unnatural love for his little blooper gun, officially known as an M79 grenade launcher. The blooper looked like a sawed-off shotgun with an extra-fat barrel. It even broke in half like a shotgun, but it fired midget artillery rounds—or so I called them—that exploded on contact. It made a *bloop* sound when fired. Red told me Sam could hit anything with it.

"Keep your eyes on your own cards, Sam," Sudsy said as he leaned back on his PRC-25 radio. Sudsy, our freckle-faced radioman, reminded me of Beaver Cleaver. He usually stayed with the CP (Command Post), with the doc and lieutenant and gunny. He had a flare for talking on the radio.

"You treat that radio like a woman, Suds," Rodgers said with a nervous laugh. Rodgers was the kind of Marine that girls would call cute. Sort of a pug-nose kind of cute. Red told me that Rodgers used to be a good Marine, but he'd heard that Rodgers was spooked now. He'd caught some shrapnel in Hue and just wasn't the same guy anymore.

I watched the card game for a while and listened to loud-mouthed Sam complaining about his luck. The men looked tired but relaxed. I couldn't have been less relaxed on a bed of nails. The place smelled like fish. In fact, the whole country reeked of fish.

My pack made a rocky pillow. I dumped out a couple of cans of C-rations, fluffed it up, and tried again. By the time the red, pink, and pastel flow of sunset had passed over our one-room, earth-floor Hilton, leaving us engulfed in darkness, most of the men were asleep.

The darkness was shattered by three violent explosions, one right after the other. Bullets of fluorescent red light rifled through cracks in the boarded-up windows. I was instantly awake. I scrambled for my rifle and got to my feet waiting for instructions. Another series of explosions shook the building. The door was yanked open, bringing in more red light filtering through clouds of dust. Confusion filled the room. Someone screamed, "Mortars!" Two men ran out the open door. The slow, fluctuating rhythm of an older machine gun opened up with a long burst. Shouting Vietnamese ran by the door. A loud voice screamed, "Guns up!" I thought I saw Red dart through the door and into the eerie red light. I followed him into a world of chaos.

Vietnamese were running in all directions. Panic had overwhelmed the compound. An ARVN ran into me, entangling the barrel of his rifle in my machine-gun ammo belts. As we struggled to free ourselves, our faces came together for one terrifying moment. He stared into my eyes and screamed, "VC!" He pulled his rifle away and sprinted in the opposite direction from the bridge. My instincts said to follow him, but just then another flare popped open above the bridge and I saw Red running into the back door of a cement machine-gun bunker twenty meters in front of me.

Behind me, on top of the three-story sandbag bunker, an old .30-caliber machine gun was going crazy, raking every inch of the surrounding barbed wire. Another machine gun opened up from the sandbag bunker on the cement piling under the center of the bridge.

ARVNs manning positions on the south side of the bridge stopped firing and ran wildly to the other side, dropping their weapons as they went. The only ARVN returning fire was the gunner on the three-story bunker. The rest were in retreat. A blast of M60 fire from the cement bunker blew one off the bridge.

I ran to the door of the bunker and screamed in at Red, "You're shooting ARVNs!"

"Shut up and feed the gun!"

I dropped my M16 and linked up a belt of ammo as fast as my shaking hands would function. Two more red flares popped open over the bridge, revealing shadowy figures crawling through the wire directly to our front on the opposite side of the road. I could see more shadows turning into people on the south end of the bridge. Red started firing twenty-round bursts southward. I tried to fire at the men coming through the wire to our front, but my weapon wouldn't work.

A ripping explosion behind us caused Red to cease firing. Another explosion to our right popped my right ear. My ears started ringing. My head felt like the inside of a bass drum. I felt warm blood trickle out of my ear and down my neck.

"Red!" I screamed. Red couldn't hear me through the constant blasts around us. The bunker filled with dust and smoke.

"Red!" I screamed again and shook his arm. "My rifle won't work!"

"Take the safety off, boot!"

I felt for the safety. It was on. God, what an idiot. Now the M60 on the cement piling opened up on the south end of the bridge. Hundreds of muzzle flashes erupted from the blackness. I put my rifle on full automatic and started firing.

"No, you idiot!" screamed Red. "Semi-automatic only. You'll run out of ammo! Link up more ammo! Quick!"

Red started firing again as I linked up another belt of ammo. A series of explosions started pounding the north side of the bridge. Then explosions walked down the road in ten-yard intervals, slowly zeroing in on the three-story bunker. Red screamed, "Mortars!" and started firing at the south end of the bridge. Shrapnel slapped against the side of our bunker, then the red light died. Red stopped firing.

Enemy muzzle flashes illuminated the darkness like hundreds of deadly lightning bugs. Suddenly the explosions stopped. Then the night was silent. A green flare popped open above the bridge and swung down slowly under its tiny parachute. Five men sprinted onto the bridge from the south end. I couldn't see any weapons. Another flare burst more light on the battle. Now I could see that each had satchel charges taped to his chest and back.

"Sappers!" Red screamed, and opened up on the five men now weaving toward the center of the bridge. The M60 on the cement piling and the .30 caliber opened up on the sappers at the same time Red did.

Orange tracers ricocheted in a thousand directions as bullets bounced around the five sappers, yet they kept coming. Then three dropped at the same time. One of them struggled back to his feet. His legs were cut from under him again. He began crawling toward the center of the bridge. The remaining two staggered like drunks, jerked spasmodically as the machine guns found their mark, then finally collapsed.

Suddenly our position came under murderous small-arms fire from directly across the road. Pieces of cement and dirt stung my face as bullets chipped away at our bunker. Whining lead tore through the gun slit. It looked like the flashes of another hundred rifles were firing straight at us.

Red ducked, bumping helmets with me. My stomach pressed against my spine. I mumbled a quick prayer. Lead smacked against the outside wall of the bunker. Bullets flattening with solid thuds ripped away precious inches of all that was keeping us alive. Then the firing stopped.

We peeked through the gun slits in time to see another group of five sappers jog onto the south end of the bridge.

I started firing, this time single-shot. I hit one; I knew I hit him, but he kept coming.

"I hit that sucker!"

"Go for the legs!" screamed Red as he opened up again. "They're doped up. You gotta knock 'em off their feet!"

Now the flashes across the road to our front were firing at the maniac manning the .30 caliber at the top of the three-story sandbag bunker. He must have two thousand rounds linked up to that thing, I thought. I haven't heard him stop yet.

I linked up another belt of ammo as Red blew one of the sappers off his feet. The M60 on the cement piling had a bad angle for hitting the sappers. That was supposed to be the job of the south-end gun bunker that the ARVNs had abandoned.

Bright white flares began popping open from above, lighting the battle like twenty little suns. When I realized where they were coming from, I cried out, "A plane, Red! Air support!"

The sappers on the bridge were being yanked and twirled like puppets with each direct hit. The lead man spun like a top, his arms flailing the air above his head, but still he came forward.

A giant sparkler moving in a small circle sizzled at us from the blackness of the jungle across the road. Red stopped firing and shoved me down, landing on top of me. Our bunker shuddered under the numbing explosion. Dirt, rocks, and dust poured through the firing slits. We lifted our heads in time to see another rocket sizzling toward the three-story sandbag bunker.

"They're inside the wire!" Red pointed as he yelled over the clamor of the screaming NVAs. Silhouettes moved across the road to our right. "Shoot anything that moves!"

I knew the positions to our right were being overrun; self-torturing thoughts of hand-to-hand combat darted through my mind. I'd rather get shot than bayoneted, I thought. God, I hate knives!

A fleeing Vietnamese ran by our door. Red turned and fired a burst through the opening, dropping two ARVNs five feet from the bunker. I couldn't believe what was happening. I stared at the dead ARVNs for a couple of seconds until Red started firing again. I watched the tracers of the M60 ripping into the sappers on the bridge. Only three still stood. Others tried to crawl forward.

At the center of the bridge, just over the piling where the M60 gun team was still firing, the three sappers put their arms around a steel support. Five seconds later a violent explosion lifted the huge steel superstructure into the air. It surged ten feet above the cement piling, twisted slightly, and crashed back down on the gun team.

For twenty seconds the firing ceased, as if the climactic destruction had ended the battle. Then an American began screaming in pain from the bridge. Until that moment I hadn't been sure it was a Marine gun team out there. "Chan!"

Red slapped me across the face. "It's not Chan! It's a CAP unit. They work with the ARVNs."

The voice of the dying Marine drifted through the damp night air. I felt more helpless with each piercing moan.

"Red, we gotta do something!"

The firing started again. Red opened up on muzzle flashes across the road. I linked up more ammo. With each lull in the shooting the torturous calls for help from the wounded Marine ripped at my sanity. Red slapped me hard on the back and then patted my helmet.

"Charlie will *de-de mow* before daybreak. It'd be suicide to go out there any sooner."

"What's '*de-de mow*' mean?"

"He'll run. Charlie has two chances against us in the daylight—slim and none."

Suddenly a noise like a sick foghorn bellowed from the sky, accompanied by a magnificent golden streak that seemed to originate from the pitch-black sky.

"What's that?" I asked.

"Puff the Magic Dragon—a C-130 with mini-guns and a whole plane full of ammo. It's supposed to cover every inch of a football field in ten seconds."

"It sure doesn't sound like a machine gun."

"No. It's like a giant Gatling gun, and each barrel is a machine gun."

I watched and listened to Puff in amazement. The

enormous stream of orange and gold tracers looked two or three feet thick. It wavered slightly with each movement of the plane or the gun. It sounded more like an angry monster bellowing than a gun firing. But the enemy was too close to us for Puff to be effective. Ten minutes later the deadly golden stream disappeared.

During the next two hours sporadic exchanges of fire continued, but as daybreak neared, the shooting slackened to an occasional sniper round. The first shafts of sunlight brought a command from the Indian corporal.

"Listen up!"

I couldn't see where the voice was coming from, but it was loud and clear.

"This is Swift Eagle! I'm going after him!"

The big Indian was on the bridge before I even spotted him. The wounded Marine had stopped calling for help an hour ago, but I still had hope. The Indian moved quickly and gracefully, like a cat. Then he jumped from the twisted bridge to the piling and out of sight. A few moments later he reappeared. I knew the man was dead.

I expected to see hundreds of dead NVA scattered about as the sun grew brighter, but this was my first lesson on just how good the enemy was at dragging away the dead and wounded.

Every inch of me itched. A layer of gritty sand mixed with sweat that felt more like glue had somehow covered my body. I wanted to see the dead men. I had to find Chan.

"Johnnie!" A voice that brought joy and relief to my heart resounded across the compound.

"Red! That's Chan! Chan!" I screamed through the door of the arid bunker. I ran out of the bunker and into a bear hug that nearly crushed my ribs.

"Well, I'm sure glad you're okay." I escaped the bear hug to see who was talking. It was the big Indian.

"This guy bugged me all night worrying about you," the chief said.

"We've been together since boot camp," I said, feeling a bit embarrassed. "He's like my brother."

Chan removed the smile from his face and went back to looking too sophisticated for a show of emotion. "Well," he said, as he took one step back and straightened his flak jacket. "I did promise your mother I'd keep you from doing anything foolish."

"Let's go," Swift Eagle said.

"Where?" I asked.

"A body count."

We followed the stone-faced Indian to the perimeter wire. There, and around the bridge and compound, we counted sixty-four dead NVA. We found one wounded in both legs by machine-gun fire. He was taken prisoner. Out of the fifteen Marines killed, twelve were from the Civil Action Patrol unit. I didn't know any of them, and I was glad I didn't. I never heard how many ARVNs died.

The official report says that the Truoi River Bridge was attacked and overrun by an estimated three hundred NVA regulars and one hundred sappers. The bridge was destroyed by suicide squads (sappers) carrying satchel charges. It says nothing about the ARVNs falling asleep on lines and then abandoning fortified positions.

THE BUSH

Twenty-four hours after Truoi Bridge was destroyed the Seabees had constructed a pontoon bridge across the river and convoys continued as usual. Forty-eight hours later the Seabees had already started construction on another permanent bridge.

Our job was to protect them while they worked during the day. Before nightfall they trucked ten miles back to the safety of Phu Bai and we went into the bush with three-man killer teams and squad-size ambushes.

Even though the bridge had been overrun, it was still considered skate duty compared to being in the bush. I didn't know the difference yet, but I had no reason not to believe it was true.

Two weeks later the VC came into Truoi Village for re-supplies of rice. When the village chief refused, they cut off his head and stuck it on a bamboo stake in front of his hut. Three-man killer teams were the best way to defend against those kinds of attacks. They were quiet and mobile. I volunteered several times for a three-man team, but was never chosen because I was still too "boot." I wasn't all that sure I really wanted to do it, but the combination of boredom and curiosity was getting the best of me. It did look exciting, and I was completely out of things to write home about. So far, filling sandbags seemed like my most notable contribution to the war effort.

Skate duty or not, it was boring slave labor as far as I

33

was concerned. Most of the bunkers had taken a beating during the battle for the bridge, and the order for the day was "fill sandbags and fortify bunkers." That was also the order for the next day and the day after that. Chan said I kept getting volunteered because I looked strong. I still had some of that stateside meat on me, and I did win the battalion push-up contest on Parris Island, but at five-foot-nine and one-hundred-sixty pounds, I didn't feel like Hercules. Still, his theory may have been partially true. The old salts looked thin and tired compared to many of the new replacements.

The only break I found in the boredom was watching traffic on Highway 1. Most of the Vietnamese traveled on foot, but sometimes a bike or a moped or even a banged-up old white school bus that leaned comically to the driver's side would rumble by. Sometimes the truck drivers in the convoys going south toward Da Nang or north toward Phu Bai or Hue would throw us a case of C-rations. If we hit the jackpot they'd toss us a crate of milk that was heading for the chow halls in Phu Bai.

Striker was on sandbag duty about as often as I was. I didn't know much about Striker. He wasn't overly friendly. He was commonplace in complexion, feature, manners, and vocabulary. In fact, his most distinguishing characteristic was a huge black mole positioned right between his eyes, just above the bridge of his nose. At the end of the second week of sandbags I was staring at that mole almost hypnotically when Striker caught me off guard by initiating a conversation.

"How come you're friends with that gook?" he asked without looking at me. He stuck his entrenching tool into the sand and sat on the ground with a tired groan.

"Do you mean Chan?"

"Yeah. The gook who talks like a professor." For a moment I considered sticking his E-tool someplace other than the sand, but I decided to be generous and postpone that action.

"Did you go to Parris Island, or are you a Hollywood Marine?"

"Pendleton."

"Hollywood Marine," I said.

"I know, I know. P.I. is twice as bad as Pendleton. I've heard it all before. But Pendleton ain't no picnic."

I ignored his defense. "You know the couple of minutes they give you before sack time to read your mail or write a note home?"

"Yeah. I never got any mail." He sounded almost angry at the remembrance.

"Chan would use that time to read his Bible. He was my bunkie, but I never paid any attention to his reading. We never had a chance to talk to each other. Well, one night the DI, Senior Drill Instructor Jones,"—I paused, remembering the terror inspired by that character— "caught Chan reading the Bible instead of his mail. He stood him at attention and punched him in the stomach so hard it knocked Chan down, but Chan got right back up. Then the DI started screaming at him about following orders and accusing him of trying to get out of 'his' Marine Corps by being a conscientious objector. Chan told him that was incorrect and that he had joined the Corps to stay. The DI told him the only Bible he was going to read was his Marine Corps bible, 'The Guidebook for Marines.' Chan told him that was incorrect. That was the beginning. The DI swore that he was going to run Chan out of the Marine Corps. They tried, but they couldn't break him. Jones finally gave up and promoted Chan to squad leader."

"They got down on a guy in my platoon once," Striker said. "They finally ran him out. Unfit for duty. He was a wimp."

"Chan's nobody's wimp. I made Chan go to Tijuana with me on our last forty-eight-hour leave before we left the States. We had a couple of other guys with us. All of us just got bombed except Chan. Some giant Mexican tried to make us pay for twenty-four drinks when we only ordered three. Pretty soon more bouncers showed up, and I ended up hitting the big one with a chair. The other two Marines with us took off, but Chan stayed right there with me and fought it out until the Tijuana police saved us. Then the Shore Patrol took us out of the Tijuana brig and threw us in their own brig. They were going to let Chan go, 'cause he wasn't even drunk, and I managed to tell 'em it was all my fault and that he was an innocent bystander, but Chan wouldn't leave me. So then the Corps took us from the Navy and threw us in the Red Line Brig at Pendleton."

"You were *there*?" Striker's face showed some interest for the first time.

"I was there."

"How long?"

"We had orders for Nam the next day so we got out in a few hours."

"Then you never had to cross the red line?"

"No," I said. "They did make us stand at attention with our faces against a wall while they hit us in the back of the head until one MP almost broke my nose."

"I crossed the red line," Striker mumbled. "If you had to take a leak, you had to cross the red line. If you wanted a drink, you had to cross the red line. If you had to throw up or wanted something to eat, you had to cross the red line."

"I heard they really put it to ya when you crossed that red line," I said.

"Yeah," Striker mused. "With clubs and boots. How'd your little Bible reader handle the Red Line Brig?" Striker asked as if he knew the answer.

"Just like everyone else. Who've you got something against, Chan or God?"

"I don't know either one. I ain't sure I trust people who sit around reading Bibles."

"I don't trust people who don't." My tone wasn't friendly, nor was the look that went with it.

"Don't tell me you believe that crap too?" He laughed. I felt my face getting flushed. I looked at Striker's tanned arms and chest. He was lean and mean, just like most Marines. It's going to be a good fight, I thought. I stood up slowly. Striker looked a little nervous as I reached my feet, still not taking my eyes off him.

"Johnnie." I turned away from Striker to see Red standing behind me holding a deadly little green claymore mine in one hand and a small roll of wire in the other. "Come over here a minute." He walked me a few feet away from Striker and began speaking quietly. "I saw what you were thinking. Don't do it." I started to explain. "And don't bother explaining. I overheard some of it, and it doesn't matter what a jerk Striker is. You don't make enemies in the bush. You've heard of fragging. If somebody wants to blow you away out there, all they have to do is drop a frag on you or shoot you in the back and say it was an accident in the heat of battle. You hear what I'm saying?" I nodded, and we walked back over to Striker. I filed Red's warning permanently in my memory bank. I knew he was right.

"You two are going out on a killer team tonight with Jackson," Red said. "If you guys set up a claymore, I want you to know how it works."

"John, do you know how that thing works?" Striker asked, motioning to the claymore in Red's hand. His tone was friendly enough.

"Not really," I said, feeling relieved the angry moment had passed.

The claymore was about the size of a 5-by-7 picture frame. It sat on four tiny legs and was slightly curved.

"Okay," Red said, giving me a friendly dislocating slap on the shoulder. He knelt down on one knee and placed the claymore face down beside the detonator.

"Connect these two wires here to the back of the clay-more first. Then string it back to your position and con-nect it to these two screws on the detonator. Got it?"

"Yeah."

"Now don't get too close. This sucker has a pound and a half of C-4 in it. Set it up after it's dark. Charlie has a nasty habit of turning 'em around if he sees you set 'em up." He paused. "How many frags you got?"

"Four."

"Here's a couple more." He pulled two grenades off his cartridge belt and tossed them to me. "Leave your pack here. And don't take your poncho, either. The gooks can hear the rain bouncing off it. Leave your helmet here too. Wear your soft cover."

"Okay, Red." My stomach started to tighten up. This was beginning to look more serious than I was pre-pared for.

"If you guys see the trip flares go off and the bridge is getting hit, don't come back in. Stay where you are until daybreak." Now I really was nervous.

A thousand years later the sun finally began its leisurely drop behind the faraway mountains of the A Shau Valley. My stomach churned like an abdominal alarm clock. I met Jackson and Striker at the gun bunker on the south end of the bridge. Jackson had taped two clips together end to end for quick loading. I immedi-ately wished someone had told me to do that. It seemed like there was always one more thing I wish I'd thought of. I knew it would be one little item on the list that I forgot that could get me killed.

As we started down the path through the village, two Marines dragged rolls of concertina wire across the road, sealing the bridge for the night. Seeing that gave me an uneasy sensation of being completely alone. Filling sand-bags suddenly seemed like a nice way to spend your time.

We walked through the village unnoticed—we hoped.

The villagers were in their caves for the night. Except for the occasional coughing of one of the hole dwellers, the only other sounds came from the river. The splash of a fish made me bite my tongue.

At the end of the village the path split in three directions. Jackson held up his hand for us to halt. We knelt on one knee.

Timing was crucial for our ambush. If we set up too early, we might be seen, and if we waited too long, we might choose a bad spot or walk into an ambush. I strained to see any movement up ahead but couldn't.

Jackson motioned to move out. Every step sounded too loud. The safety of the bridge felt a million miles away. I kept looking behind me, but the only thing following was my own fear. Jackson took the path that led away from the river.

Our pace slowed to one quiet step at a time. A branch fell from a tree on our right and splashed into the river. We all dropped to one knee. I could see no sane reason for going one foot farther from the bridge. Jackson stood up. He motioned us to move out again. I wanted to tell him that if all this was just to scare the boot, not another step was needed. My knees were jelly.

I wanted somebody to know what I was going through. Right now my friends are cruising around Steak 'n Shake trying to pick up women. This is crazy. No one will ever believe this. What do I do if we get hit? I have to quit cluttering up my mind, I thought.

The deepening night steadily took any vision I had had at the start. I kept Striker in sight, but Jackson was part of the blackness ahead. I wanted to stop. We kept going. A woodsy noise behind me started my heart pounding. I walked backward for twenty meters. The paranoia of being stalked from behind sent goose bumps up my spine. I turned back around. Now Striker was gone. The urge to call his name got as far as my throat before I managed to control it. I started walking faster.

A quarter moon slipped out from behind a large dark cloud. The jungle blackness turned misty blue. It was like trying to see through a heavy fog, but it wasn't a fog. It was just another eerie Vietnam night, dense with humidity. Now I could see Striker and Jackson.

Instead of feeling better, the dim blue light made me jittery. Suddenly I felt conspicuous. Sweat dripped into my eyes and stung them with salt. The path looked like it might lead all the way to the dreaded mountains.

We stopped at the edge of a clearing about twenty-five meters square. The path led through its center and into thick jungle on the other side that appeared as a solid black wall. In the center of the clearing another path crisscrossed ours. Most of the paths led to rice paddies that the villagers worked each day, but some went through or around the paddy fields and all the way to the mountains.

The new path led in a direction away from the bridge, southwest, toward the A Shau Mountains. The men always joked about that area being a gook R&R center. It didn't seem very funny right now. Jackson knelt down on one knee. He motioned for us to do the same.

"This is it," he whispered.

"How about over there, behind those bushes?" Striker pointed to some knee-high shrubs ten feet from where the two paths crossed. It looked like a logical place but was well into the clearing and rather naked.

"I'll go first and check it out," Jackson whispered.

"Make sure we're hidden from both paths," added Striker.

Jackson crouched as he scampered into the clearing. His feet rushing through the foot-high saw grass made too much noise. He disappeared behind the bushes for a moment then raised one hand and motioned for us to follow.

Striker went first. He made too much noise too. Once Striker had ducked out of sight, I followed. My first few steps were quiet but slow. Then I ran for the cover of the bushes, making more noise than Jackson or Striker.

We set-in three feet away from each other. Our cover was perfect for watching the paths without being seen. I tried to remember all the things I'd been taught, but all I could focus my mind on was the merciless attack of gigantic mosquitoes. Jackson gave Striker a bottle of insect repellant. Striker put some on his face, neck, and hands, then leaned toward me.

"Put some on, but not too heavy. The gooks can smell it if the wind is right."

Jackson leaned over Striker and handed me a watch with the face down.

"You got first watch. Don't let the luminous hands show or we're all dead." Jackson smiled. His smile was more luminous than any watch. "Wake Striker at 2400 hours."

As soon as they closed their eyes I felt like I was the only target in Vietnam. Every bush and every tree began looking like an enemy soldier. I tried to calm down by thinking of how miserable I felt. It was no use. I was too excited to be miserable.

The quarter moon slid in and out of occasional clouds, seesawing visibility from ten feet to three hundred. Between each lapse in visibility trees and bushes seemed to move. All the John Wayne war movies I'd ever seen began to haunt me. The Japs always disguised themselves as bushes. I started to wake Striker up but didn't. The Vietnamese had probably never even seen a John Wayne movie.

Jackson and Striker had pulled their shirts up and retracted their heads like turtles in an effort to evade the constant whining of mosquitoes. I checked the watch. Only twenty-five minutes gone. It felt like twenty-five days, but so far so good. Not a single bush had snuck up on me yet. Maybe the night would go by without incident.

One more scan of the clearing dispelled that hope immediately. The shadowy figure of a man, crouching as he cautiously moved in, step by step, emerged from the blackness of the jungle. My heart thumped so strongly I could feel my chest moving.

I clicked my rifle off safety and felt for my spare magazines.

Striker slapped at a mosquito. I quickly put my hand over his mouth. He froze stiff, his eyes opened wide.

"Gooks," I whispered so low I wasn't sure he heard me. He rolled quietly toward Jackson and gave him a nudge on the shoulder. They looked at me. I pointed at the shadow. They both came up on their left elbows and peaked over the brush that hid us.

Three shadows were now visible leaving the thick jungle and proceeding across the clearing. They weren't on either of the trails. They were coming straight at us. We took aim. Fifteen meters away they veered slightly away from us. Now a large group of figures appeared at the edge of the clearing. We held our fire.

My eyebrows were back to my hairline. I could see at least forty shadows moving into the clearing. Jackson held out his hand and motioned to get down. The faint whisper of an aircraft high above stole my mind for an instant, and for an instant I prayed to be on that plane, or any plane.

I melted myself into the ground, and I prayed silently, Yea though I walk through the . . . Oh, God forgive me, I can't remember the words!

The rustle of feet swishing through damp saw grass pounded into my ears. I could hear the booming of heavy artillery off in the distance, probably out of Phu Bai. Thirty seconds later two rounds exploded, judging by the sound, about two thousand meters away. The feet started moving faster.

I wanted Red to be here. Flashbacks of boot camp blended with fear. One slap of a mosquito and my life was over. One sneeze. One ill-timed twitch. I remember when Private Allen slapped that sand flea in front of me. The DI kicked him in the shins and knocked him down. Then he made the whole platoon lie down and he screamed at the top of his lungs, "Private, you have just killed your entire platoon!"

My arm was aching like crazy, but I didn't dare move even my eyes to see why. I could hear the enemy huffing and grunting as they filed by. I could feel each second individually. I felt like I'd spent days lying here with my face in the mud.

Finally silence. No more feet shuffling by. I wanted to look up. Suddenly a gripping terror seized control of my mind. The gooks were standing over us. They'd shoot me in the head when I looked up. Two minutes passed.

"All clear." To me Jackson's whisper was the Mormon Tabernacle Choir singing, "Hal-le-lu-jah." Somewhere bells were ringing, and the sun would come up tomorrow.

I looked up and straight into Striker's eyes. He had a tourniquet grip on my arm.

"My trousers are wet," he said as he released me. "And it ain't rainin'."

My back hurt, my legs were numb, and the blood still wasn't back in my arm. My neck cracked; it felt better. Then it hit me. It grabbed my funny bone and squeezed it just like Striker had been squeezing my arm for the last eternity.

"Your trousers are wet?" I looked into Striker's muddy face. He nodded yes. It started with a snicker then grew to a contained laugh then out of control. I laughed so hard I snorted. Tears of sheer delight gushed uncontrollably down my face. Jackson leaned over Striker and shook my shoulder.

"Don't . . ." The sentence turned into a chuckle. Then Striker began laughing. I covered my mouth with my arm to hide the noise, but it only made me laugh harder. Jackson's chuckle grew louder. Smilin' Jackson could laugh louder and harder than anyone I'd ever met. I felt an urgency to quiet him down before he got going, but it was no use. I was out of control. Jackson rolled onto his back, his knees pulled in to his stomach as if he were in great pain, and laughed. Great, big, fat, from-the-pit-of-his-stomach belly laughs.

Jackson sat up in a panic.

"Oh God! Grenade!"

In the span of two seconds we crawled, hopped, and ran ten meters away. We were hugging the ground again when the grenade went off, spitting dirt all over us. Striker and I sat up immediately after the explosion with rifles at the ready. Jackson chuckled. We stared at Jackson in disbelief. Jackson's chuckle turned into a cackle. Striker shook Jackson by his shoulder, which only made him laugh harder and louder.

"If you don't stop, I'm going to butt-stroke you," Striker growled.

"Okay, okay," Jackson replied, the words squeezing between the snickers. "It was my grenade. I pulled the pin when the gooks were walking by."

"We better get out of here!" I said, trying to keep my panic to a whisper.

"Keep cool," Jackson said with a pat on my shoulder. "They ain't turnin' that big column around. They'll figure somebody tripped a booby trap."

"Just the same," Striker whispered with a quick look around, "I don't wanna stay here!"

Jackson thought for a moment and pointed back toward the bridge. "Okay, let's move back closer."

It was a nervous two-hundred-meter retreat, but I felt better after the move.

By the time the sun came up I was ready to write a letter home. My friends would never believe this one, but I wanted to tell them anyway. I especially wanted to tell Chan.

Two big deuce-and-a-half trucks sat at the north end

of the blown-up bridge. Corporal Swift Eagle stood beside one of the trucks, looking in our direction.

"Move it! Hurry up! We're movin' out!"

Chan leaned out the side of the lead truck and waved. I trotted up and started to get on board.

"Where do you think you're going?" said Swift Eagle.

I looked at Chan.

"Where are *you* going?" I asked.

"S-2 school. The Marine Corps has expressed their desire that I acclimate myself to the Vietnamese language. Don't worry, I'll return in two or three weeks. You take care of yourself, buddy."

"You too, Chan," I said, rather dumbfounded.

"Move it! Move it! Get your gear together. We're saddling up!" the big Indian was shouting at me.

Chan's truck pulled away. We waved one last time. I felt alone. I wasn't all that hungry, but my stomach sure felt empty. I kept watching until the truck rounded a bend and was out of sight.

"Move it! Move it!" I turned around.

"Hey, Chief!"

"Yeah," he said as he tied his jungle trousers securely around his boot tops. "You better do this too, boot. It won't keep all the leeches out, but it stops some of 'em."

"Where's Chan going to school?"

"Phu Bai first, then down to Da Nang at China Beach." He looked up. "It's nice—real nice! About as good as R&R."

"That sucker," I mumbled. I knew it was envy and that I should be happy for him, but I wasn't. First time we hit the bush and he gets R&R.

"Hey, cheer up!" Swift Eagle said. "At least he won't get killed at China Beach."

"Right, Chief." I decided to be happy for him even if it made me sick.

"Saddle up!" I ran to the north-end gun bunker to grab my pack, helmet, canteens, and machine-gun ammo.

The old gunny was leaning against the bunker with his pack and helmet on. My gear lay beside him.

"God! What a night, Gunny."

"Hurry up and get your gear on, son."

"We must have had one hundred gooks walk right by us! Right by our noses!" He acted as if he didn't hear me.

"How old are you, John?" He handed me my flak jacket and spit out a shot of tobacco.

"Eighteen, Gunny. Why?"

"Just curious. I got a boy with a baby face like yours. He's eighteen too. He's in his senior year. Didn't you finish high school?"

"Yeah. I graduated last June. I started school when I was five."

"When did you turn eighteen?" He handed me my cartridge belt and canteens. I wondered what he had on his mind. This was the first time he'd ever talked to me.

"October 12th."

"Did your parents sign for you to get in the Corps?"

"Yeah. It took some fast talking, too."

He shot a stream of tobacco juice at a large anthill beside the bunker then stepped up close to me, put his right hand on my shoulder, and stared me right in the eye. Deep wrinkles stretched across his tan forehead and all around his dark blue eyes. He suddenly looked very old and solemn.

"You can't be eighteen anymore, John. You have to think older if you want to come out of this hole alive. Do you know what I'm trying to tell you?"

"I think so, Gunny."

He bent over, picked up my helmet, and put it on me.

"There ain't many Marines better than Big Red. You do what he says when he says it. Swift Eagle, too. That Indian is all Marine. Watch him and learn."

"Is this as tough as World War II, Gunny? They told me you were on Iwo Jima."

"I was at Chosin Reservoir, too. This war is the worst

yet. We ain't tryin' to win, and we ain't tryin' to lose. We could stop it in a month if we invaded the North." He took a couple of quick steps as if he were too angry to stand still. "Every war stinks, but I ain't seen this kind of stink before. You stick close to Red, you'll be okay." He slapped me on the back.

"Saddle up!"

My stomach started churning. I missed Chan already. A sense of foreboding smothered my excitement as the small column meandered through the village.

Two thousand meters out we crossed the last rice paddy. One hundred meters beyond that we crossed a small muddy strip of water that looked ankle deep. On the first step the muck was up to my chest. The rancid odor clung to me for the next few miles; unfortunately, that wasn't all that clung to me. Big black leeches stuck to anything they touched, anything going through the water. They'd suck blood until they swelled up like a balloon, then they'd drop off. Red turned around in time to see me trying to pull a leech off my neck.

"Don't do it! If you pull it off, the head stays in your skin and you get infected. You have to burn 'em off." He lit a match and touched it to the leech. It fell off.

The terrain rose slightly and changed from the swampy areas in and around the paddies to hard, rocky, rolling hills with not a tree anywhere. My pack straps were ripping into my collarbone. The four 100-round belts of machine-gun ammo already had my neck bleeding, and stinging flies were feasting on the blood. I tried to walk fast to get in front of Red, but the weight of my gear made it hard to walk at all.

"Red," I called quietly from behind him.

"Yeah."

"These flies are killing me, man. My neck's bleeding." He slowed his pace until I got beside him.

"You're packing too much gear, boot!"

"I already know that!"

"First time we cross a deep river, ditch that E-tool."
His expression turned to disbelief. "Hey, you jerk!
You've got the gun ammo facing in!"

"What?"

"The bullet casings should be facing your neck, not
the bullet points! Well, you can't do anything now but
turn the belts over when we stop." Red managed to yank
my collar up, shielding my bloody neck from the flies and
direct contact with the ammo. It helped, but not much.

After four hours of humping in the general direction
of the mountains that surrounded Tra Ve, I hurt everywhere. My feet managed to cause enough pain to take
my mind off my shoulders, back, and neck, but not for
long. Finally we climbed to the top of a small, rock-
strewn hill and set up a perimeter.

No one knew where we were going. Somebody
shouted, "Dig in!" I pulled my E-tool off my pack and
tried to puncture the hard ground. A parking lot would
have been easier.

I finally gave up on the idea when I noticed I was the
only one shoveling. Red was already heating up a can of
meatballs and beans.

"Aren't you diggin' in?" I asked, wondering why he
had told me to ditch my E-tool.

Before Red opened his mouth, the hollow thumping
of a mortar round leaving the tube echoed across the hilltop, bringing a wave of quiet over the chattering Marines.
Some men looked up, while others flattened against the
rocky surface of the hill.

The first round exploded against the base of the small
hill's southern side. The second round hit fifteen meters
up the slope of the southern side. I stuck my face into the
dirt and put my hands over my helmet. I wanted to hide,
but there wasn't even tall grass available. The third
round hit the crest of the hill. I heard a scream. I clawed
into the rocky earth with my fingernails. I heard another
thump, followed by a faint whistle. Then a violent explo-

sion shook the ground I was trying to become a part of. I peeked from under my helmet just in time to see another explosion ten meters to my right. Rocks and dirt came down on my back. The mortar rounds walked across the top of the hill like a giant's footsteps, mangling anything in their path.

I shoved my face into the dirt and waited for the pain.

"Guns up! Guns up!" The command came from the other side of the hill.

Red jumped to his feet with the M60 in one hand and ammo belts in the other.

"Come on, boot! Guns up!"

I got to my feet with my M16 and two belts of ammo for the machine gun. Red shouted, "Gung-ho!" at the top of his lungs and darted up the slight incline toward the crest of the hill. His shout went through me like a shot of adrenaline. Suddenly I wasn't terrified anymore. The emotional high that comes when life or death is on the line swept all fear to the back of my mind. An odd sense of exhilaration, almost pleasure, pounded through my system as we weaved across the top of the hill. More explosions behind me heightened the thrill. I was Superman and John Wayne. Nothing could stop this dash. I heard myself screaming, "Yeee-hii!" like a cowboy on a bronco.

I could see the lieutenant ahead, pointing at another hill one hundred meters south. Red hit the dirt and opened up on the hill. As quickly as it had started, it stopped. The mortars ceased. We had no target.

One man was wounded. Sudsy, the radioman, called for a medevac. The wounded man's name was David Blaine. He was from Kentucky. His butt was peppered with shrapnel. He didn't seem to mind a bit. It was a painful ticket out of Vietnam. I felt a bit of envy. I started daydreaming of ticker-tape parades and a hero's homecoming.

"Hey, John! That's a hard-Corps way to lighten your load!" I turned away from the bleeding Marine to see who was calling me. It was Red. He was holding something up and laughing.

"What is it?" I moved closer to inspect the object of his laughter.

"I think you need a new pack." Red tried to restrain the laughing when he saw that I didn't think it was all that funny.

My pack was in shreds. A direct hit. My writing gear, food, and my little Instamatic camera—gone. Red gave my helmet a couple of pats.

"Don't worry about it. You better thank God you didn't have it on. Marine Corps packs aren't worth crap anyway. We'll get you an NVA pack like mine." I looked at Red's pack. I had admired it since I first saw it. It was bigger than ours. The straps were made of a much softer canvas, more comfortable. Only an old salt would have a pack like that; Chan and I knew that the first day we saw it.

"Where did you get it?"

"Hue City. It's in good shape, too, except for this one M60 hole here."

Red was still looking for the hole when I spotted a piece of my own pack twenty meters down the side of the hill. As I started toward the remnants, a sharp burning pain high on my right thigh stung me so badly that I bent over.

"What's wrong with you?" asked Red.

"I don't know." I felt the warm slow trickle of blood running down my leg. Two small holes in my trousers near the groin were the only evidence I needed.

"Red! I'm wounded. I've been hit!"

"What? Where?" Red dropped his pack. In a flash he was kneeling on one knee in front of me.

"Unbutton your pants, stupid! Let's see how bad it is."

"I wonder why I didn't feel it sooner?"

"It just happens that way sometimes."

"Wow! My own little red badge of courage!"

"This could have been real tough on your love life. Are you hit anywhere else?"

"Will I get a Purple Heart, Red?"

"Are you sure you aren't hit anywhere else? What's this?" He pointed to a tear in my left chest pocket. "What's in that pocket?"

"My Bible."

"Pull it out."

I unbuttoned the flap over my pocket and pulled the small Gideon Bible out. A hole right under the word "Holy" sent a stream of goose bumps down to my toes. The hole went three-quarters of the way through the little book. A splinter-sharp piece of shrapnel one-quarter inch long had made it all the way to the book of Hebrews.

"Could that have killed me?"

"It took us an hour to find out what killed my last A-gunner. A tiny sliver of shrapnel went under the back of his helmet and into his brain. It was in his hair, so we couldn't even find any blood, but it killed him."

"Will they medevac me?"

"No way. Not for those two little holes. Go see the doc. Tell him to put something on it before it gets infected."

I did what Red told me to do. The doc, our corpsman, tweezered out two splinters of shrapnel while I looked through my little wounded Bible. On the inside cover someone had written a long passage in red ink. It was Chan's handwriting; I didn't know anyone else who could print that small. I wondered when he had written it. I started reading it, and each line made me feel a little better.

Romans 8:35–39

Who shall separate us from the love of Christ? Shall tribulation, or distress, or persecution, or famine, or nakedness, or peril, or sword?

Just as it is written, "FOR THY SAKE WE ARE BEING PUT TO DEATH ALL DAY LONG;

WE WERE CONSIDERED AS SHEEP TO BE
SLAUGHTERED."
    But in all these things we overwhelmingly conquer
through Him who loved us.
    For I am convinced that neither death, nor life, nor
angels, nor principalities, nor things present, nor things
to come, nor powers, nor height, nor depth, nor any
other created thing, shall be able to separate us from
the love of God, which is in Christ Jesus our Lord.

                        Romans 8:28
    And we know that God causes all things to work to-
gether for good to those who love God, to those who
are called according to His purpose.

    "Are you okay?" the doc asked. He looked up and
seemed to be studying my face.
    "Yeah. I'm fine." His concern surprised me. "I'm just
reading something really neat out of the Bible. You should
hear this."
    "No thanks," he said with the slur of a spoiled snob.
He was a Navy man from Massachusetts, and was gener-
ally disliked for his attitude of resentful superiority, but
for some uncharacteristic reason I didn't get mad at him.
I found myself wondering what his parents were like.
The doc threw on some red stuff that burned and a
couple of Band-Aids. I gave him a thanks that I didn't
mean and headed back to the gun position.

    A chopper picked up Blaine twenty minutes later. The
moment it lifted off, Swift Eagle shouted, "Saddle up!" A
collage of thoughts rambled through my mind as the
hump through the bush started again. I was a Spartan on
my way to Thermopylae. We looked like Spartans. Red
looked like one. Everyone looked meaner than me. Their
eyes were serious, almost menacing. They all had mus-
taches. I had peach fuzz.
    I started scuffing my boots as we walked along. One of

the best ways to recognize the grunt Marines was their boots.

The terrain turned hard and hilly with little vegetation. At 1900 hours the seventeen-man column stopped. We dropped to one knee and waited to be placed in ambush position. Corporal Swift Eagle swept through the column, taking three men at a time and quickly placing them in position for the night. When he finished we had a textbook L-shaped ambush.

It was that eerie time of the day. The lighting was just right for your eyes to play tricks on you. A pinkish yellow twilight filtered across the brown and green earth, casting odd shadows that made me nervous.

Tactically we were on our own except for possible artillery support from Phu Bai about five miles north. There was supposed to be an enemy battalion out here roaming around. The logic of sending seventeen Marines to make contact with an NVA battalion had escaped me, but I was only a private first class. I was contemplating the prospects of finding an NVA battalion when Red woke me up with a stiff elbow to the shoulder.

"Do you see movement?"

"Where?" I asked.

"Straight ahead. Keep looking straight ahead."

I strained to see what he was now aiming at. Then I saw movement. Shadowy figures, silhouetted by evaporating sunlight, looked to be moving thirty meters away. I felt myself trying to crouch lower as I took aim. I covered my mouth and whispered in the direction of the Marines on our left.

"Gooks!"

I started linking up ammo for the gun. Suddenly green tracers shot across our position from the left flank. Then another burst of fire came at us from straight ahead. Seven khaki-clad NVA appeared from the shadows in front of us. They were led by an officer who suddenly ran toward us firing a pistol. The others carried AKs. They looked surprised, maybe as surprised as we were. A couple turned and ran from us, but the others followed their leader. Red opened up first, making us the only real target they had. The officer was lifted off his feet and blown backward with the first twenty rounds. The gun stopped firing. I started firing my M16, but the targets disappeared. All firing ceased. I knew Red was hit. My face was wet with blood, and it wasn't mine. He was slumped forward onto the gun.

I rolled him off the gun. Two dime-sized holes sunk into one cheek. His eyes were open—lifeless and blue. I could hear myself calling for a corpsman. My voice sounded dreamlike. For an instant I thought I was dreaming: I'd wake up and find none of this had really happened. Swift Eagle flattened out beside me. He looked at the back of Red's head with no expression. Doc slid in beside us, breathing hard.

"He's dead, Doc," Swift Eagle said.

"Red?"

"Yeah. Put his poncho over him. I'll get an A-gunner for the boot."

"He only had a month to go, Chief." Doc's voice sounded far away.

The night crept by sleeplessly, congested with weird, fully awake dreams of home, friends, and the Marine Corps. I felt numb. It started drizzling. The sound always reminded me of French fries in a pan.

By first light it was still raining. The air smelled fresh and crisp. It was a stateside rain, not the normal pounding rain of the monsoon that sounds more like a war than the war itself. Raindrops formed tiny puddles on Red's poncho. His huge Viking boots stuck out of the poncho like out of a blanket that's too small. I was thankful for the rain. It kept away the ants and flies and hid my tears. How could he be dead? Men like that couldn't just die. He told me if you got past the first two months you'd make it. I wanted to pray; I needed it now, but I just didn't know God well enough to do it right, I thought. Chan always told me you had to talk to him regularly if you wanted to get to know him. I missed Chan. I felt more alone than I could remember ever feeling. The others weren't crying. Maybe they didn't know yet. I remembered the gunny's warning about being eighteen. I looked around again and the lieutenant was walking my way. His young Annapolis face couldn't hide the loss. No tears, but he was frowning. He pulled back the poncho, grimaced, and covered him again.

"You're the gunner now, Marine. Keep it clean. Every man here depends on it. Red said you'd do all right. Don't let him down." His words sounded rehearsed.

"I won't."

"Look, John, I don't know what to say. I thought the world of that big redhead. You've been dropped into a real tough spot. I'm here to help in any way I can. If you have questions, I want you to come to me. If I don't know the answers, we'll go to the chief or gunny or whatever it takes. Do you pray?" he asked bluntly.

"Yes, sir," I said, surprised at the question.

"Start praying, John. He'll get us through this mess." He gave me a pat on the helmet.

"Yes, sir." I immediately felt much closer to Lieutenant Campbell than I ever had before.

"I'll try to get you an A-gunner with a machine-gun MOS as soon as I can. I'm supposed to get the next one that shows up."

"Lieutenant!" Sam was calling from twenty meters in front of us. "We got one confirmed. I'm claiming the pistol."

"Hey, stow-it-below-Marine!" Striker yelled. "The gun got him. It belongs to Red."

"Red's dead," he said.

Sam pulled out his K-bar. It looked sharper than any knife I'd ever seen. He ripped the dead man's shirt open and began carving "A 1/5" across his chest. I could hear

Sudsy sputtering out coordinates over the radio. It lent a perfect background to Sam's bizarre ritual. Sam pulled an ace of spades card out of the black band that he wore around his helmet. He took a small metal clip off one of his bandoliers of M79 rounds and tacked the ace of spades into the forehead of the dead officer.

"Johnnie." I pulled my eyes off Sam to see who was calling me. It was Sudsy. "Here." He threw me Red's NVA pack. "Take this, too." He tossed me Red's .45-caliber pistol and holster. "You're the gunner now, right?"

"Yeah."

Sam the Blooper Man gave the forehead of the dead NVA officer one last tap and walked over to Red's body. The muffled popping of helicopter rotors signaled the approach of the medevac chopper. Sam pulled the poncho away from the face of the corpse.

"Not too bad. He can still have an open casket—just plug up these two holes and put something on the back of his head."

Swift Eagle walked forward, took the poncho from Sam's hands, and covered the corpse.

"Okay. Sam, you and Striker load him on the chopper."

Sudsy tossed out a green smoke grenade to mark the landing zone. When the chopper landed, a chunky little man with glasses jumped out as Sam and Striker loaded Red for the last chopper ride.

The chunky guy said something to the lieutenant. Then the two of them came over to me.

"John, this is PFC Doyle. He's boot. He's 0331, so he'll be your assistant gunner. Teach him what he has to know as fast as you can." The lieutenant turned and walked away before I could speak. I knew my mouth was hanging open as I stared at PFC Doyle in disbelief. "Teach him what he has to know" kept echoing through my stunned brain. I didn't know any more than he did, I thought. My God, if ever there was the blind leading the blind!

"Hi!" Doyle stuck out his hand. I shook it, and a nervous but friendly smile pushed up his fat cheeks. He sure didn't look much like a Marine. I'd never seen anyone come out of boot camp with that much baby fat. Had to be a Hollywood Marine, I thought.

"Your MOS is 0331?" I asked.

"Yep, that's me." He pushed his glasses back on his pug nose and they promptly slid back down. I tried to remember some of the things Red told me to do.

"Well, the most important thing you have to remember is this: When you hear 'Guns up!' make sure you're on my tail no matter what."

"Okay." He hesitated. "What happened to that guy they put on the chopper?" he blurted quickly, his eyes open wide with curiosity.

"I'll tell you later. Take those dog tags off and put 'em in your boot laces. You know how to feed the gun and clear a jam, right?"

"Yep. Can do."

"Don't forget the Halazone in your water and the malaria pills. And don't forget salt tabs. Got it?"

"Yeah. I'm scared." Doyle looked at me like I was supposed to tell him what came next.

"I know. Don't worry about it. Just make sure you react the way an A-gunner should. You'll get killed a lot quicker by panicking. Where are you from?"

"Denver, Colorado. See?" He pointed to his camouflage helmet cover where he had printed COORS in large black letters. I knew it. Camp Pendleton.

"Saddle up!" Swift Eagle shouted.

"Well, here we go, Doyle."

The umbilical cord got severed in a harsh, uncaring way as far as I was concerned. Just yesterday morning I felt close to God. My life was probably saved by my

Bible, and I knew in my heart that only fools believed in luck and accidents. Now I was marching into the bush feeling betrayed, bitter, and all alone. Chan had left me. Now Red. The big red Viking was gone. I tried praying for help but couldn't.

Four hours later we plodded up a rocky gray bump in the green terrain and set up a loose perimeter. Word came around to chow down. I felt too low to eat but decided to try. I missed Chan more than ever. He could always tell me where to read in the Bible, that one specific place that would answer my problem, whatever it might be. I needed that a lot more than I needed this disgusting can of congealed ham and lima beans I was gagging down. Doyle gulped down the last bite of his second can of C-rations.

"Doyle, do you know the Bible?" I asked.

"Just a little. Why?" He pulled another can out of his pack.

"The body they were putting on the chopper was my friend." Suddenly a lump the size of an egg developed in my throat. I turned away to keep Doyle from seeing his leader cry like a baby.

"Yeah. I sort of figured that out. He had 'Guns up!' printed on his helmet just like you do."

I swallowed the lump in my throat and looked at the grayish haze clinging to the steep mountains to the west.

"Sometimes I feel like God's dumpin' on me," I mumbled.

"Well," Doyle said. "I don't know the Scriptures very well, but I have an uncle who's a minister. He once told me this parable that Jesus said, I think. I don't know exactly how it goes . . ."

"Saddle up!" Swift Eagle shouted. The men started putting their packs on.

"Finish your story," I said. "But make sure you bury that C-ration can. The gooks use 'em for booby traps."

"This parable was about a potter who made pots for

different purposes. Well, the potter is God, of course. This one pot is a spittoon or something, and he doesn't think it's fair because this other pot is holding the king's gold, or something. Now, I probably got the story all screwed up, but the gist of it is, what right does the pot have to cry about being a spittoon to the potter? The potter can do anything he wants to. It's his clay. Then he told me that some people blame God for every bad thing that happens, and when good things happen, they call it luck."

I thought about Doyle's rendition of Jesus' parable for the next hour as we inched closer to the threatening mountains. It didn't sound very scriptural, but it made sense.

I felt closer to my chunky A-gunner, but still strangely alone. I remembered the writing in the front of my Bible. I put the stock of the machine gun on my left shoulder and held one bipod leg with my left hand so I was free to pull the Bible out of my shirt pocket with my right. I read it over and over as we humped along. Soon I started feeling pretty good again, or at least I stopped feeling so sorry for myself.

Dusk came upon us before I was ready. The gloaming hour turned the hot blue-white sky into striking shades of red, pink, and blue. The danger that nightfall brought usually overshadowed the glorious sunsets, but it was impossible not to notice.

We stopped along a small trail. The lieutenant moved from man to man among the kneeling column, pointing to positions for the night ambush. By the time he reached us, Corporal Swift Eagle loomed beside him.

"Lieutenant," Swift Eagle said quietly.

"Yeah, Chief." They both knelt down on one knee to talk.

"It might be a good idea to set in here until it gets black and then move about twenty-five meters."

"Why, did you see anything?"

"No, sir."

The careless splash of a shot of tobacco signaled the presence of the gunny. He knelt down beside the lieutenant.

"The chief thinks we should set in and then move again. What do you think?"

The gunny shot another stream of tobacco juice to the ground. "It's the chief's fourth tour. He's got time in grade over both of us." The gunny drew his syllables out like a Southern farmer.

"They've probably been watching us all day." The lieutenant seemed to be talking to himself. "And we have made contact already. You might be right, Chief. Better to be safe. We'll set in here until I give the word in about twenty minutes, then we'll move twenty-five meters east. Does that sound right to you?"

"Sounds good to me, sir," Gunny replied.

"Yes, sir," Swift Eagle said.

I liked knowing what was going on for a change. I'd listen to that big Indian anytime he chose to speak.

Ten minutes later the sunset color show disappeared. Our position, now engulfed by darkness, felt dangerous. A sense of urgency swept over me. Then we moved, rather clumsily at first. The clinking of a mess kit carried through the still, humid night. Someone to my right stumbled over a rock with all the delicacy of a drunken bull. The hollow clump of a helmet striking the rock-hard earth identified another Marine Corps klutz. Doyle's breathing got louder with each noise until at last we reached the new position on slightly lower ground, where our only cover was a gradation of small natural trenches, the kind caused by rainwater runoff. Yesterday's mortar attack had made me thankful for any indentation in the earth I could find.

By 2200 hours most of the perimeter was asleep and it was my turn to turn in. My eyelids felt like they were being weighed down by sandbags. I tapped Doyle on the shoulder. He didn't budge. I tapped him again.

"Your watch," I whispered and pointed at my wrist. He sat up, looking groggy. I shook him again. He nodded and motioned me to stop with his hand. I went down and seemed to just keep going and going, all the way home, but not to Saint Petersburg. To South Charleston. Dad was there, alive, and he wasn't blind. He kept calling for me to hurry up, but the faster I ran the farther away he was, until I stopped. I was in front of the old log cabin out in Lincoln County. It was snowing, and the mountains up and down the holler turned gray and bleak. I ran into the cabin for warmth. Shafts of blue light streaked from the cracks in the walls, crisscrossing the hard dirt floor. A potbelly stove blazed with heat in the center of the room, but the room was still freezing. Someone was crying. They kept saying the same thing over and over, sobbing with each word. "The baby's freezing! Junior, he's freezing!" It was Mom. She was frantically gluing newspapers over the cracks between the logs, but the more she put up, the colder it got, and I shivered and kept shivering until I shook violently. . . .

"Wake up! John! Wake up, man!" Doyle was shaking me in near panic and whispering into my ear. "I hear something," he whispered and pointed to our front.

At first I thought he was just jumpy. I stared into the darkness until the sleep began to clear from my eyes and brain. Twenty meters to our front, silhouetted against a purple and black sky, the helmeted head of an NVA soldier moved slowly toward our old position.

"I see one!"

A large hand seized my shoulder. My heart stopped cold. "Don't open fire till I do." It was the chief, of course; no one else could be that quiet. He slipped to the next position without a sound.

The wait was on. A few moments later, rustling weeds to our left warned of more men crawling in the direction of our old position. No one opened up. Doyle pointed to silhouettes of at least three men straight ahead. Still no one fired. My hands started shaking. Doyle was trying to turn his teeth into powder. I put my hand over his mouth to quiet him.

"Link up some ammo. Be quiet." I whispered so low I wasn't sure he heard me. He rolled quietly from his stomach onto his side and began linking up a belt.

A single burst of AK47 fire shattered the silence. An instant later a host of chattering AKs joined in. Muzzle flashes erupted from three sides of our old position as at least twenty AKs sent a murderous barrage of fire into it. Bullets ricocheted off hard ground, whining through the air in every direction.

Still no Marine fired. Flashes two hundred meters away marked the beginning of a mortar barrage that lasted five minutes. Our old position had already been plotted. The mortars were probably supposed to hit us first, followed by a ground assault, but in the confusion the NVA didn't realize they were the only ones firing.

The mortar rounds swept through like a giant scythe. Two machine guns crisscrossed fire, sending green tracers ricocheting in all directions. I was dumbfounded. They were having a war all by themselves, and we had box seats. The flashes of exploding mortars provided a terrifying strobe-light effect.

Still the word to return fire did not come. At 2235 the mortars ceased fire. Screaming NVA stormed the abandoned position, firing as they ran. Their own deafening firepower was so constant they still did not realize that no one was firing back, and the friendly thunder of big 155s at Phu Bai gave a hollow background echo that went unnoticed by the attacking NVA. Suddenly I realized why we weren't firing. We wanted them where they were.

Still, I wanted to open up. I wanted to for Red. The baneful whistle of friendly artillery rounds grew sharper and sharper until I cringed, feeling that final hiss as much as hearing it. Flashes of white light followed by ripping explosions, dirt, rocks, and screams mixed in a chaotic montage of war. Rocks pelted us like hail. Somewhere from behind me Sudsy was shouting, "Fire for effect! Right on, Bro! Fire for effect! You got it, Momma! You got it!" The barrage felt like it went on for an hour, but it was probably closer to ten minutes. Then it ended as quickly as it began. One final bright flash, an explosion of rocks and dirt, quiet.

"Is it over?" Doyle's whispered voice sounded like a scared child.

"I think so."

"Jesus! My first firefight and we never fired a shot."

A heavy, sulphurous cloud settled over the scene like a fog. I couldn't imagine anyone living through that destruction, but a forlorn moan told me someone had. The remainder of the night passed without incident.

The first shafts of light replaced my sense of apprehension with a morbid curiosity. All around our perimeter men stretched their necks to see what could be seen. It was the same feeling I got in funeral homes. Part of me wanted to look in the casket, and part of me felt repulsed at the thought.

The hard ground looked churned, as if a giant had gotten angry and stabbed the earth. Rocks the size of baseballs were strewn everywhere. The perimeter was stirring behind me. A cough, the klick of a safety, a canteen being downed. The sun wasn't fully up, and it was already stinking hot.

"We're going out for a body count! Spread out! On line!" I turned to see who was shouting this insanity. The lieutenant stood with one hand pointing to where he wanted the line to start. No way, I thought. He had to be kidding. I looked at Doyle and laughed.

"Next he'll want us to fix bayonets."

"Fix bayonets!"

Doyle forced a nervous laugh. I wanted to tell him not

to worry, but I was worried. I had a bloody machine gun. What was I supposed to do in a bayonet fight?

I looked back toward the center of the perimeter. Lieutenant Campbell stood next to Sudsy, the gunny, and Doc. They always looked less tired than the rest of us. They sat in the center of the perimeter, the CP (command post). Four people in one position equaled twice as much sleep as I was getting.

Lieutenant Campbell looked downright excited. It wasn't any secret, even to boots, that killing more gooks than the other platoons could mean a promotion. The Corps called it "Shoot of the Month."

The M60 machine gun was a superior weapon. It could be fired from a tripod, which was too heavy and which no Marine Corps gunners ever carried into the bush, or the bipod, two attached legs that swung from under the barrel, or it could be fired from the hip. The recoil from firing would actually help hold the weight of the barrel up and the gun on target. I could put out 550 rounds per minute with a maximum range of 3,750 meters. I was sold on the gun. But in spite of all this, going into hand-to-hand combat with a 23.16-pound machine gun, plus ammunition, was like fencing with handcuffs and snowshoes. I was petrified.

"Move out on line!" The lieutenant pointed his rifle at the craters. We moved slowly. "Shoot anything that moves!"

Somewhere a bird started chirping. With each step the gun got lighter, until it felt as light as a pretzel. The bird stopped chirping. I strained to see the first bodies. Something moved in the weeds. Suddenly I was firing a twenty-round burst into brush straight ahead. I stopped. Everyone had dropped to one knee, ready to fire at anything. There was a long, silent pause.

"Move out!"

We moved forward again, this time even more cautiously.

"What shootin'!"

I looked at Doyle in disbelief. How could he talk at a time like this?

"Look!" he said. He pointed his rifle at the front half of a now deceased large gray snake.

"What'd he hit?" yelled the lieutenant.

"He blew a snake in half," replied Doyle in a rather astonished tone.

"Move out!" Lieutenant Campbell said.

The search ended with only three bodies found. Shredded web gear covered with blood lay strewn about, indicating more kills than three, but as usual the NVA had done an incredible job of removing their dead. Sam found a spare leg. He thought it was funny. He took the bloody stump and shoved it into the crotch of one of the stiffs. He laughed at the three-legged corpse until tears filled his eyes.

"Moronic Marines," the doc mumbled. He sure had a sarcastic way of saying things, I thought. It was only a matter of time before somebody planted a fist in his mouth if he kept it up.

I looked at Sam. He was still laughing. I wondered what he was like before the war. Had he ever felt sympathy? Maybe this was just his way of coping.

We spent the rest of the day on a hill two thousand meters north of the bodies. The break from the daily march felt great. The last hours of the day looked like a 3-D movie. The sky billowed in pink and red and violet. The kind of day that made me feel infinitesimal. It looked like a Cecil B. De Mille backdrop.

An hour before darkness we split into two squads of eight men each and headed back toward the corpses. Because the NVA had a habit of returning for their dead, we decided to develop a habit of waiting for their return. Doyle and I were put with the chief, four riflemen, and Sam the Blooper Man. Our squad went east, and the other squad went west. We circled around the rocky terrain and ended up twenty meters east of the NVA corpses. I wasn't sure where the lieutenant's squad was.

The hour felt ominous—that hour when it isn't day or night but some gray, primitive zone between the two. My nose caught the whiff of something foul. I wondered if the bodies were rotting already. I started to ask Doyle if he could smell it, but then something moved near one of the artillery craters.

"Did you see that?" I asked.

"No. Where?" He sat up.

"Something moved from that bush to that bush." I pointed where I saw movement. My heart started pounding like a jackhammer. Doyle took aim in the direction I pointed.

Before either of us saw another movement, the unmistakable *bloop* of Sam's M79 grenade launcher sucked away the silence. A bright flash followed by a crisp, small explosion blinded me momentarily. Then silence.

The night ended quietly. At first light I called to Sam.

"Sam, I'm comin' over."

"I'm over here." He gave a wave from behind a small clump of earth. I walked over to Sam's position and found him putting a notch on the stock of his M79. He looked up with his pitted face gleaming in pride, smiling through rotted teeth.

"I got another one, John." He pointed at a body fifteen meters to our front.

"I saw movement over there just before you fired."

"Go check him out. Got him right between the eyes."

I walked out to look at the body. Doyle stood over the already sun-dried corpse. Immense red ants bored into the large hole between the dead man's eyes, foraging for food.

"What a shot!" Doyle mumbled. "But I thought the M79 would do more damage than that."

"So did I."

"Did you see this one over here?" Doyle pointed to one of the three corpses from the night before. He had swollen up like a balloon. The buttons on his khaki shirt had popped off.

"Don't go too close. Red told me they'll blow up sometimes and send the guy's insides all over."

"Who put the ace of spades card on that one?" Doyle pointed to the corpse with three legs.

"Sam the Blooper Man."

"What a character!" Doyle said as he removed his thick-lensed glasses and proceeded to clean them on his shirt.

"He sure is."

"He told me not one machine gunner has rotated out so far." He carefully adjusted his glasses over one ear at a time and looked in my eyes for the truth.

"What?" I stalled.

"He said since he's been here not one gunner has done his thirteen months and rotated home. Is it true?"

"I guess so. They told me the same thing."

"Doesn't that bother you?"

"I try not to think about it, but sometimes it sneaks up on me."

"How can you not think about it?" snapped Doyle.

"Not all those gunners are dead. Most were probably just wounded. To tell you the truth, that's what scares me more than dying. I don't want to go home without any legs. I'd just as soon die. That's enough of this crap. If God wants you, you're goin' one way or another."

"I guess that's true, but being a gunner seems to be a surefire way of rushing the process."

"Getting a little wound might not be so bad. I think that a lot. I mean, I don't want to get hurt or anything, but I have a chick at home named Nancy. I got a couple of 'em, but she's my favorite, a raving knockout. Trouble is she gets chased by half of Saint Pete. I daydream of her reading about me in the newspaper and getting all upset, but with my luck my little wound would be a fifty-cal. round upside the head."

"Yeah, I think about that stuff too. I always think about getting off the plane and getting the hero treatment. My old high school band playing the Marine Corps Hymn—you know, the whole bit."

"With women waiting, lots of 'em!" I added.

"You can't have a decent hero welcome without women." He laughed. I laughed too. "John." He paused. "Think we'll make it? I mean, you know, being gunners and everything."

I was stumped. I didn't want to freak Doyle out, and I wasn't real sure I wanted to admit the obvious. We both had a whole tour in front of us, and we were going to have to finish that tour as gunners. Our chances didn't look real good. I shook my head to stop thinking and grabbed my pack.

"Let's have a cup of coffee before you get me all depressed. I'd rather talk about women. I heard they're wearing mini-skirts that would make a grown man cry!"

After some coffee and a can of horrible C-ration eggs we started toward the mountains again. We marched all day, spotting nothing but scenery. The terrain grew harder and greener, rising and falling erratically as we inched closer to the foothills of the ominous mountains. We kept moving as the sun dipped behind the dominating peaks. Gigantic bomb craters scarred the landscape. The earth looked gray and dead. Some of the craters were thirty feet across and fifteen feet deep.

Doyle tapped me on the shoulder. "What makes a hole like these?"

"Had to be B-52 strikes," I whispered.

We stumbled along a rocky trail as the deepening night replaced any vision left over from the dusk. Doyle and I were in the center of the sixteen-man column, the position from which we could respond to a "Guns up!" call from either end. It was on nights like this that I relished the best part of being a gunner. I never walked point, and I never walked tail.

Without warning, successive cracks of AK47 fire reverberated from the front of the column. Quickly the firing increased until it sounded like we'd made contact with a battalion. Everyone instinctively hit the ground. Doyle had a grasp on my foot. He repeated, "Oh God, oh God," in a panic. Bullets ricocheted all around, whining as they went overhead, and thudding into the earth nearby.

"Guns up! Guns up! Guns up!" The call sounded more urgent as each man picked it up and passed it back. I was already moving, crouching, stumbling, and running into the darkness ahead.

I felt an arm under my foot, then a curse. I started up a small knoll. Now I could see muzzle flashes.

"Get down!"

"Lay down some fire!" It sounded like the lieutenant's voice.

I fell to the ground just on the other side of the small knoll and started firing at the flashes directly ahead. Immediately, more flashes opened up from our left. I carried a fifty-round belt in the gun at all times. The ammo was gone quickly. I turned and screamed for more. No one was there.

"Doyle! I need ammo!"

Enemy fire increased on our left flank. I tore a 100-round belt from around my shoulders and loaded the gun. An enemy machine gun opened up on the left flank and a bit below us. Our high ground was saving us. I started firing at the enemy gun, hitting low at first, then walking my tracers up to the target. The green tracers of the enemy gun arced high into the dark sky, then ceased.

"You got him!" someone shouted.

Bullets thudded and flattened all around me. I crawled back over the knoll for cover, and then a sudden, unaccountable silence cloaked the battlefield. I wasn't sure which was worse. At least when they were shooting I knew where they were.

We backed up twenty meters, moving like blind men to our new position. There we sat in a perimeter and waited nervously for the safety of sunlight. I passed the word around the perimeter for Doyle. He finally showed up, mumbling something about falling into a hole. I decided to wait until morning to talk about his disappearance. Part of me wanted to punch his lights out, but I knew I should give him a chance to explain. I wanted him to know that men had been shot for less in Vietnam. Morning finally arrived.

I woke him up with a solid thump to his helmeted head.

"You better have a good reason you fat little—"

"I fell into a crater! One of those B-52 craters! It knocked my glasses off! By the time I found 'em, we stopped firing!" I pondered his excuse, trying to see a lie in his face.

"Honest!" he said, holding up his right hand as if he was swearing in.

"I want to believe you, Doyle. I almost got killed last night because I didn't have an A-gunner. Life and death are about a hair apart in this armpit of the world. You have to be dependable."

"I am. I swear! I fell in a hole!"

I paused, staring at his dirty, chubby face.

"Okay. I'll drop it." I wanted to believe Doyle. I liked him. He was a little scared of being a gunner, but he was quick to laugh and as jolly as a man could be over here.

We searched for bodies but came up empty. I felt an odd sense of disappointment. Although I may have killed someone, only confirmed counted, and I had no confirmed kills. I wanted one badly. It didn't make sense to me. I didn't even go hunting when I could have back home because I didn't like shooting animals. Yet here I was itching to blow some North Vietnamese into pieces.

Sam found traces of blood, and Swift Eagle found a Chinese Communist grenade. ChiComs looked like the old potato masher. Chief said they were more concussion than shrapnel.

The sun seemed to wrap itself in last night's clouds; the rain was near. The lieutenant and the gunny pinpointed a pimple on the grid map for a resupply LZ. Three hours closer to the mountains, the tiring march ended on a small rocky hill. We set up a quick perimeter. Sudsy spit out the coordinates into his radio.

I carved out a small niche in the ground and chowed down. Soon the backfiring echo of a Huey gunship penetrated the hot, still air. It banked sharply, circled our position, then made a larger circle, trying to draw enemy fire. A CH-46 helicopter floated in after the Huey finished checking out the LZ.

"Stand by for cover fire!" Swift Eagle screamed across the top of the hill. Four men unloaded supplies, and the chopper lifted off without drawing fire.

I tried to keep my attention on the surrounding hills, but it wasn't easy. I had a feeling that mail came with that chopper, and I wanted to hear from home so bad I was ready to ask the chief about smoke signals.

"Your manners are sadly deficient, as always," said a voice from behind me. "Well, aren't you going to invite me into your home?"

I turned, already recognizing the voice. "Chan!" I jumped to my feet and we traded bear hugs. "God, it's good to see you!"

"I presumed it would be. I find I'm curiously pleased by your presence also, but I'd rather be back at China Beach."

"China Beach! You mean there really is such a place?"

"Oh, it's nice, too. It's like being back in the world. White beach, beautiful blue water. You barely hear the artillery." He looked around quizzically. "Hey, where's Red?"

"He's dead, Chan. I'm the gunner now."

Chan removed his helmet. He slumped down as if I'd let the air out of him.

"I don't know what to say." He looked dazed. "What . . . How did he . . . I just can't believe it!" He grimaced as if in pain.

"Yeah. I know."

"When?"

"Right after you left. That first night. We set up an ambush, and Red opened up first. He got about a twenty-round burst off and that was it. Two AK rounds hit him right here." I pointed to my cheek just under the eye. Chan's eyes looked frosty. He lowered his head. I wasn't sure if he was praying or just fighting back tears. Then I felt that familiar lump swelling up inside my throat. I wiped away the first tear and tried to talk.

"This is Doyle. He's my A-gunner. He's boot."

Chan looked up, slightly teary-eyed, then stood and shook hands with Doyle.

"Heard a lot about you, Chan," Doyle said with a friendly handshake.

"I'm taking over as A-gunner, Doyle," Chan said. "The lieutenant informed me that you're now assigned to the chief's squad. Just temporarily until some replacements arrive; then you're back with us." I couldn't tell if Doyle was glad or sad at the news.

Corporal Swift Eagle ended the awkward moment when he emerged abruptly with the mail.

He tossed us five letters. Three were mine. Doyle got the other two. We ripped them open and started reading.

"It's funny, the conception people have of this war," Doyle said with a chuckle. "My girl wants to know if I'm in a fort." He laughed.

"Valerie's mother"—Chan paused and looked at the ground, shaking his head as if in disbelief—"Valerie's mother," he began again, "told Valerie that I was over here having the time of my life chasing little Vietnamese girls."

"That figures," I said. "Listen to this. 'Dear Son: Your dad and I worry about you in that awful place. I think of you and Chan in your little pup tent camped under the stars each night and pray for your safety.' "

"Chan, why didn't you put up the tent?" Doyle asked sarcastically. Chan began to laugh. His laugh was contagious. I started laughing too; it was like old times again.

Jackson strolled over to us with his beacon-light smile already on.

"Man, you can sure tell the laughers are together again. I bet you two laugh through this whole war. I never saw two grown men laugh so much."

Chan gained control long enough to stand up and slap Jackson on the back.

"It's good to see you again, Smilin'." Chan turned to Doyle as if he were introducing Jackson. "This is the happiest smile in Southeast Asia."

"The gunny wants one of you guys to come get your C-rats," Jackson said. "I think you better hurry; we're movin' out." He turned away to a chorus of boos.

Twenty minutes later our packs were on our backs, heavy with new food. We got more ammo than we wanted to carry. I felt ten pounds heavier as the walk began. It started raining. An odd glow covered the mountains to our front, a yellowish tint like that given by cheap sunglasses. Then the yellowish tint disappeared as enormous black and gray clouds rolled sheets of rain across the mountain peaks. The rain lashed against our tiny column so powerfully that for an instant we stopped, shielding our faces. The rain changed from lukewarm to ice cold.

By nightfall the pounding storm had beaten against my helmet until all I could feel was a concussion-size headache. We crossed a swift, chest-deep river, carrying our weapons above our heads. Once on the other side word filtered back to set up a perimeter. Chan and I sat down shivering in the mud.

"What are you stopping for?"

I peered through the water pouring off my helmet to see Corporal Swift Eagle standing over me.

"They passed the word back to set up a perimeter."

"How are we supposed to hear Charlie over that river?" The chief didn't wait for my answer, possibly because the question wasn't directed at me. He sloshed off in the direction of the lieutenant's CP. In ten minutes we moved another fifty meters away from the river. I settled into a nice soft bed of mud, pulled myself inside my flak jacket like a turtle, and fell asleep while Chan took first watch.

At 2300 hours Chan shook me away from a blazing fireplace and a beautiful lady I was just getting to know.

"I thought you might want to know you're drowning," he whispered. I didn't want to open my eyes, but I did.

He was right. The rain hadn't stopped, and I was quickly going under. I felt cold and stiff. Before I maneuvered my head out of the mud Chan whispered again. "Somethin's up!"

I sat up to see what Chan was looking at. I heard someone step in water. Then the muffled thud of a plastic M16 falling into the mud. The rain was still too heavy to see more than four or five feet on either side. White zigzagging lightning bolts streaked across the black sky. Jackson and Striker were standing with their packs on, ten feet to our left.

"Chan, what's going on?"

"I don't know."

"Jackson," I whispered.

"What?" came the reply from the darkness.

"What's going on?"

"Saddle up."

"That's just outstanding," Chan said. "They're moving out without us!"

"I can't stand all this concern over my life," I added as we scrambled to get our gear on. I crawled around in the mud on my hands and knees to make sure we weren't leaving anything, then sloshed over to Jackson.

"Why didn't you tell us we were moving out?" I asked.

"I thought Sudsy told you."

"What's up?"

"Sudsy got word that a gook battalion, maybe more, is coming this way."

"Did you say 'more'?"

"Maybe more. Comin' our way. Sudsy said we're getting our butts out of here, ASAP."

Chan adjusted his pack straps, then patted himself on his shoulders and chest.

"Oh, no!" he gasped. "I left the gun ammo!" He raced back to retrieve the belts of machine-gun ammo. The column started moving out.

"Chan! Hurry up! We're moving out!"

"I found them!"

"Hurry up! They're already gone!"

"Okay, okay!"

We caught up to the column as it moved back toward the river. A violent thunderclap followed closely behind each brilliant streak of lightning. We started back across the jungle river. This time the water reached my chin. The current swept Striker's feet from under him. He went under. Jackson grabbed him by one arm and pulled him up. His helmet had been swept away, but he had managed to hold on to his rifle.

As we reached the river bank each man pulled the man behind him out by grasping his rifle. Jackson pulled Chan to solid ground, then Chan turned and held out the butt of his rifle. I grabbed it with a shaking left hand and staggered up the muddy bank, balancing the gun over my right shoulder. I turned to help the man behind me. No one was there.

"Chan!"

Chan turned to see what I wanted.

"Are we the last ones in the column?" A brilliant rod of lightning showed the river empty of everything but raging whitecaps.

"I guess so."

"The gun ain't supposed to be on the end of the column!"

"Quit crying and hurry up. Or would you prefer being a column all by ourselves? I'll get behind you."

The incessant rain felt as though it was coming down harder than before. My skin was wrinkled and freezing. We followed a barely discernible trail running parallel to the river. Sagging and draping trees, bent from the storm, formed an eerie wet tunnel.

Just as I caught up to Jackson, Chan tapped me on the shoulder.

"Pssst!" I turned to look back, nearly clobbering Chan with the butt of the M60 resting on my shoulder.

"Yeah?"

"Are you sure we're the last ones in the column?"

I stopped and looked back into Chan's face. "You know we're the last ones in the column. What's the matter with you?"

Chan gave me a little shove.

"Keep moving!"

I was beginning to think his normally witty mind was waterlogged. Five yards later he tapped me on the shoulder again.

"Pssst!"

"Chan, I don't—"

"Pass the word up. We picked up an extra squad." His voice was calm. Too calm. I peeked over my shoulder.

"What'd you say?"

"We picked up an extra squad." I looked back.

"Are you . . . ?" A vivid streak of lightning danced across the pitch-black sky, revealing a paralyzing sight. Twenty meters back, the safari-helmeted heads of at least ten NVA bobbed along behind us. My heart stopped. My feet didn't. I quick-stepped up to Jackson and tapped him on the shoulder. I suddenly felt near panic and couldn't speak. I inhaled all the air I could shove down my lungs then blew it out. Why hadn't they already blown us away? If we could see them with each lightning bolt, why couldn't they see us? I tapped Jackson again.

"Pass the word up. We picked up an extra squad!" He looked over his shoulder.

"What?"

"No kiddin' man! Pass it up! Hurry!"

A thousand questions raced through my mind, but none of the answers made any sense. Where was their point man? The only possible answer was that they believed they were behind their own men. I felt very cold. I started shivering uncontrollably. I bit my lip until it bled in an effort to snap out of it. These things didn't happen in real life. I remembered the movie about D-day, the scene where Americans and Germans passed each other without noticing. That was a movie. This was real.

The next minute dwindled by painfully slowly. With each crack of lightning the fear that they would recognize the shape of our helmets increased. Jackson looked over his shoulder and covered his mouth.

"Prepare to fall off to the side of the trail. Hit 'em as they pass."

My heart sank into my stomach. I passed the word to Chan. I tried to take the gun off my shoulder without being conspicuous. I only had a fifty-round belt linked up. Striker fell off to the left of the trail, then Jackson. I dropped to the side of the trail. Chan followed. Chan pulled the pin on a grenade and held the spoon in with his hand. I pointed the gun back down the trail and started praying all this mud and rain wouldn't jam it.

Then the incredible happened. Fifteen meters back the NVA fell off to the side of the trail too. I didn't understand it. A shot of lightning hit a tree nearby. Chan jumped, nearly dropping the grenade. We looked at each other in disbelief.

"Jackson! Pass the word up. They dropped off too."

A few moments later word came back to move out. Panic gripped my stomach. I think I started to urinate; either that, or the rain was getting warmer. I felt ashamed and tightened my stomach to stop myself. We stood up, bowing our heads in an effort to look shorter and hide the shape of our helmets from the flashing thunder. I kept the gun on my hip this time.

"Pssst. They're following!" Chan's whisper sent visions of hot lead ripping through my back. What are we doing? If the lieutenant was back here, he'd come up with a better plan than move on. Suddenly some grim possibilities became graphically clear. We might be in the middle of that NVA battalion. I felt a tap on my shoulder.

"They're staying about twenty meters back."

"Why don't you walk backward and show off that Chinese face?" He didn't laugh.

The column veered right, off the trail. We started moving faster. The terrain got steeper with each step. We were going up a hill covered with thick brush and thornbushes. Jackson's voice came from the darkness ahead.

"Run for it!"

"Run Chan!"

The thorns tore through my trousers, ripping at my soggy skin. Rain smashed against leaves and brush, sounding like grease in a frying pan. I stumbled and crawled and clawed up the dripping hill in near panic, sliding back one step for every two forward. Near the top Jackson stuck out his big friendly hand and pulled me to him. Chan was right on my heels, still clutching his grenade. Swift Eagle appeared beside Jackson.

"Hurry up! Set up the gun!" I fell to the ground and

took aim back down the hill. The chief pulled the pin on a grenade and screamed, "Now!" On that command everyone threw grenades down the hill. I opened up with the gun, firing into the darkness, probably hitting nothing more than rain. Fifteen sharp explosions rattled the bottom of the hill. Then silence. Only the rain could be heard. The night ended in a nervous perimeter around the top of our newfound friend, an unknown hill in a land of unknown hills.

The hot sun was more welcome than usual. The morning body search brought negative results, except for Jackson, who found a nest of snakes. One particularly aggressive snake chased him uphill for fifteen meters. It was the fastest I'd ever seen a man run uphill, especially Jackson, who wasn't usually in a hurry to go anywhere.

For no sane reason the day started by crossing the same river for the third time. We did it just in time, too— some of us had almost dried out from the night before. After three hours' humping, we finally reached the first of the densely forested mountains that I had gazed at and curiously dreaded since my first day on the bridge.

The temperature dropped ten degrees as we entered the cover of the massive, sheltering trees. We climbed up a conspicuously well used trail for two thousand meters, when the column stopped. The point man found an American Schwinn bicycle lying on the side of the trail. I knew they used bikes to haul supplies down the Ho Chi Minh Trail but knowing they were using American bikes bothered me.

Thirty meters from the Schwinn the sharp single crack of an AK47 ripped through leaves and branches and splintered into a proud old oak tree on my left and just above my head. The column dropped to one knee, scanning the canopy of tall trees in front and above.

"Why me? Why's the little scumbag takin' a potshot at me?" I was talking to myself as much as to Chan.

"You take things too personally," said Chan, staring at the treetops above. "If you'd give the gun to someone else, they'd probably be more than happy to shoot at him. I don't know what you're worrying about anyway. The little scumbags, as you've aptly named the enemy, couldn't hit a barn from the inside. If they aim at you, I'm the one who's in trouble."

"You're probably right. I feel much better now."

Chan turned his head away, then looked back at me suspiciously out of the corner of one eye. Every twenty to forty meters up the trail another sniper round slapped through the leaves nearby. By the third round no one bothered to duck. The trail led around the mountainside to a heavily wooded overhanging cliff. A picturesque waterfall cascaded from above, smashing into a beautiful small round lake three hundred feet below. The trail skirted into a natural indentation in the mountains, allowing us to avoid the plummeting waterfall, then descended into a valley and back up another steep mountainside.

At a point where the trail leveled off, we entered a tiny village of four grass huts. Inside the first, Sam found three half-empty bottles of Vietnamese beer and three bowls of rice. The second hut held two tons of rice, thousands of rounds of AK47 ammo, and enough C-4 plastique explosive to blow up a major portion of Da Nang. The third was empty, but in the fourth was the big surprise of the day.

The fourth hut was a shelter over a dirt stairway that led down and into the side of the mountain. Candles were burning, providing the only light in the damp underground room, which looked to be about thirty feet long and fifteen feet wide. It was furnished with ten bloodstained, six-foot-long wooden tables. Chan found a small wooden box filled with medical instruments, morphine, and bandages.

"It would give me immense pleasure for my premed

class at Tennessee to see this!" Chan fingered the instruments as if he'd found gold.

"Okay, let's get out," Lieutenant Campbell said. "We're going to blow it!"

We continued to search the area while the demolitions were set. Fifty meters from the underground hospital we stumbled across another incredible find. Built across a small ravine was a replica of Truoi Bridge, with every bunker, including some concertina wire to practice crawling through. The setup was detailed. I wondered how many months they must have practiced the attack on the bridge.

We destroyed what we found and, to everyone's relief, headed back down the trail and out of the mountains. Part of me wanted to stick around under the cool shade of the giant trees, but my sane half realized we had probably come upon a battalion headquarters. I couldn't figure out why we were there, or what sixteen Marines were supposed to do if we did find that many NVA. I had heard Sudsy talking to B Company so I knew they too were roaming about out here somewhere, but what good would they do us in this kind of terrain? We could kiss it goodbye before help found us.

By 1500 hours we had crossed the same river for the fourth time and reached an area of rolling, rock-strewn hills with no trees in sight. The temperature zoomed well over 110 degrees, with not a single cloud to slow the merciless rays.

A faraway whistle stuck in my ear. I felt groggy from the heat. At first I thought I was hearing things, but it quickly grew louder, too loud to be my imagination. It became shrill, like a dog whistle. Whatever it was, it was coming fast, bewilderingly fast. The column stopped. We looked up, all eyes gazing in dread, all mouths gawking in disbelief. I pulled my shoulders up, trying to cover my head as my knees started to bend instinctively with the approaching whistle. Then I actually saw them. Three small black objects blurring by twenty feet overhead, forcing air out of their way like tiny jets. The sight froze us in place. Then like a rocket burning out, the sound stopped and a ripping explosion followed.

"Hit the dirt!"

Shrapnel whished by. I clutched the shuddering earth. Rocks landed all around. More whistles. I could hear someone cursing. Sudsy. Then the lieutenant. Someone tugged on my foot. I pulled my face out of the dirt and looked back. Chan's face was spotted with bits of loam that were sticking to his sweat. "Did you see that?"

"Yeah!" I answered. "I didn't know you could see artillery rounds."

"I didn't either. But it's logical, presuming your position in proximity—"

"The people who see 'em probably don't get to tell anybody," I interrupted.

"Precisely."

I heard the closing whistle of another artillery round. I held on to my helmet and started praying. A shuddering explosion ripped into the earth thirty meters away. Then another. A rock the size of a bowling ball crashed into the ground beside me with a back-breaking thud. I prayed faster. The explosions stopped.

"You stupid son of a—! You're shelling Alpha Company!" Lieutenant Campbell's curse could have been heard in Phu Bai without the aid of Sudsy's radio.

It was over. Someone cursed the Marine Corps. Someone else cursed Vietnam. Shots echoed through the steaming heat. I saw flashes on the crest of a barren hill one hundred meters to the left.

"Guns up! Guns up! Guns up!"

I grabbed the gun and ran zigzagging toward the voice as little clouds of dust spit out of the ground around me. Then I heard the gun. "That's an M60!" I dove to the ground, flipped the bipod legs down, and took aim at a wavering stream of orange tracers floating my way.

Chan slammed to the earth beside me, knocking a solid grunt of air out of him. I opened up. Chan linked up a belt of ammo like a pro, holding it out of the dirt with his left hand and firing his M16 with his right. The enemy tracers stopped. I kept firing in twenty-round bursts.

"We got 'em ducking!" Chan shouted as he linked up another belt.

"Get 'em, Johnnie!" someone screamed nearby, then yelped like a cowboy. "Blow 'em off that hill!"

"Cease fire! Cease fire! Cease fire! It's B Company! They're Marines!" Sudsy screamed. I released my sweaty grip on the gun, and my insides churned in panic.

"Did I kill any Marines?" I shouted as I jumped to my feet and ran at Sudsy. He kept talking into the radio. "Are they hit?" I grabbed him by the shoulder. "What's going on, Sudsy?"

"They thought we were gooks!" He turned from me and spoke into the field phone again. "No, that is negative. No one was hit in Alpha Company." He looked back at me, pulling the phone away from his mouth. "They thought we were gooks! They called in arty and opened up!"

"That's brilliant! Just brilliant!"

"Saddle up!" Lieutenant Campbell shouted, his grimacing face red with anger. He jerked the field phone out of Sudsy's hands, turned Sudsy around with a push, and pulled the antenna on the PRC-25, strapped to Sudsy's back, all the way out. "Alpha one, Alpha one, this is Alpha two . . . over!"

We started off again. This time back toward the mountains. I was beginning to feel like a dusty green yo-yo. If we crossed that river one more time, I would know for sure that everyone had lost their minds. Dusk, the time of the day I was learning to hate, crept up on us before we reached the river. The column stopped. The silhouette of Jackson turned its head and covered its mouth.

"Psst. We're setting up a perimeter."

Before I turned to give the word to Chan, an automatic burst of AK fire sent us diving for the ground. Fiery green tracers sputtered out of the darkness ahead. I started to move into position to return fire. Bullets pounded the earth around me. I froze stiff waiting for the pain. Hot whining lead sucked the air near my right ear, and dirt stung my face. It sounded like hundreds of bullets whistling and flattening into the earth around me. I covered my helmet with my hands and waited for the bullet that would scream through my skull. I didn't want to die like this. At least I wanted to be shooting back. I looked up from the dirt. A tracer round hit close to my face. The sizzling phosphorescent tip broke from the lead and fried into my flesh. It felt like someone had put a cigarette out on my cheek. I started to move again. Chan grabbed my pack and shoved me down. Then silence. It was over. A painful moan came from the front of the column.

"Corpsman!"

"Corpsman up! We got wounded up here!"

"Okay, let's get in a perimeter!" I looked up to see who was barking orders. Swift Eagle stood over me.

"Chief, who got hit?"

"Thomas."

"Who?"

"The point man."

"Is it bad?"

"Don't know. Sam said two in the belly."

"He's the only one hit out of all that?"

"Looks that way. I want the gun facing the direction they fired from. I think we walked into the flank squad of a large unit."

Somewhere to my right I could hear Sudsy calling for a medevac chopper. Twenty minutes later helicopter rotors whirred overhead. The gunny popped a green flare, lighting up a landing zone for the chopper.

"We should just carry a portable neon sign to mark our exact location," Chan murmured.

He had a point, but Thomas was a dead man if we didn't get him to a hospital unit. His chances didn't sound good even with a medevac. I didn't know him very well. Chan thought he was married. The moment the chopper touched ground three men gently lifted the wounded Marine in. Gunny stomped out the flare. My night vision was gone. I was totally dependent upon my hearing. I didn't like it.

A few minutes later someone on my left whispered, "Saddle up." I couldn't believe my ears.

"We'll be stumbling around like blind men out there."

"Let's write LBJ," Chan said.

"Okay by me."

The perimeter turned into a column, and we plodded into the blackness ahead. Mosquitoes were tearing me up. I wanted to splash some bug juice on but didn't dare put the gun on my shoulder. I was scared, and I wanted to be able to pull that trigger fast. Somehow, Jackson, the new point man, stumbled onto a trail. We followed it up a large rocky hill, down the other side, and halfway up another that was overgrown with scrubby bushes. At that point, it leveled off and skirted around the hill. We followed it for fifty meters and stopped.

"Set up a perimeter on the side of the hill," whispered a voice. I was too tired to care. No one had had any real sleep in days. I was exhausted.

Swift Eagle grabbed my arm. "Put the gun down there." He pointed to a large bush ten meters on the downhill side of the trail. "We're ambushing this trail, but the flank is all yours."

Chan and I set the gun up behind the large bush facing downhill. Within ten minutes we were sound asleep. I knew it was wrong, and so did Chan, but staying awake felt impossible. The moment I leaned back against the hillside, a heavy dreamless sleep fell over me like a powerful drug.

"All right, listen up!" It was Corporal Swift Eagle. "The lieutenant's ticked off today. People fell asleep on line last night."

"Did you fall asleep, too, Chief?" I asked naively. His piercing black eyes were harsher than the answer I didn't get. He turned and started to walk back up the hill then stopped and turned back to us.

"Prepare to saddle up."

Chan slapped me on the helmet.

"You're insinuating the Warrior could fall asleep on line."

"Saddle up! We're moving out right now!"

"Somebody sounds overly anxious this morning," mused Chan.

Two hours later that statement haunted us. We force-marched farther and faster than we ever had before. I felt a sense of urgency in our pace. We finally reached an area with a flat terrain and small patches of trees that looked like undernourished pines. There I saw the first signs of civilization I'd seen in seventeen days: four grass huts huddled together. Two hundred meters beyond the huts we passed what appeared to be a Buddhist shrine, then we reached a rarely used dirt road that seemed to snake off to nowhere.

Chan tapped me from behind. "Did you hear that?"

"Yeah! Now I do. What is it?"

"Sounds like a tank."

Around the first bend in the dusty road, parked behind and under a clump of trees, sat two huge American tanks. One already had its engine rumbling.

"Now that's the life," Chan said enviously. "Why didn't we get into tanks?"

"The tour guide said we'd see the country better on foot."

"These guys go out once every six months whether they have to or not."

"Hurry up! Saddle up!" Lieutenant Campbell shouted. "Get aboard!"

"No thanks," Striker said louder than he meant to.

"Move it, Marine!"

Sam the Blooper Man pulled me up and onto the nearest steel monster. I pulled Chan up. A moment later the ride began. It was exhilarating. It was the first time in my life I'd ever been on a tank. Two hundred meters down the road two more of the big machines pulled out in front of us, kicking up thick clouds of dust that turned us all beige.

"Wow, man!" Sam hit me with a sharp elbow. "This looks big. You might get your first confirmed today."

CONFIRMED

"Do you grunts have any idea just how bad you smell?" the baby-faced tanker shouted over the rumbling diesel. "How long have you been in the bush?"

"Seventeen days!" I shouted back.

"It becomes less repugnant after a couple of weeks!" Chan added.

The tanker looked at Chan questioningly. "They told me you guys stay in the bush two months at a shot."

"So they say," I replied.

"Made any contact?"

"We made contact every single day."

The young tanker turned completely around inside the turret hatch, banging his elbow on his .50-caliber machine gun. He winced, then cursed.

"I must bang myself on this thing ten times a day." He rubbed his elbow. "Did you say you made contact for seventeen days straight?"

"Yeah," I said.

"Wow! I haven't seen a Charlie yet."

I suddenly felt rather salty. Downright pleased with myself. Another cloud of dust from the two tanks ahead settled on us like a brown fog. It stuck to our sweaty faces and turned instantly into mud. I felt like I was in World War II, racing toward Rommel over the desert for a tank battle.

"Chan, do you still have your little camera?"

"Of course."

"Let's take a picture of the tank behind us."

"Oh, brother. Look, Baby-san, is it a permanent ingredient of your basic nature to become excited about everything?"

"Just take the picture, will ya? And I want a copy when we get home."

Chan snapped the picture just as our tank pulled off the road and slammed on the brakes. The gunny jumped off first, shouting as he landed, "Get off! Move it! Move it!"

I jumped down and stumbled into a column already forming.

Freckle-faced Sudsy trotted up to us. "Lieutenant wants to know if you'd mind switching to an M16 for this sweep? We got a gunner with no gun in Third Platoon, and they're setting up a blocking action for the sweep."

"He actually asked me?"

"Yeah." Sudsy blew a small bubble from what had to be an ancient piece of bubble gum. "He said you gunners are a strange breed, once you get used to a gun."

"Well, I sure ain't that used to it yet."

"Ol' Red sure was," Sudsy said. "The guy you're giving it to is up front." He turned and started back toward the front of the column with Chan and me following.

"What did you mean, Red sure was?" I shouted over the rumbling of diesel engines.

"The lieutenant tried to get the gun away from Red once when we were up at Hai Van Pass and ol' Red wouldn't let him have it."

Lieutenant Campbell looked happy to see us. He was talking to the gunner from Third Platoon.

"Thanks, John. We'll get your gun back to you right after this sweep. This M16 is going to be a lot easier to carry across that field." He handed me the plastic M16 as I gave the M60 to the Third Platoon gunner. I felt like I was abandoning an old, trusted friend. The little M16 rifle felt like a toy. The lieutenant held Chan's rifle while he removed four hundred rounds from around his neck.

"Is this a major operation, Lieutenant?" Chan asked.

"A spotter plane saw a lot of fresh dirt out there. It looks like they may be doing some digging." He looked at me and smiled. "I bet it feels good to get rid of that gun, doesn't it?"

"No, sir."

"What?"

"I'm better with the gun than the M16."

"He's telling the truth, Lieutenant," Chan added. "Don't ask me why. Our instructor at Lejeune said he was a natural gunner."

"I'll get it back to you as soon as this sweep is over." His face looked happily puzzled. He patted me on the back and turned to look for Sudsy.

A few minutes later the sweep started across a treeless field. The huge steel monsters led the way, churning deep paths into the moist earth for fifty meters. Having tanks in front of us was a new phenomenon. Hiding behind a thirty-ton caterpillar with cannon gave me a new sense of confidence.

That confidence was short-lived. We reached a ledge with a twenty-five-foot drop that no tank could possibly negotiate. The tanks lined up along the ledge overlooking a relatively flat, unwooded area. Small ridges of earth covered with brush dotted the terrain like some gigantic gopher had pushed up long mounds of dirt.

We climbed down the embankment, fanned out on line, and proceeded cautiously across the field. Suddenly my foot sank into an ankle-deep hole and I fell forward. I caught myself with my rifle. I realized immediately what I'd done. The barrel of my rifle, the notoriously jammable M16, was rammed full of mud.

I wanted to tell someone, but we were past the point of talking. Visions of meeting the enemy, pulling the trigger, and nothing happening flashed through my head. Then an even worse vision of the barrel blowing up in my face flashed across my mind.

One hundred meters across the field I smelled a faint whiff of smoke. I wasn't sure if anyone else smelled it or not. Chan, looking straight ahead, moved slowly fifteen feet to my right. I looked quickly to my left. Jackson had come to a stop. He was looking down into a large hole in the ground. Ten feet in front of us was the first of the long mounds of dirt, six feet tall and about thirty feet long.

I didn't like the embankment in front of me. I looked at it, then at Jackson, and then back at the embankment.

"Ohhh, gooks!"

Jackson turned away from the hole and jumped backward. Three shots followed in quick succession. I dropped to one knee. Green plastic flew from the hole, followed by a small cloud of smoke. Three men jumped out of the hole carrying rifles. I opened fire as they scrambled over the embankment. My rifle worked! The last one staggered at the top of the embankment then fell forward to the other side. We ran forward, taking cover against the embankment.

I pulled a grenade off my cartridge belt, pulled the pin, and tossed it over the embankment. A moment later Chan did the same. We leaned against the dirt, bracing for the explosions. I put in a new clip of ammo. Suddenly I realized that they could be doing the same thing. My grenade exploded, then Chan's. I ran around to the end of the mound and fired the entire clip full automatic into the prone bodies of two of the NVA and dove back behind the mound.

I yanked the empty clip out and jammed another full one into the M16. Adrenaline shot through my system. My hands were shaking. I gasped for air like a panting dog. I pulled another grenade off my flak jacket, straightened the pin, pulled, and threw it over the mound. Gunpowder smoke filled the air. My second grenade exploded. I darted around the end of the mound again, unleashed an eighteen-round burst, firing from the hip, and jumped back behind the mound.

Marines were screaming something twenty yards to my left. I pulled out the empty clip and reloaded. My fear had been replaced by the sheer thrill that comes with a life-and-death situation. The thought of getting shot when I stepped around the mound had not even occurred to me until Swift Eagle slid in beside me breathing hard and looking mad.

"Don't fire that way again! Some of your rounds almost hit the First Platoon. They're flanking the gooks. Are you trying to get yourself killed, boot?"

"I don't know what happened, Chief. I just really got into it."

"You keep playing John Wayne and you're not going to make it out of here."

"Cease fire! We're movin' in!" Lieutenant Campbell ran over to Swift Eagle and me. "Okay, Chief, let's see what we bagged." Swift Eagle turned and shouted, "Give us cover! We're going in for a count!"

We ran around the mound and spread out. I could see one body but not the other two. I wondered if they got away—but how could anyone survive all those grenades?

"Here's one, Lieutenant!" Swift Eagle shouted and pointed at a body I didn't see.

We moved forward cautiously.

"Are you sure there were just three?" Lieutenant Campbell asked.

"That's all I saw, Lieutenant," I said, not daring to move my eyes from straight ahead.

"Where's the third?" I looked to my right. Swift Eagle stood over a khaki-clad corpse. "This one's been shot. He's yours, John." The Indian's expression didn't change. Business as usual. "Looks like a kid."

I walked over to the chief and stared down at the dead man. He was face up. His single-shot Russian SKS rifle lay beside him. It was a grotesque scene. Singularly odd.

The skull was split in half, like a watermelon. The morbidly yellow face lay fully intact but separate from the rest of the skull and looking up with a ludicrous expression of almost childish shock. I felt riveted to the ground. I wanted to pull my eyes away but couldn't. I could hear voices drifting in and out around me. The gray brains of the dead man slid lazily onto the ground, carried by a tiny river of dark-red blood. My mouth tasted like bitter cotton. Sweat streamed out of every pore on my body.

"Quit admiring your work and see if he's got any papers on him." I didn't recognize the voice, but it struck a nerve. I turned around slowly. By the time I faced the voice, tears were trying to force their way out of my eyes. I dropped the M16 and started toward a short, stocky corporal with a thick brown mustache. Someone grabbed me in a bear hug.

"Don't!" It was Chan. "It's not worth it!" He turned to the corporal. "What platoon are you in?"

"First."

"I would suggest that you take your posterior back to First Platoon before I decide to let him put his foot up it."

"I gave that jerk an order to check the gook's papers, and he better—" The corporal stopped in mid-sentence with the help of a pincer-like grip from a large reddish-brown hand now attached to the back of his neck. Swift Eagle turned the corporal's head toward him like it was a hand puppet. The big Indian nodded his head in the direction of First Platoon, released the corporal's neck, and stared down at him with his icy black eyes. The corporal slid away like a wounded dog with his tail between his legs. Not another word was spoken.

Chan released me from the bear hug. I walked back over to the dead face. For a moment I felt sick, but it passed. I leaned down to search his pockets, holding my breath to keep from getting sick. I found a thin brown wallet wrapped in green plastic. I tossed it to Chan.

"Check this out."

I took a deep breath and searched his shirt pockets. They were caked with quickly drying blood. From inside his left shirt pocket I pulled out a scratched-up Timex watch.

"He was only fourteen," mumbled Chan, still looking at a paper from the dead man's wallet.

"Fourteen?"

"Yeah."

I didn't have to turn to see who made the next remark. "Well, at least you know there's someone in this war younger than you are, Baby-san." The coarse laugh that followed identified Sam the Blooper Man.

"Hey, Doc!" shouted the gunny. He was leaning over one of the NVA. "Get over here. This one's still alive."

Doc jogged over to the gunny. I wandered over to see how bad he was. He was shot through the back and out through the chest and stomach. One ear was shot off and bleeding badly.

"He might make it if we medevac him." Doc peered down under his glasses at the bleeding NVA. He sounded disinterested. His Massachusetts arrogance showing itself again. He'd made no secret of the fact that he joined the Navy to stay as far away from Vietnam as possible and to avoid being drafted into the Army. He considered himself a genius and Marines cretins. In all his genius he neglected to discover that the Marines don't have medics. The Navy provides corpsmen for that duty. It felt good to see the arrogant snob as dirty as the rest of us.

Chan strolled over to the wounded NVA, bent down on one knee, and checked his wounds. "He can make it, Gunny. If we hurry. The wound's not sucking."

"Thanks, Chan," Gunny said. He turned and looked up at Doc. "You better watch it, Squid. You don't want to get on my bad side. Sudsy! Let's get a medevac in here ASAP!" He spit a shot of tobacco on Doc's boot. "Sorry."

"Check this out!" Jackson appeared from the other side of the mound holding something in the palms of his hands. "I went down in that hole to see what was smokin'. These guys were smokin' dope!"

I'd never seen marijuana before except for a couple of goofy movies in high school. Sam forced out a hoarse laugh.

"Now that's a bad trip, man!" An odd smile spread across Sam's pitted face.

"Hurry up and get that medevac in here, Sudsy!" Gunny shouted.

"He's on his way, Gunny."

Jackson flipped the marijuana into the air and did a quick-step over to one of the dead men's SKS Russian sniper rifle. He laid his M16 down and snatched up the bolt-action Russian rifle.

"Who gets the rifles, Lieutenant?"

"John gets one."

"Can I have one? There's three of 'em here."

"I guess so. Make sure you tag it before that chopper gets here."

My eyes drifted back to the dead face. It looked even more yellow than before.

"Hurry up, John. Tag the SKS you want. It's single shot; you can bring that dude home when you rotate." Jackson's voice sounded far away.

"He doesn't feel well," Chan said. "I'll tag it for him."

"Fourteen. It's a shame, isn't it?" Someone put his hand on my shoulder. I managed to pull away from the dead face to see who was talking. His name was Jack Ellenwood, a corporal with the Third Platoon. He stood a good four inches taller than me. His face looked round but he wasn't chubby. Just the slow soothing tone of his voice calmed me. He sounded honestly regretful, as if he knew exactly how I felt. "You probably shouldn't stare at it any longer, John. As it is, I imagine you're going to remember this scene the rest of your life."

"How did you know my name?"

"You took over Red's gun, didn't you?"

"Yes."

"I've heard you're going to be as good as he was."

"No way. Red was a Marine's Marine. I could never be as hard-Corps as Red."

"I had a good friend who looked exactly like you when he got his first confirmed. Only difference was he puked. We came over together. I named my new baby after him. Want to see a picture?" Jack didn't wait for an answer. He took his helmet off and produced a thick black wallet. His face was already beaming with pride and he hadn't even found the picture yet. "Here. Here it is." He patted me on the back and gave up fighting back a giant grin. "Isn't he something?" It was the usual: a fat little baby on a blanket looking up.

"Yeah, he's great. What's his name?"

"Red."

I wasn't sure what to say. Finally I managed the only word that made any sense.

"Thanks, Jack."

"Are you married?"

"No," I said.

"That's good. Kamikazes shouldn't get married; besides, you don't look old enough."

"I'm not. Why 'kamikaze'?"

"That's what I call gung-ho gunners. All you're missing is the plane." He laughed. A hearty laugh. The kind that makes you feel good just to hear it. Then I felt a solid slap on the back of my flak jacket.

"Are you okay?" It was Chan.

"Yeah, I guess so. Chan, do you know Jack Ellenwood?"

"Third Platoon, right?"

"That's me." Jack stuck out his hand and Chan shook it.

"Thanks for talking to Baby-san."

"Pay no attention to him, Jack. Chan is my A-gunner and built-in big brother since boot camp."

"His mother asked me to take care of him." Chan's smirk nearly made me laugh.

"You know what's really bothering me?" I asked.

"What?" Jack said.

"I've been wanting to get my first confirmed. I mean, I wanted it like it was a game or some sort of competition. I wanted to kill another human being, and now I have, and he was all of fourteen years old."

"John," Chan said calmly.

"No, Chan, I mean it. I wanted a confirmed like I always wanted a touchdown and never got it. But that's not the worst of it. I just don't feel as bad about killing a kid as I should."

"How bad do you think you're supposed to feel? He'd have blown your brains out and bragged about it all the way to Hanoi," Jack said, then spit as if the thought had angered him. Chan slapped me on the shoulder.

"Why don't you get over there by yourself and read your Bible? You have to pray about it."

"Right now I don't feel like I have the right to open that book," I said.

Chan put his arm around my shoulder and walked me a couple of steps away.

"In Philippians God tells us to 'be anxious for nothing but in everything by prayer and supplication with thanksgiving let your requests be made known to God. And the peace of God which surpasses all comprehension, shall guard your hearts and your minds in Christ Jesus.' " Chan paused and looked me in the eye. "Look, buddy, I'm not trying to preach at you, but the word of God is the only thing that's going to help you."

"I don't want to hear that stuff right now!"

I couldn't believe I was actually barking at Chan when deep down I totally agreed with every word he had spoken. He looked at me patiently.

"Later," he said with a pat on the shoulder.

"Saddle up!" the old gunny bellowed like he meant it.

"Let's get a perimeter around this position. Choppers comin' in!" Gunny turned toward me. "Johnnie-boy, go get your gun."

"Don't call me Johnnie-boy!" I snapped. Immediately I was sorry. I liked the gunny, I wasn't mad at him. I wasn't sure what I was mad at, but I was angry enough to fight. The gunny looked shocked, then the leathery wrinkles tightened.

"Move it, PFC!" He turned back to the wounded NVA. I wanted to say I was sorry but I couldn't seem to force a friendly word out.

By the time I returned with my M60, the whirring rotors of the medevac chopper were bending the knee-level saw grass. A moment later the three bodies were loaded and we moved in column back toward the road. Four deuce-and-a-halfs sat waiting for us with engines running. The tanks had split up, with two leading the convoy and two bringing up the rear. I had no idea where we were going, but the general hope was Phu Bai.

The ride was bumpy and dusty. There wasn't much conversation. Nearly everyone in my truck had closed his eyes. Sometimes the tired faces of my comrades frightened me. They all looked so much older than they were, harder than they should have been. I was glad I couldn't see my own face. It no longer felt like the face of Baby-san.

We finally reached Truoi Bridge. I started getting my gear together, but the tiny convoy didn't stop. Streams of Vietnamese carrying everything from chickens to bicycles scurried off the road and out of the way. They were all headed south toward Da Nang. Probably refugees from Hue, I thought. It had to be over 110 degrees, yet some of the Vietnamese wore coats and shirts on top of shirts.

Soon Phu Bai was visible up ahead. If we didn't pull in to Phu Bai our other choices looked grim. Hue was a few miles farther up Highway 1, then Quang Tri, Khe Sanh, and a couple of other meat grinders I least wanted to visit. The convoy turned. A couple of the men sighed out loud. Then the excitement of civilization brought on some serious thoughts.

"Beer!"

"Women and beer!"

"Women?"

"Yeah, I heard there's a USO show at Phu Bai."

"Yeah, I heard that too from a corporal in Third Platoon. Australians!"

A few minutes later we piled out of the trucks in front of the same tent in which Chan and I had first met Big Red. Seemed like years ago, I thought. A group of ten boots, still dressed in stateside utilities, stood in formation nearby. They gawked at us like we'd just stepped off a spaceship. I remembered being on the other side of that look. It was frightening, yet thoroughly exciting.

I'd be a liar if I said I wasn't rather impressed with myself. I looked hard—so hard, in fact, that my baby face was barely noticeable. A grenade hung off every available space. Four hundred rounds of machine-gun ammo crisscrossed my flak jacket, which was no longer green but beige from the sun and dust. My NVA pack stood out among the tiny Marine Corps packs. A .45-caliber pistol hung low on my right hip. It was balanced by my K-bar on my left hip. Last, but anything but least, was the gun. It added that final homicidal ingredient.

"I look pretty bad, don't I?" I asked Chan.

"No worse than usual," he said with a smirk.

"No. I mean I look pretty hard-Corps, don't I?" I said chuckling.

"Surprisingly hard-Corps for someone who couldn't kill a cow." He started laughing.

"It wasn't a cow. It was a water buffalo!" I said.

"Hard-Corps." He smirked again.

We stood gabbing in formation for a solid two minutes before Sam the Blooper Man spotted the boots who couldn't take their eyes off us. He couldn't resist the old ear routine. I knew it was coming when his eyes lit up like a vampire in a blood bank. I gave Chan a nudge and nodded toward Sam. Chan's Snoopy-like grin stretched into place as we waited for the reaction.

Sam strolled casually over to them, put his M79 under his left arm, and asked for a cigarette. The boots seemed to back up a step or two like they didn't want to be too close. I realized why. It was the smell. We stunk. One of the young boots handed Sam a cigarette. Sam got a light from another, took one big puff, then removed his helmet. He unpinned the sun-baked human ear from his helmet cover and held it out to the boots, asking anyone if they wanted a lick. The young Marines all took another step back. They frowned as if they were about to get sick, then looked at Sam in wonder when he shook off the flies and put the ear in his mouth and sucked on it.

"Listen up!" Lieutenant Campbell shouted. "That means you, too, mister!" he shouted at Sam. Sam put on his helmet and walked back to our formation. He pinned his ear back on his helmet. "I don't want anyone getting lost. Stay in the area. You're allowed to hit the enlisted men's bar and chow hall, or sick bay, of course. There is a possibility that we might have to saddle up quickly, and if you ain't in one of those places then you're AWOL. Leave all frags with Sudsy. Dismissed."

"Chan, have you got any money?" I asked.

"I've got one American dollar, but we're not allowed to spend American money."

"I don't believe it!" A strong slap on my back followed the strangely familiar voice with the Boston baritone. "You two are still together?" I turned to see who I wasn't having a conversation with. Chan recognized the freckle-faced back-slapper first.

"Mike Flanagan?" Chan asked in disbelief.

"One and the same," he replied with a hearty laugh. Flanagan was a good-natured Irishman we'd known in boot camp.

"Where did you come from?" I asked.

"Weapons Platoon."

"In Alpha Company?" Chan asked.

"Yep. I just got assigned to Second Platoon."

"That's us!" I said.

"Far out!"

"Yours, I presume?" asked Chan, pointing to a 3.5 rocket launcher Mike held under one arm.

"Yep, she's mine. Well, I should say ours." Mike stepped aside to introduce his A-gunner. He looked a lot like Doc. Round glasses made him look like a professor. His face was pale, his mouth small and tightly closed like it was hard for him to speak. "This is my A-gunner, Lance Corporal Benjamin Allen." Benjamin said nothing. I nodded hello. "And these two are buddies from boot camp."

"And Camp Lejeune," I said.

"It's great to have you on board, Mike. But tell me something. Why would they send you out with that primitive tube?" Chan asked, pointing at the bazooka. Mike looked insulted.

"Yeah, why don't you stay with mortars and avoid this crap?" I asked.

His freckled face lit up as his voice lowered. He looked around to make sure no one else heard. "Scuttlebutt says they might send you guys tank hunting!"

"What?" said Chan in total disbelief.

"No, I'm serious. They knocked out a couple of Russian T-34s just this week south of Da Nang."

"Are you serious?" I asked.

"It's true," said the nonspeaking A-gunner with the professor face. He caught me off guard. I was beginning to think he couldn't speak at all.

"Well if we suddenly move toward Da Nang, I hope you guys are accurate with that tube," Chan said.

"I've got to have a drink at the Animal Pit before some

fool says, 'Saddle up!' " I said and gave Chan a pat on his helmet.

"Okay, Baby-san. I'll go with you to make sure you find your way back."

"Let's go, 3.5 rocket team. But you're a pro runner, aren't ya, Mike? Are you still trying to stay in shape?" I asked.

"Sort of, but this is a special occasion, and my next Boston Marathon is a long way off."

"Chan doesn't drink much either, but he's drinking with me this time."

The bar sat about one hundred yards from our tent. I'd never seen it before, but all we had to do was follow the dust of most of the platoon. The building had sandbags up to a tin roof. A sign out front read 101ST AIRBORNE. It didn't surprise me. Any small luxury I'd seen so far always belonged to the Army. The Marine Corps prided itself on giving back to the Pentagon half its allotted funds. That's why we still used Korean War–era helicopters, World War II packs, and bazookas.

An MP stood out front to guard a row of weapons.

"No weapons allowed inside." The Army MP made sure we knew the rules.

We set our weapons down and walked in. Three Marines from our platoon sat at the bar. Army men sat at tables. It could have looked like any bar back in the world if the grungy-looking Marines weren't part of the scene. Jimi Hendrix blared from a red and blue Wurlitzer in one corner. A pinball machine with an assortment of bells lit up another. A large brown, white, and blue Schlitz sign on the back wall provided most of the light for the dimly lit bar. Two black and white blowups of President Johnson shaking hands with Army generals hung behind the bar. Swift Eagle sat at one end of the bar by himself, separated by five chairs from the other Marines. We positioned ourselves there.

"I hate going to bars with this little turd," Chan said to Mike, referring to me.

"I beg your pardon," I said indignantly.

"Why's that, Chan?" Mike said with his Boston accent showing.

"The last time I made this mistake I was thrown in jail in Tijuana."

Mike bellowed out a laugh and choked out the words, "Are you serious?"

"Yes, I'm serious," Chan said.

"Now wait a minute, you guys," I said. "There's a reasonable explanation for these accusations."

"Yes. And the reasonable explanation is that he struck a giant Mexican bouncer with a chair," Chan said. Mike started laughing harder.

"Now wait a minute. You're only hearing one side of the story."

"That's right. After that, he managed to involve the entire bar in his brawl, got us arrested by the Tijuana police, the Navy Shore Patrol took us from them, then Marine Corps MPs took us from them, and we'd still be in the Red Line Brig in Camp Pendleton if we hadn't had orders for Vietnam."

"Are you finished, Chan?"

"No, but the details are too painful to remember."

Before I could properly defend myself, Sam the Blooper Man pulled up a stool next to us and bought us a round of beers. He wore a smile that only his mother could love. Showing off those rotten teeth should have warned me that he was up to something.

"Bartender! Here's ten bucks MPC. Drinks for every Marine in the house!" Sam shouted over my shoulder. He pulled up a stool next to Mike. "Who's your friend, John?"

"Sam the Blooper Man meet Mike Flanagan and Benjamin Allen, our new bazooka team."

"3.5 rocket team," Mike corrected.

"So that's your bazooka out front?"

"Yeah," Mike said.

"See those five Army guys sitting over at that table by the pinball machine?" We all turned to see the Army guys and turned back to Sam. "Well, they were just out front laughin' at the Corps over that bazooka." Mike looked back at the table.

"I wonder how hard they'd laugh if I tore that '101st' sign off the wall and broke it over their heads." Mike spoke dangerously loud.

Things were beginning to look like Tijuana all over again. With twenty to thirty M16s right outside the door, a bar fight didn't feel like a real smart idea to me.

"Don't worry about a thing, Mike." I didn't like the way Sam said that. "The Army has these new blooper rounds that I been wantin' for months. They got all kinds of 'em. Some explode and send out hundreds of steel ball bearings and some are flares. All kinds of new stuff, and naturally the Crotch won't see any of 'em until the next war. Bartender! Another round for every Marine in the house!"

"Does that mean them, too?" Our overweight Army bartender pointed at four Korean Marines who were seating themselves at a table behind us at that very moment.

"Are those ROKs?" Sam asked loudly, as though the first three beers had done the job.

"I think so," the beer-bellied bartender answered.

Sam raised his glass. "Give 'em a drink!"

"Are they White Horse Division?" Mike asked.

"I don't know," I answered.

"I'll ask 'em," slurred Sam. He jumped off his stool, walked up to the Koreans' table, and slapped one of them on the back like he was an old friend. A few seconds later all four stood up and walked over to us, with Sam leading the way.

"I want you guys to meet my friends." I wasn't sure who Sam was talking to. As a matter of fact I wasn't sure Sam had any friends. "This is Sergeant Kim. He speaks perfect English."

The short, stocky Korean bowed politely then stuck out his hand. He caught us by surprise. No one moved to shake hands with him. I reacted just as he was prepared to remove the offer.

"Sorry. I didn't know Koreans shook hands. My name is John Clark."

The sergeant bowed again then stepped aside to introduce someone else. "This is Master Dong Keun Park. He is very famous master of Tae Kwon Do. He is here to train South Vietnamese troops." A short Korean in the center, even stockier than Kim, bowed politely. I found myself bowing back. Tae Kwon Do is a Korean version of karate.

"American Marines very good fighters!" Master Park said then stuck out his hand. This time everyone reacted. He shook each hand. His chunky paw felt like a club covered with calluses. Master Park spoke in Korean. I couldn't understand what he said, but it was forceful.

Kim bowed again. "Master Park says Koreans are honored to fight beside American Marines." He bowed again. Then all four Koreans bowed.

During the introductions I hadn't noticed that Sam had left the bar. He came through the door just as the Koreans bowed for the last time. He still had that evil smile stuck on his face, but I wasn't sure what he was up to. We toasted to the Koreans, then they toasted to us so we toasted them again and they toasted us again. Things moved along rather merrily.

"Who stole my M79 ammo!" A large, angry voice shattered the merriment. A giant in Army fatigues blocked the doorway. I leaned away from the bar to get a better view. I thought he was standing on top of something. He wasn't. "I know it was one of you thievin' Marines! Who was it? Who has my ammo bag?" Now I knew what Sam was up to. The giant looked impatient. The soldiers in the bar stood up, their chairs squealing against the wood floor as they pushed them aside.

"This is the last time I go to a bar with you," Chan said in a muffled tone. "I knew this would happen."

"Me! I don't have anything to do with this," I said.

The giant walked over to us like he just got off a horse. I quickly debated in my mind the pros and cons of turning Sam in. Couldn't do it, not to the Army.

"He's even larger than the Mexican!" Chan whispered. "We'll need a bigger chair!"

The giant stood between us and the Koreans. He looked down at each of us, then suddenly reached to his right, grabbed Sam by the throat, and started squeezing him purple. Mike jumped off the stool to help. The giant shoved him down with one hand. Just as quickly the giant's right leg buckled and he fell to one knee. Master Park snapped his foot back from the giant's knee, then without lowering it to the ground snapped off a second kick to the side of the giant's head. His huge head bent sideways from the force of the Korean's tiny, spit-shined combat boot. The giant dropped over like a fallen redwood. For an instant I thought his neck had snapped. The other three Koreans formed a half-circle, each in a different fighting posture, facing the remaining Army men still standing on the other side of the bar, all with shocked expressions. No one moved. One Army man sat down. Then another. Finally everyone. Master Park knelt on one knee and put his ear to the giant's chest. "He is not dead."

"Wow! That was great!" I said.

"Did you see that kick?" Sam put in.

The door of the bar opened wide, bringing in more light than I wanted to see. Sudsy poked his face through columns of dust and light. "Hey! Any Marines in here from Alpha 1/5?"

"Yeah! Come on in, Suds!" Sam shouted.

"Saddle up! We got choppers waiting on us right now!"

"What?"

"We're comin' in on a hot LZ! Prepare to fire as soon as we disembark!" Lieutenant Campbell shouted over the noisy, twin-rotor CH-46 assault choppers. From cozy bar to hot LZ, it felt like a bad dream. The rear end of the chopper opened up like the tailgate of a pickup as we neared the LZ. "Don't forget, we're here to rescue those useless Green Berets, not shoot 'em!"

I faked a laugh. My stomach turned inside out. I looked at Chan for reassurance. His face looked like my stomach felt. The chopper dropped quickly. My stomach felt worse. I peeked out of one of the round portholes in the side of the chopper. Yellow smoke swirled up from a muddy rice paddy wedged tightly between two steep mountains.

A bullet smacked through the helicopter. The pilot leveled off fifteen feet above the paddy.

"Look out!"

"Get out! Jump out! This is it! Disembark!" the copilot screamed at the top of his lungs. Somebody gave me a shove toward the open tailgate. I stumbled forward under the weight of my gear. The chopper swung left, throwing me flat on my stomach. I looked up. The chopper was empty. I scrambled for the opening, carrying the gun under my right arm. I could feel the chopper pulling away. I held my breath. I jumped. The fall felt endless. Bits of blue sky and green trees shot past me. I could hear the cracking of AKs around me, then I hit. My helmet smashed into my head. Blood streamed down my face. A sharp pain ripped up my spine. I didn't know if I could move. I wiped the blood from my eyes and looked down. I was in mud up to my thighs that smelled like a sewer. Bullets hit the mud around me with a sucking sound. It felt like quicksand. I dropped the gun and rolled back and forth, then crawled and pulled myself free. Marines returned fire from the edge of the paddy behind the cover of five small trees at the foot of a mountain on my left. I grabbed the gun and ran for the trees. Suddenly I realized I was alone in the middle of the paddy. I ran faster. The mud grabbed at my boots. Chan called from the trees. Five yards from the trees I dove and rolled behind a small mound of dirt. The firing stopped.

Lieutenant Campbell shouted us into squads. Miraculously our only casualty was some corporal's canteen. An AK round tore it right off his cartridge belt. Ten minutes later all three squads swept up the steep mountain. An hour later we reached the top. We found nothing.

"All right, let's check that other mountain!" The gunny's command made my feet ache.

Five hours and two mountains later Sudsy got word over the PRC-25 that the Green Berets were safe at home with no casualties. The enemy had disappeared too. The men were incensed. Some of the best swears I'd ever heard ricocheted up and down the column. Most swore to deck the first person they caught in one of those stupid green hats. It was all new to me. First chopper assault on a hot LZ. First rescue of Green Berets. Evidently it wasn't the first time for the salts in the platoon.

"One of these days those suckers in their fag hats are gonna get all of us killed!"

I was so tired I almost paid no attention to the gripe walking up behind me in the column. It certainly wasn't the first one of the day, but when the voice swore something in a strange language I looked over my shoulder to see who it was.

"Swift Eagle? What'd you just say?" I asked, surprised at his rare show of emotion.

"Nothing important," he answered without looking.

"How many times has this happened?"

"A couple."

"Why's everybody so ticked off?" I asked as he moved up beside me.

"It's a setup." His piercing black eyes seemed to stare straight through me. "The gooks throw a few mortars into a Green Beret outpost, let them scream for help, then ambush the help. It's the oldest trick in Nam, but they never learn."

"I thought they were pretty good, for Army."

"Ah, they're good troopers, but they keep putting these clowns out here by themselves where they don't do a bit of good and get everybody else killed tryin' to save 'em."

Now I understood. If the chief said it and was even willing to talk about it, then it must be fact.

"Chief, what'd you think of that fight in the bar?"

He nodded. "The Koreans are great."

"Have you ever been on an operation with those guys?"

"No. Once, on my first tour in country, my platoon came across nine dead gooks. None of the gooks had been shot, and they looked all beat up. A couple of knife wounds here and there but no bullet wounds. We started searching the stiffs and these eight Koreans came out of the bush."

"How'd you know they were Koreans?"

"One of 'em shouted to us first so we wouldn't blow 'em away. He spoke perfect English. Anyway they killed 'em all with Tae Kwon Do and knives. They take less casualties that way than with guns. The gooks don't stand a chance going hand-to-hand with those guys."

I had a few thousand questions for the chief now that I had him talking, but we reached the spot for the chopper pickup. We set up a quick perimeter around it. Fifteen minutes later two CH-46s started circling the LZ. Green smoke covered me as the first chopper settled down. Twelve Marines hurriedly filed into the rear of the helicopter. I held my breath, waiting for that first AK to open up from the surrounding mountains. The painfully slow helicopter finally lifted off. Still no fire.

Our chopper landed thirty seconds after the first was airborne. Still no fire. I ran up the small ramp, cringing, waiting for that first shot. I collided with Chan as I lunged for my place on the six-man bench attached to the inside wall of the helicopter. The chopper lifted off. Twelve of us sat facing each other. Each face was strained, anxious to get out of range.

Once we were above the mountains, relief swept over the tired faces in front of me. A bright afternoon sun streaked through the round portholes. I leaned back and looked at Chan.

"Boy, I really hurt my back when I jumped out of this thing."

"Is that how you cut your forehead?" Chan asked. He leaned back, looking exhausted.

"Yeah."

"It's odd that you didn't fracture something. I'd like to find out who that pilot was," Chan said.

I leaned back and closed my eyes. When I opened them we were landing in Phu Bai. My stomach growled.

"I'm starving!" I said.

"Eat some C-rats," Chan said.

"I'm saving my stomach for real food in Phu Bai."

"Yes. Let us make an effort to reach the chow hall instead of a bar this time."

"Right."

We walked off the chopper and found ourselves facing a big, snub-nosed, camouflaged C-130 cargo plane. At least one hundred Marines were filing into the rear of the big plane.

"All right, I want you men to get in that line over there!" The lieutenant pointed to the C-130. "The regiment is moving to An Hoa!" he shouted over the helicopter engines still idling behind us.

I dipped into my pack and pulled out a can of beans 'n' franks.

PAY BACK

The Fifth Marines had moved to An Hoa Valley on April 1, 1968. We'd been there for two weeks now. It was like getting used to a new neighborhood. After being up around the DMZ, I thought we would catch some slack, but every day was the same, humping all day in one hundred or more degrees of heat and setting up ambushes at night.

An Hoa Valley made a natural supply route for the NVA coming off the Ho Chi Minh Trail and across the Laotian border. The Laos-Vietnam border region consisted of mountains and jungle as rugged as any in the world. The thick jungle canopy blacked out the sky in some areas. The valley was just as miserable or worse. Knee-deep mud, leech-infested rice paddies, fields of waist-level elephant grass, and small rolling hills. Every inch of it dangerous.

The enemy's main target in I Corps Tactical Zone was Da Nang. An Hoa Valley happened to be the most accessible attack route. The enemy had taken a pretty good beating up north around the DMZ, and they were shifting their main effort to the central provinces, with Da Nang as the ultimate target.

The valley was a maze of booby traps. My paranoia of going home without legs grew more intense each day. Dying seemed almost easier. Rarely did forty-eight hours go by without someone tripping a grenade. Even worse were the booby-trapped artillery rounds. Every artillery barrage has some rounds that don't detonate. The Viet Cong would find them and booby trap them.

We changed the point man regularly so no one would have to play human mine sweeper too often. The best point man was Jackson. A keener sense of direction didn't exist.

Lieutenant Campbell stood up in the center of the perimeter and spit out some coffee. It started raining. Two bad signs, I thought. I wanted to eat something before we started out again, but my stomach wasn't up to lima beans. I settled for water; nothing like the taste of Halazone water to start off a day. Halazone tablets were supposed to purify the water. If I put a couple in my canteen, I didn't get dysentery, but I remained very close to sick. Sometimes dysentery ignored the Halazone. There's no feeling that compares with crapping your way through a fifteen-mile hike in the bush. My cramping stomach told me it was going to be one of those days.

"Saddle up! Take the point, Jackson." The lieutenant's command was echoed around the perimeter by Corporal Swift Eagle.

Jackson stood up, gave me a mischievous wink and a nod toward a new boot replacement named Buford Unerstute. A chopper had dropped Unerstute off a week before, but I hadn't met the guy yet. Sudsy said he was totally spooked and a real hick. Jackson stretched and yawned and called for the lieutenant, making sure that Private Unerstute could hear him clearly. I nudged Chan so he wouldn't miss anything.

" 'Bout how long does a man live after a bamboo viper gets him?" Jackson asked sincerely.

"How long would you say, Gunny?" Lieutenant Campbell asked, rubbing the four-day growth on his chin.

"I've seen 'em go awful quick." The gunny stuffed in a mouthful of chew. "Staff Sergeant Morey saw a Marine in China die in ten minutes. I've seen 'em chase a man fifty yards through the bush."

"How about that gunner in Third Platoon?" Sudsy added. "They couldn't pry that snake off after it bit him."

A moment later a green flash shot across the perimeter and then back again. On the second pass I spotted the reason for Private Unerstute's amazing speed. Jackson's pet green rubber snake was clamped by its fake bloody teeth to the seat of Unerstute's trousers, which were two sizes too big. Unerstute was doing his best to run right out of them. He started running in circles with his stomach pressed forward and shoulders bent backward to keep the snake's bite from reaching skin. He high-stepped in circles like a drum major, with his mouth open but no sounds coming out. Finally Jackson caught up with him and yanked the snake off. I laughed until my eyes filled with tears. I looked at Chan. Huge happy tears ran down his face too. It felt so good I wanted to thank all the participants individually, but there wasn't time, and now the laugh was over.

I turned my attention to the painful matters at hand. Getting my mind and body up for a morning romp through the mud was a chore. The Bataan death march was probably worse, but around the fifteenth mile I started having my doubts.

The night rain had me itching from head to toe. I moved around like the tin man in *The Wizard of Oz*. My back hurt, my feet were rotting away, and I had dysentery. In other words, it was a normal morning with the U.S. Marines in the armpit of the world, Vietnam.

We headed in the direction of the base camp at An Hoa. A thousand meters later the sharp explosion of a grenade at the head of the column brought us to a halt. I knew it was Jackson, but I hoped it wasn't. I'd always liked him. He smiled so much he'd been accused of being my black twin. We'd been nicknamed the "White Teeth Brothers."

Anger swept across the faces of the column. The gunny sent two men ahead to see what had happened.

The rest of the column sat down, as silent as the jungle it-self. Only the staccato sound of the rain bouncing off my helmet broke the dead silence. The ground vibrated with a second explosion.

The man in front of me turned. "Get into a perimeter. Pass the word."

We spread into a hasty perimeter. Swift Eagle called for his squad. Seven men ran forward. I grabbed Chan.

"They need a gun team."

Chan was already up and removing his pack.

"Let's go," he said.

I stood up. A friendly hand pushed me back down. Corporal James stood over me.

"Stay here, John. I already sent Paunchy's team up." Sanchez was the platoon's only other gunner, known as Paunchy Villa because he was short, chunky, and Mexican-American. A huge black mustache that covered his mouth, and machine-gun ammo crisscrossing his chest, made the image complete.

We waited. Ten minutes passed. Still no sounds.

"Hold your fire! We're comin' in with wounded!"

Friendly helmets poked through the tangled brush. Two men carrying one wounded Marine by his feet and arms struggled through knee-deep mud. It started rain-ing more heavily. I couldn't see Jackson yet. Then more helmets came through the brush. Three men carried an-other wounded Marine, his face streaked red and white with blood and rain. Then Swift Eagle burst through the brush with Jackson over his shoulder.

"Corpsman!"

Doc rushed over to the chief and helped him lay Jackson down gently.

"How are the others, Doc? Cudar looked bad." Swift Eagle's expression never changed, but his tone was serious.

"Cudar's dead," the corpsman answered without look-ing away from bandaging Jackson.

I shouted at the chief, "How's Jackson?"

Sudsy tossed a green smoke grenade into the center of the perimeter and started spitting coordinates into his radio faster than any mouth in the Corps.

"Hey, Doc," I shouted. "How's Jackson?"

"He's okay."

Twenty minutes later a rickety Korean War–era helicopter with a giant purple heart painted on both sides followed the swirling green smoke to the ground. It landed with a splash, throwing mud into the faces of the men who rushed toward it with the wounded. A boyish face peered hesitantly from the hatchway of the old chopper. The baby-faced replacement jumped out, sinking into mud up to his knees. From the far side of the perimeter someone started cursing. Sanchez ran at the chopper, screaming curses half in Spanish and half in English. "I told you I'd kick your butt!"

All eyes turned to the center of the perimeter. The chopper lifted off with the dead and the wounded as Sanchez reached the freckle-faced boot who was still stuck in the mud. Sanchez sloshed up to the replacement and started slapping him senseless with both hands. The freckle-faced replacement regained his balance from the assault and managed to wrestle Sanchez to the ground.

Two men from Sanchez's gun team finally pulled them apart, only to have both men lunge at each other again. This time they hugged each other like lost brothers.

Sudsy got the scoop on the story and passed it on as we moved out again. The replacement's name was Simmons. He and Sanchez were best friends from the same Indianapolis high school. Sanchez had told him to join anything but the Corps. Normally the whole scene would be worth a couple of laughs, but Jackson was the seventh casualty in ten days, and we hadn't fired a shot. It was hard to smile. Out of the other six casualties, two were probably crippled for life and Cudar was dead.

My skin felt like cellophane holding in anger. I wanted

revenge. I was beginning to hate. I forced any thoughts of God out of my mind. I didn't want my hatred softened.

The rest of the day drifted into obscurity, like the day before and the day after. Each hour went by one step at a time: watching for trip wires with every movement, trying to put your foot exactly where the man in front of you put his. It felt like the kid's game of avoiding the cracks in the sidewalk, the only difference being the penalty. Hitting the crack in this game might cost you a portion of your body.

Someone in Alpha took the fatal step every day or so. Sudsy picked up medevac calls over his radio and kept us posted on the bad news. The news never came easy. We all had friends in the other platoons. I felt helpless. Agonizingly helpless. The feeling was becoming too common. Morale bottomed out.

We had started out as individuals. We looked at things in different ways. Some feelings weren't different; they were contagious. Feeling the wet, sticky debris of what was a friend a second earlier hit you in the face after he steps on a 155 round sends hatred through a man like very few things can. The hatred builds when there's no fighting back.

After weeks of this we no longer looked at anything differently. We became a unit. An angry unit, with no exceptions. We had one intention. Find the little slimes and "take names." I hadn't heard that phrase so much since boot camp. It meant find the enemy, in this case the 308th NVA Regiment, and kill so many of them that they would no longer be considered a combat unit.

Craving for revenge infected us like a virus and built steadily with each new casualty. I wanted to kill as many as possible. I looked forward to it with lust. I felt older each day, eighteen going on forty.

April 30th. We started humping back toward An Hoa. I knew what was up. They brought us in to base camp every couple of months for new jungle utilities (clothes), weapon repairs, ammo, and one hot meal. We usually went back to the bush the same day. No sense spoiling us.

Three thousand meters later Private Jones fainted from heat exhaustion. It wasn't unusual. If anyone forgot their salt tablets, the heat would get them. Doc rushed by me to tend to Jones, and from the look on his face I wasn't sure if it was a mission of mercy or murder.

"Take your time, Doc. I need the rest," I said as he stumbled over the M60 beside me.

"He didn't forget his salt tabs!" fumed the young corpsman. "He just wants out of the bush!"

I looked at Chan as Doc stormed on to the front of the column.

"Boy, he's ticked at the Corps today," I said.

"I don't blame him," Chan said. "He joined the Navy to avoid combat. Did you get a chance to talk to that boot Simmons?"

"Yeah, I did. He said the Beatles put out a new double album, and protesters and fags were holding hands in marches, and skirts were so short he couldn't talk about it. I love legs!"

"He asked me why everyone was so angry," said Chan. "I told him how many men we lost this month. Poor guy, I think I scared him to death."

"We must really have picked up his spirits," I said.

"What do you mean?"

" 'Cause I told him if he didn't get killed the first three months he'd make it."

"Saddle up!" The eternal order sifted through the column.

The march to An Hoa felt like an angry funeral procession. The only thing missing was a casket. I tried not to think about the lost friends, but it was no use. Even my eyes felt violent. The faces near me looked about as unfriendly as I felt. It should have been a routine resupply march. It wasn't. Except for the constant marching, nothing felt routine.

The timing was all wrong for a twenty-four-hour trip into civilization where typewriter pushers, rear-echelon pogues, and base camp artillerymen were having an interesting trip to the Far East. They drank cold beer, ate hot meals, slept out of the rain, smoked dope, played with village harlots, and wrote the folks back home more war stories than Ernie Pyle. I was jealous and bitter, and I knew it.

As we entered the village of An Hoa, we looked as if a giant rock ape had dragged the platoon through the swamp by its heels. Vietnam had its own unique way of ripping, rotting, and eating away your clothes, your body, and your sanity. There was constant rain, mud, blistering heat, and hungry insect life. There was the stink of the Vietnamese jungle and the sickening sweet smell of rotting dead. A touch of malaria was burning my body. The bottom of my left foot looked like raw hamburger from a rotting fungus infection. And of course there was the fatigue. Marching all day and fear of death at night induced utter weariness always.

Some of the men were half naked. I was one of them. I had torn the seat and crotch out of my trousers because of dysentery. No stopping for head calls. I drained as we marched. More than clothes got tattered; I was walking on my morale.

The men's faces looked drawn with fatigue. Each had the same menacing stare—like drunks about to get nasty. Some had full beards. I envied them. I wanted to look as mean as I felt, but I couldn't grow one yet. Others just looked hard. We hadn't used soap and water for a couple of months. Toothbrushes cleaned and oiled your weapon. Your weapon was your life. As the old gunny so aptly put it, "Our breath could knock a buzzard off a crap wagon from twenty yards."

Our appearance and odor were nothing new, but the

tight, murderous faces had just been unwrapped. It went beyond the gung-ho Marine look. Revenge became personal. Each brow pinched as though straining under a heavy invisible burden. Anger clearly stamped into each face. Not one man smiling.

It was visible to the children of An Hoa. I'd never once seen them miss a chance to beg C-rations off returning Marines. Not this time. They ran at us as usual, some yelling, "You okay, GI?" others just yelling like any kids in a school yard. They stopped cold on the edge of the dirt road as if sensing danger, staring silently at our faces filing by.

A group of ARVN soldiers stood laughing together near the barbed-wire gate that separated the village from the camp. They spoke that language that has no pause, just a continuous chatter that grated on one's nerves. It was like a scratch on a blackboard to my ears.

One of the ARVNs pointed at us and cackled with laughter, like we were clowns in a parade. His uniform was tailored and starched. A voice behind me yelled at Sam, "Hey Sam, what good's an ARVN?"

Sam shouted from the rear of the column, "An ARVN ain't worth a pimple on a Marine's rear end!"

The ARVN stopped laughing and shouted, "*Du-me*, Marine. *De-de mow*, Marine!" I wasn't sure of the exact translation, but it didn't mean "Have a nice day."

That lit an already short fuse. I hit the laugher with the butt of my M60. For a second I felt good. I watched as the rest of the ARVNs got clobbered by the men around me. By the time the lieutenant reached the scene, seven ARVNs lay in various positions of semi-unconsciousness. I was sorry for what I'd started.

The lieutenant stomped out his cigarette. He looked mad. He turned away from the battered ARVNs and scanned across the silent faces of the Marines.

"Swift Eagle! Are any of 'em dead?"

"No, sir."

"What happened, Corporal?"

"They wondered what it was like to defend their own country, sir."

"Are you saying, Corporal, that they requested a demonstration of Marine Corps hand-to-hand combat techniques in order to better defend themselves and their country?"

"Yes, sir!"

"Very well. Move out."

For the first time in a week a smile stretched across the hard face of the platoon. I felt a little better, but not much. I liked Lieutenant Campbell more now than I ever had before.

An Hoa base camp consisted of one portable airstrip made of pierced steel planking. One artillery unit, one chow hall, one bar for officers, one bar for office pogues, and rows of large, dust-covered tents for troops coming and going. A few small, slightly more permanent structures dotted the camp for various supply purposes. The camp was hidden away behind three large rolls of concertina barbed wire, sandbag machine-gun bunkers, and an array of trip flares and claymore mines.

After a quick formation we got two free hours to sleep before the big event—hot food. The big, dusty tents were lined with cots. Not as soft as the mud I was used to, but a luxury I wasted no time in taking advantage of. I slipped into a lovely coma only to be slapped into consciousness by the roar of what was unmistakably an angry Indian.

"Pogues!"

My eyes opened like I'd been stabbed with a cattle prod. Men instinctively jumped from their cots to the ground while others with their eyes still closed groped for their weapons. Swift Eagle stood at the open end of the tent with clenched fists.

The chief rarely complained, but when he did it seemed intelligent to keep your distance and be agreeable. He had been wounded seven times and had a couple of medals for bravery, for what specific action I never knew. This was his fourth tour in Vietnam, all four as a grunt. He refused to stay in America.

Sam stood up, fidgeting with an unlit cigarette. "What's wrong, Chief?" he asked hurriedly as he glanced outside the tent.

The Indian looked at Sam indifferently. "Those typewriter pushers are wearing camouflage utilities! Not a single grunt in Alpha has camouflage!"

"I noticed that too," Sam said. "Maybe they're hidin' from all that ink. Let's kick butt on a couple of pogues our size and go back to the bush in style."

The chief just stared. He didn't talk much, but when he did it was short and to the point. An Indian John Wayne if ever there was one. The blacks in the platoon put it best: "He's the dude who keeps you out of the green plastic bag."

Everyone in the tent looked ready to do anything he said. Just then two MPs and a frail-looking man wearing nothing but his boxer shorts and brand-new jungle boots burst into the tent in a rage. Boxer Shorts looked like he'd been mugged by a bear. He glared at every face in the tent, which wasn't easy considering one eye was a throbbing purple plum and the other swollen shut, with the eyebrow covering the eyelid. He evidently didn't see what he wanted and stormed out, cursing, raging in a frenzy toward the next tent, with the MPs glued to his rear end.

A grin tried its best to crack through the stonelike face of Swift Eagle. All eyes riveted to the chief. I personally had yet to see him actually smile, though some of his expressions seemed more pleased than others.

He took a quick glance outside the tent, then reached inside his shirt and proudly pulled out a brand-new set of camouflage utilities. The tent erupted in a gut-busting, sorely needed belly laugh. I laughed until I cried. Then I saw it. A confirmed, documented grin broke across the stone face of the Indian.

Twenty minutes later the company stood at attention in front of the top sergeant for full inspection. Beside the top stood the frail office pogue sporting another new set of starched camouflage utilities. A fine pair they made, camouflaged from head to toe, and with a Marine Corps shine glistening off their new jungle boots. Corporal Boxer Shorts now had eyes as black as his boots. I bit my lip to keep from laughing. The top sergeant breathed in heavily and stuck out his lower lip.

"No man will enter the chow line without a Marine Corps cover on his Marine Corps head. There will be another inspection before chow. Any man with unshined boots and improper Marine dress will not enter the chow line." The top rambled on with his insanity. Men began shuffling their feet. Others started spitting and kicking at the dirt like angry children being scolded. It felt like any positive gains we may have acquired by getting a day's rest had just been negated.

Chan looked at me with a blank stare. "Ghastly timing. He is obviously uninformed." Chan sounded almost sad. He turned his stare back to the top sergeant, who was beginning to shout through his list of commands.

"Every man will have a haircut and shave. . . ."

By the end of the inspection the mood was complete. Completely hostile. We got one piece of good news. We'd be staying in An Hoa overnight.

At midnight I was awakened by the explosion of two grenades.

"Did that sound close?" Swift Eagle asked the question for me. No one answered.

Outgoing artillery serenaded us the rest of the night. The next morning in formation the lieutenant informed us that the top sergeant had been fragged. He wasn't dead but had lost both legs. I knew there would be an investigation, but even Sherlock Holmes couldn't find fingerprints on a grenade.

It sure wasn't the first time a Marine got murdered by another Marine, but in this case it left a bad taste in my mouth. It would have been better if he had died. The whole incident had the smell of pettiness.

Talking was at a minimum on the way out of An Hoa. If anyone knew who fragged the top, they were keeping it to themselves. Whoever it was had to be worried. Justice could be swift and cruel in Vietnam. If the identity of the person or persons was discovered, their next firefight would probably be their last.

The top sergeant wasn't exactly popular, but he was still a Marine. He had been through World War II and Korea.

Ten miles out we found ourselves sloshing through seemingly endless fields of rice paddies. It looked like a treeless desert of knee-deep mud and blood-sucking leeches. We tightroped along the paddy dikes of an especially wide paddy, trying hopelessly to keep our feet dry. Halfway across, a sniper started taking potshots at us. The distant sound of his AK47 told me he was too far away to hit anything. No one paid any attention except the new boot, Private Simmons. Simmons dove into the mud face first. I laughed until my eyes watered.

An eternity later we came upon a small oasis of solid ground with trees, bushes, and overgrown hedgerows.

Chan nudged me from behind with his M16. "This farmer must have truly appreciated his solitude," he said.

"I don't blame the little hermit. If I lived in this hole, I'd want to be as far away from people as possible." I slung the M60 machine gun off my shoulder as we neared the oasis. "That shade sure looks good. It has to be a hundred twenty today."

"At least that," Chan said. "My brain feels like an overbaked potato. I hate this helmet. We should be wearing soft covers instead of these ten-pound pots."

Chan rambled on, uncharacteristically, about the intense heat.

"My, my, PFC Chan," I taunted. "Feeling a bit feisty today, are we? Maybe you thought you were joining the Navy."

Chan gave a response that sounded Chinese, though he swore he couldn't speak the language.

We acted like sailors who'd been at sea too long, each man stomping the firm ground of the oasis, shaking off the mud, and feeling for the weight of huge clinging leeches. I headed for the best shade I could find. Chan pointed to a small group of banana trees with giant, long green leaves just on the other side of what was once a well-kept hedgerow.

The hedgerow surrounded a narrow, overgrown graveyard. Creeping tentacles of brown and yellow vines seemed to be feeding off the oval grave mounds. It looked ghoulish, but it was a perfect position for covering the right flank.

Just as we reached an opening in the hedgerow someone shouted from behind us, "I want your gun team over here, John!" I knew the owner of the voice without looking.

"What possible difference can it make?"

"Just move it, Marine."

Chan and I looked at each other in disbelief. I wanted to tell the lieutenant that he sounded like a ten-year-old but didn't.

"Sanchez! I want your team over there with John."

Sanchez gave the lieutenant a quick thumbs up and headed toward us, with Simmons and the rest of his gun team close behind.

Sanchez mumbled a tired "Semper fi" as we passed each other. Chan and Simmons exchanged the customary thumbs up.

"Now aren't you glad you came over?" Chan said as Simmons shuffled along behind Sanchez.

"Wouldn't have missed it for the world," Simmons replied enthusiastically.

The rest of the gun team were too tired to take their eyes off their feet.

By the time Sanchez reached the opening in the hedgerow, Chan and I had gone twenty meters in the opposite direction. A popping explosion threw me to my stomach. I blinked my eyes clear and quickly looked behind me. Chan lay motionless, flattened to the ground. Blood trickled down the top of his camouflaged helmet, dripping over the greens and browns. I couldn't speak. He looked dead.

The helmet moved. He pulled his face out of the dirt, spitting a healthy portion of it at me.

"You jerk! I thought you were dead!"

"You don't have to sound so disappointed. I thought so too!"

"Are you okay?" I asked.

"Yes, how about you?"

"I'm fine, but somebody ain't." I motioned toward the hedgerow. Part of it was now a large crater.

Chan turned to look. Pieces of bloody flesh hung from the back of his flak jacket. I stood up, nudging Chan with my foot.

"You got blood all over you," I said.

"*I* do?" Chan retorted. "You should see *your* back. You look like you've been sprayed with red paint."

I felt something on the back of my neck. I reached to slap it off, thinking it was a bug. It stuck to my hand. I held it out to see what it was. An unrecognizable fragment of a man dangled from my fingertips. Vomit came into my mouth. I spit it out quickly, hoping no one would see. No one did.

Chan stood up. We started slowly toward the hedgerow. I saw Sanchez lying ten feet from the crater. The crater was exactly where I had stopped to argue with the lieutenant. I felt cold. Goose bumps swarmed over me.

Chan looked down and shook his head. "Had to be a 155."

I walked over to Sanchez. He lay face down. I rolled him over. His eyes opened; he looked fully conscious. I turned to Chan. "He's alive!"

"Praise God," Chan said quietly, then shouted, "Corpsman up!"

Doc reached us quickly, with the lieutenant close behind.

Sanchez looked up alertly. "I'm okay, Doc. Help the others. I'm okay. I'm okay. Simmons! Go check Simmons!"

Doc began sobbing uncontrollably. He tried to remove bandages from his pack. Chan took the pack from the shaking corpsman and removed bandages and morphine. As he leaned over Sanchez to administer the morphine, my heart fell into my stomach. His legs were gone. Severed six inches below the waist. I hadn't even noticed. Strangely enough the bleeding didn't look too bad.

Sanchez kept insisting he was okay. No one told him he wasn't. He grabbed Chan's arm with more strength than I thought possible from a man in his condition. "Find Simmons!"

I couldn't hold back the tears. I turned and headed for the crater to find Simmons. Arms and legs lay about the crater. "Four men missing," a voice behind me said. I found a hand hanging from the branch of a small tree by the threads of what was once a forearm. A flak jacket held the upper torso of one man together, but the legs, head, and dog tags were gone. No one could be identified.

We gathered the pieces together and placed them in a poncho. By the time the medevac chopper arrived, Sanchez was numbed with morphine. The rest of us were numb with hate.

The doc and Chan lifted Sanchez into the chopper. He was pale but still awake and still asking for Simmons. The chopper lifted off grudgingly, its engine straining with the weight. As it floated out of sight Chan sat beside me and pressed the bridge of his nose with his forefinger and thumb. He slumped forward. He looked the way I felt. I handed him a canteen.

"No thank you," he said without looking up.

"Go ahead. It's that Kool-Aid sent in the last care package."

"No thanks."

"It's grape."

He peered at me with one frosty Chinese eye, then broke into his Snoopy-like grin. He dropped his chin to his chest and stuck out his hand palm up. "Give me the canteen." He snatched it and took a big swig.

"Will he make it?" I asked.

"I think so. The hot shrapnel cauterized the vessels, causing minimal blood loss." Chan looked up, his eyes fighting back tears. "I feel so frustrated I can't stand it."

"So do I, but we'll catch 'em, Chan. When we do, it'll be pay-back time."

"Pay back is a medevac." Chan's tone was low and serious.

"That's right, buddy, and they're in a world of it when we find 'em."

Chan held out his hand and gave the M60 two pats like it was a pet dog, then turned his hand palm up.

"Give me five on it, bro."

I slapped his hand like a black man and it felt good. The threats gave us momentary relief, but not enough.

Corporal Swift Eagle walked by with harder steps than usual. He looked more Indian, more intense. His face was darker red than normal. He halted a few feet from us and shouted, "Saddle up!"

"Wonderful! Just wonderful. Let's go see how many booby traps we can find today."

I didn't see who said it but found out by following the chief's glare. It was Private Doyle. His M16 sat in front of him disassembled for cleaning.

"Shut up and get that rifle together! We're moving out. Now!" Swift Eagle sounded like he looked—mad.

"This Marine—" Doyle tried to file one last complaint. It ended abruptly. The big Indian glided several feet and with one hand lifted Doyle by the lapel from a sitting to a standing position. Then he released him and walked away. There were no more comments.

I spent the next four hours enjoying the scenic beauty of the armpit of the world. No one talked. Every ounce of energy became vital as the day grew hotter. Just before I decided to faint, the column stopped. The man in front of me turned and said, "Five minutes," then collapsed to the ground with the rest of the platoon.

I passed the word to Chan and stumbled forward to get some salt tablets from Doc. Sudsy sat next to the doc, fondling his radio as usual and listening to another platoon's transmission.

"That's a roger, Alpha One, single medevac, over."

"Who got hit, Suds?" I asked.

He looked up with a frown. "Lieutenant Hawthorn, Third Platoon. He got ticked at the point man when he refused to go into an area that looked booby-trapped. Sounded like he took the point himself. Tripped a 155. Cut him clean in half."

I took the salt tablets and the bad news back to Chan. A couple of swigs of water and someone said, "Saddle up!" I didn't know where we were heading, but for the first time all day I started caring.

At dusk we set up an ambush in a dried-up area known as the Arizona Territory, four miles northwest of the An Hoa combat base. The night drifted by to the customary serenade of distant artillery fire, but still no contact with the enemy. The next day started like the day before.

"Saddle up! We got fifteen klicks to go today!" Swift Eagle's command started my feet talking to me. Obscenity after obscenity.

Chan handed me the rest of his coffee. "You emit the odor of a rice paddy," he snickered.

"You ain't no bloody rose yourself," I replied.

Chan gave my boot a nudge with his. "How's the foot doing?"

"It's killing me."

"You're going to lose that foot to jungle rot if you don't stop the infection."

"Why don't you write me a prescription, young Dr. Chan, and I'll drive on down to the drugstore and get it filled. Maybe I better call in sick today."

Chan looked at me, rolled his eyes toward heaven, and raised one hand. "Lord, help me communicate with the mentally ill."

On most days we could have had a good chuckle. Some said we laughed an inordinate amount. Others thought a Section 8 was in order. Laughing kept me from panicking. The mood was different this time. I couldn't fake a laugh. A quiet storm raged inside the platoon, with no way out. The faces around me were slowly turning to granite.

We marched all day, stopping for one meal. I spent that time burning off leeches. The pace quickened in the afternoon. The Vietnamese called us elephants because we hacked through the bush making a lot of noise, but I thought we looked more like a caterpillar. Today the caterpillar shifted into fourth gear. No one talked. I felt an odd hint of excitement.

Boredom returned a few miles later. The sun felt closer. My helmet made an excellent frying pan, and my brain was reaching over-easy. The mind escapes boiling by fantasizing. We called it "world dreaming." Sometimes it was air conditioning or driving a car again. Sometimes strawberry shortcake and ice cream. My fantasies usually had long legs; chocolate ice cream was always optional.

Fantasies had to be tempered with caution. It was wise

to always be aware of where your foot was about to land or of the dark spot in the tree fifty meters ahead.

With dusk the mountains came closer and closer. They finally swallowed the sun from view. We stopped as we reached the last rice paddy at the foot of the ominous, haze-covered mountains. An arm up ahead motioned us forward and into a circle. A peculiar and dangerous procedure. We gathered around the lieutenant. It felt like a huddle. A rifle butt stuck me in the ribs as we crowded in closer to hear him.

"All right, listen up. Intelligence says we got a major group of VC and NVA comin' between those two mountains and possibly across this coordinate tonight. I know these things are usually screwed up, but this one looks legit."

The lieutenant's tone induced enthusiasm. I went quickly from excited to scared and back to excited again.

Sam mumbled. "We're takin' names." The old gunny joined in with a subdued "Semper fi." Suddenly I felt a different kind of fear—the fear that they wouldn't come our way.

"All right, listen up." The lieutenant knelt on one knee and began drawing a primitive map in the dirt. "We're going to use an L-shaped ambush, with the gun on the left flank." He looked around the huddle of faces until he found the chief's. "Swift Eagle, I want the gun team and two riflemen set up over there." He pointed to a small tree and shrubs on the left of the rice paddy directly in front of us. "We can't lose the gun. It's the only heavy fire we got left, so let's keep the heat off the gun. I want the rest of the men behind this tree line with five meters between each position, two men to a position. Any questions?" No one spoke.

We waited until the sun disappeared before moving into ambush position. The dark, menacing mountains, blanketed with lush jungle foliage thick enough to hide the entire North Vietnamese Army, watched every move we made. The riflemen positioned themselves behind the tree line two hundred meters from where the bottom of the mountains melted into the flat paddy fields. We set the gun up one hundred and fifty meters from the mountains and to the left of the riflemen.

It would be a textbook L-shaped ambush, just like we practiced in North Carolina. Looked great on paper. Just one small problem. If the gooks came from the wrong direction, we might get turned into fertilizer. I started saying my prayers. Explaining to God all the wonderful contributions to society I could make if I weren't fertilizer took imagination and a lot of gall. My prayer had plenty of both. God must not have been impressed.

Swift Eagle appeared from somewhere, cutting the prayer short. "Murph and McQueen are gonna be on your left for cover fire. Don't open up until we get 'em in the middle of the paddy." The chief turned away, vanishing into the darkness as silently as he came.

Murph and McQueen acted nervous. It was considered a "crap detail" to get stuck near the gun. They moved a few feet away and settled in without a word. A few minutes later they moved a little farther away. We didn't take it personally. It was common knowledge: The gun would be the first target, because its tracers would make it the only visible target.

"Chan," I whispered. "I hate these tracers!"

He looked into my face and tilted his head. "But why, John?" He then proceeded comically with his memorized version of the Marine Corps handbook. "Tracer rounds are a necessary evil. They pinpoint enemy targets for riflemen and point out enemy positions to fighter pilots or helicopters viewing a battle from above."

"Oh. I feel much better now. If only the tracers didn't form a bright golden arrow pointing right at lovable little me."

The night grew black. I couldn't see my hand in front

of my face. The air felt thick. I hated not being able to see.

A rare, pleasant breeze bounced off my sweaty face. Suddenly the moon popped out of a cloud, lighting the landscape. I could see all the way to the mountains. I'm ready, I thought.

Chan started linking up ammunition and stacking it on my pack to keep it out of the dirt. He gave his M16 the once-over, put his magazines within arm's reach, and began straightening grenade pins. It reminded me to do the same.

The first two hours of the beautiful moonlit night went by as monotonously as always. Ants and mosquitoes were using me as a midnight snack. The quarter moon drifted through small transparent clouds, illuminating the vast flat paddy. The mountain peaks looked black, sinister against the dark blue sky.

Chan rolled toward me with his canteen out. "How about some Halazone Kool-Aid?" he whispered.

Before I managed a reply Chan stiffened like a dog ready to bite. His eyes opened wide. Tension sliced through the boredom like a silent alarm. The backache I was going to complain about dissolved. The mosquitoes that were sucking me dry vanished. My body tightened.

I strained to see what Chan was now aiming at in the direction of the mountains. A barely discernible piece of darkness began to move. Another shape appeared from the trees just behind the first. They looked to be one hundred twenty meters to our left and twenty to our front.

A third shadowy figure emerged. Then a fourth. My stomach churned. A muscle cramp hit me in the rear end. I rolled over to straighten my leg.

"Chan, check the ammo, quick." He lowered his rifle and made sure there were no kinks in the ammo belts.

Drops of sweat trickled from my forehead to my chin faster than I could wipe them away. Chan's face glittered with tiny moon balls of perspiration. He started piling the grenades in front of us. He covered his mouth and whispered.

"Still see 'em?"

"Yes. Hope those jerks beside us see 'em." I shielded my mouth on the side facing the rice paddy, leaned toward the riflemen on our left, and called as quietly as possible, "Psst, you see 'em?" A few seconds passed. No reply. "Chan, those morons are asleep!"

A few more seconds passed. Silence. Not even a snore.

"Yeah, we see 'em now!"

I sighed. Chan looked at me, rolled his eyes, and exhaled heavily.

"No screaming-eagle crap."

Sweat dripped off my palms. I tried unbuttoning the holster of my .45-caliber pistol. My hands felt shaky, almost spastic.

Chan nudged me and squinted. "You don't think they're getting that close?"

"I sure hope not. I don't think this sucker works."

We gave each other a quick hard look. The realization of what we just said sank in. I said a quick, open-eyed prayer.

The four shadows turned into four men fifty meters away and closing. I followed the lead man with my gun sights, making sure my finger stayed off the trigger. One early finger could get us all killed.

From the corner of my eye more movement. More shadows. Stinging salt sweat penetrated my eyes. The line of shadows grew longer. My bladder felt like exploding. The column of shadows grew longer and closer. Ain't no way I'm wetting my pants, I thought.

Twenty meters in front, crouching and looking in all directions, the four gooks walking point crept by like they were stepping on unbroken eggs. The moon silhouetted their safari helmets. NVA regulars. As they crept by us I couldn't breathe. I started gasping for air. I stuck my face into my arm to suffocate quietly. I've been holding my breath, God how stupid. Chan nudged me without speaking. I let him know I was all right with a thumbs up, but I wanted to admit being stupid.

More shadows. The moon bathed the landscape in an eerie blue light. I felt hot and cold and sweaty all at the same time. Chan held the first fifteen inches of the ammo belt in his left hand with his M16 rammed into his right shoulder. His forearm started twitching like a muscle spasm was getting him. I didn't like it. An early round could get us overrun.

The four NVA walking point were within twenty meters of our line of riflemen, and the column was still filing out of the brush at the foot of the mountains. The usual chatter of the jungle insects vanished. I could hear my heart trying to push blood out of my ears.

Chan released his rifle and reached into one of his huge trouser pockets, producing a small can of oil. He began squeezing it onto the barrel of the M60 as he whispered so low I only heard two words: ". . . whole company."

I was afraid to answer, afraid the whisper wouldn't work. A cough or a sneeze would get us all killed. Memories of being tortured in boot camp for slapping a sand flea fluttered through my mind. The DI had said the entire platoon was dead because of that noise. God, even Parris Island was beginning to make sense. I knew I was in trouble.

Shadows kept multiplying from the foot of the mountains. Every other man in the column was bent over to the waist, lumbering under the weight of huge packs. The men in between the carriers walked more upright, with smaller packs, and carried rifles. I had a human supply train in front of me. This would be pay back, long-awaited pay back.

My stomach still churned. In a few seconds I'd kill a lot of people. My stomach bellowed loudly, then rumbled with more than enough noise to carry to Hanoi. A brackish taste filled my mouth. I wanted to spit, but there wasn't any saliva.

Doubt strangled me. Fifteen of us were about to ambush a column of gooks I couldn't see the end of. A quick violent shiver shot from my neck to the base of my spine.

Bloop. Sam's blooper gun! I pulled the trigger. Orange tracers spiraled away from me. My first target exploded backward, arms and legs flailing. I laid on the trigger for what seemed like eternity. Frantic screams screeched from the rice paddy, piercing even the explosions. I could feel the screams more than I could hear them. The NVA scrambled for cover that wasn't there. Some ran from the machine-gun fire and directly into the row of M16s, while those at the front of the column retreated into a shower of lead from the M60. The crossfire was a human lawn mower.

I swept the machine gun from one end of the column to the bottom of the mountains. The phosphorous ends of the tracer rounds broke off the bullets and sizzled like miniature sparklers as they found their mark.

Chan changed clips in his rifle as fast as he could. The barrel of the M60 glowed red, then white. Adrenaline and fear pushed me, while my whole body vibrated to the rhythm of the gun; I became one with my weapon, and we were killing. The barrel became transparent from the heat of continuous fire as I poured another hundred rounds into the rice paddy.

A fluorescent lamp couldn't have pinpointed my position any better than that glowing barrel. I knew the barrel might melt and jam, but I couldn't stop. I felt like I did in my first fistfight, scared to stop swinging for fear of getting hit.

Chan dropped his rifle and started frantically feeding ammo into the gun with both hands. Sam's M79 blooper-round explosions sounded consistent, almost automatic. His loading speed was phenomenal.

Louder, more powerful explosions of grenades and

ChiComs sporadically thundered above the blooper rounds. The speedy bursts of M16 fire mingled with the slower, more powerful cracking of AK fire in a chorus of insane chaos.

Total confusion engulfed the rice paddy. A few NVA fired back. Others dragged dead and wounded toward the safety of the mountains. A flare sizzled into the dark sky, arcing over the paddy, then popping into a tiny sun and drifting down. The lights were on. The miniature red sun added a 3-D effect to an already bloody picture.

Chan screamed and reached for his rifle. Three gooks were running at us, bobbing and weaving in a suicidal charge to knock out the gun. They fired full automatic, spraying bullets all around us. They were screaming. I swept the stream of tracers from left to right, bearing down on them like a sputtering laser beam. A ChiCom blew up ten feet in front of us, stealing my night vision with a white explosion. Incoming bullets kicked dirt into my eyes and mouth. The barrel melted. The gun jammed. The sweeping laser stopped along with my breathing.

I fumbled for my pistol like a drunk in a shoot-out. My vision turned spotty. I heard Chan firing. The grunts on my left opened up full automatic. Blurred images of two men ten meters away came through the spots in my eyes. Their heads jerked back like poorly manned puppets, legs crumbling last, not knowing the upper half was lifeless.

Silence. The loudest silence of my life. My heart pounded the breath out of me faster than I could bring it in. The bloodlust evaporated into the gunpowder air. Pay back. The frustration turned into fatigue . . . Chan . . . "Are you hit?"

"No. Are you?" he asked.

"No. I'll be okay when I see the sun."

"Praise the Lord," whispered Chan.

The night became deathly still. The moon slid behind thick, dark rain clouds. The sting of ants and mosquitoes returned. I felt like talking to Chan, but I knew better than to relax now. I leaned against my pack and stared into the rice paddy.

I felt tired and dull and years older than eighteen. My energy and emotion dripped out of me along with the sweat. My mind escaped to home for an instant. Soft images flowed peacefully through my mind with a harmony of happy scenes. My mom, my stepdad, Paul, and Christmas and Pass-a-Grille Beach and Nancy in a bikini. I'll go to college, I thought. I'll get an apartment with Sid or Ben or Joe. Maybe I could still play football at a little college somewhere. The happy images vanished as the last groans of a dying man drifted through the dank night air. I opened my eyes and waited for the sun and wondered if I would hate the night when I got home.

Dawn finally came, lifting pressure from me with each inch of the yellow sun peeking up behind us. The first movement came from the chief. He moved smoothly from position to position until he made his way to us. He looked to be always in perfect balance.

"We're going out for a body count. Keep us covered." He turned to the tree line and gave a wave. As the chief started into the paddy, Doyle and Striker came out of the tree line with their rifles on their hips. Swift Eagle stopped. He looked over his shoulder at Chan and me. He gave a nod and a thumbs up.

"You did good." His stoic face showed the same expression it always did—none; but his piercing black eyes left no doubt. We had just gotten the seal of approval. We were salts. Old salts.

A body count was grim business. Each corpse told a different story. I wanted to look. I didn't know why. I felt like a morbid tourist gawking hungrily for a glimpse of blood.

The three Marines approached each unmoving body with equal caution, kicking each one hard to get a groan. Doyle hustled around from body to body, picking up rifles and grenades. Swift Eagle waved nonchalantly toward the tree line. The lieutenant came out with Sudsy and his radio close behind. Once in the center of the paddy, Sudsy pulled the pin on a smoke grenade and dropped it. Chan mumbled something as the green smoke billowed into the pale blue sky.

"What?"

"Someone got hit."

"Who?"

"I don't know, but why else would they be spotting for a chopper?" he replied.

The lieutenant looked toward us and shouted, "Guns up!"

We gathered up our packs, grenades, and the little ammo that was left and ran into the rice paddy. As we reached the lieutenant, Swift Eagle pointed at a blood trail leading into the nearby bush.

"We count nineteen, Lieutenant, but we'll find more if we follow some of these trails."

"Take Striker"—he paused and looked around—"and the gun team and follow that trail, but don't go more than a hundred meters away."

A helicopter appeared overhead and began circling down toward the smoke. Chan beat me to the obvious question. "What's the chopper for, Lieutenant?"

Just then Corporal James and Unerstute lumbered out of the tree line carrying a body wrapped in a camouflage poncho liner. The greens, browns, and black of the liner were stained dark with dried blood. The jungle boots of a dead Marine hung limply from one end of the liner. I should have been hardened to the sight of dead comrades by now, but I wasn't. The dead enemy were frozen in a grotesque silence. Some clutched invisible weapons that comrades had pried from their dead hands. Some fought death with open mouths, screaming in silent anguish, while others conceded to it with serenity. They looked curiously black and white, like an old Civil War photograph, as if they had never really been alive. Dead Marines maintained the painful color of loss to me. Red freckles on a young white face and cold dead blue eyes. A letter not finished.

"Who was it?" I asked quietly.

"Billings," the lieutenant said abstractedly.

"I never even met him," I mumbled.

"Doesn't matter now. I want you and Chan to go with the chief and Striker. If there's nineteen here, we must have bagged a load of 'em last night."

"My barrel melted last night," I said.

The lieutenant looked at me angrily. His lower lip disappeared as if he wanted to bite it.

"I thought that was the longest twenty-round burst I've ever seen." He looked away, shaking his head in disgust. "That's the kind of fire discipline the Army employs, John."

"Yes, sir."

"I should send you over to the Seventh." He smiled and looked at the chief. "Old Bill's gunners don't like firin' in the dark." He looked back at me. "Tough night."

The old Korean War–era helicopter floated down to the smoke grenade that was spreading green vapors around like a fog. It looked like the last landing for the rattling, choking machine. Sam crouched over the dead man a few feet from the chopper's giant rotors. He pulled an empty, bloody pocket inside out. He was going through his traditional last-minute search for anything from cigarettes to dry writing paper. It gave me the creeps, but Sam could defend his unwholesome practice by rattling off an endless list of invaluable items that he personally kept out of the hands of pogues in the rear.

"Hey, Sam!" I called as I stumbled over the stiff hand of a dead gook. "Hold that chopper!"

"Move it, Marine!" the chopper gunner shouted at Sam as I reached the chopper door.

"Hey!" I screamed over the noise of the rotors. "I need an M60 barrel real bad. You got a spare?"

The door gunner ignored me and yelled at Sam, "Hurry up, dude! Get that stiff on here. We're not staying for tea!"

Feeling a bit insulted, I tried again. "I need an M60 barrel!"

The gunner leaned out of the door and replied with a nasal New Jersey accent, "This ain't no supply train, girene."

Sam and Doyle picked up the stiff, sidestepped up to the open hatch, coordinated the toss with a three-count, and heaved the body in. The door gunner struggled to drag the dead weight away from the hatchway, grabbing the end of the poncho and pulling. He turned to cover it with a large green canvas. I seized upon this moment to remove the barrel from his door gun. He turned, realized immediately what I'd done, and started to curse. His voice sank in mid-sentence when he noticed the barrel of Sam's blooper gun pointing at his nose. Sam smiled through his rotted teeth like only Sam could.

"Don't speak, jerk face. Just take off. We need the barrel a little bit more than you do."

I guess the door gunner could sense that Sam was a bit strange. He said nothing, and motioned thumbs up to the pilot. The helicopter got away without being fired on.

I gave Sam a pat on the back and hustled back to the chief. We followed the bloody tracks of what was obviously someone being dragged into the bush. Fifty meters in, Swift Eagle held up his hand. He bent forward slightly. He looked like an Indian sneaking up on a settler. He motioned for us to come forward.

At the chief's feet lay two bloody, khaki-clothed NVA soldiers. One was dead. Very dead. Bullet holes ran from his face to his ankles. He was being dragged by means of a hook jammed under his chin and through his mouth. The man doing the dragging wasn't in much better shape. Both legs dangled from the thigh area by some skin and a few tendons. He was bleeding to death but still found the strength to reach out with his left hand, grab a handful of elephant grass, and pull himself a few inches forward. Then with his right hand on the hook, he pulled the dead man a few inches forward.

He didn't know we were watching. We couldn't speak. It didn't seem real.

The chief broke the silence. "Okay. Pick the live one up and drag him back."

Striker and Chan grabbed his arms, but his grip on the hook would not loosen. Swift Eagle finally pried it free, and we started back.

Striker was impressed. "Jesus Christ!" he said. "Did you believe that? Jesus Christ!"

Chan gave Striker a cold, haughty look.

"Jesus Christ! Jesus Christ!" Striker repeated with more emphasis each time.

Chan stopped walking. I could feel his anger growing. "God already knows about it, Striker. If you like his name so much why don't you try praying?" Having said his piece, Chan strengthened his grip on the wounded NVA and began walking again.

Striker looked puzzled. The big black mole between his eyes disappeared as his bushy eyebrows came together in a frown. "I didn't know Jesus Christ was the same as God." Striker's muffled tone sounded like a little kid who had just been scolded.

Chan looked shocked, then almost sad.

"Why don't you let me tell you about Jesus?"

"Tell me about this guy we're carrying," Striker sneered. "He believes in Buddha. Tell me why Jesus is any better than Buddha?"

"Buddha's grave isn't that far from here," Chan replied quickly. "He's dead. His body is still there. He was a schmuck just like you and me. Humanoid. Get it? Muhammad is the same story. He's dead as a doornail. He was just a man."

"Well, just how's this poor sap gonna know who this Jesus is? And what about all your kinfolk in China?"

"Yeah, Chan," I asked. "What about people in Africa or on some island in the middle of nowhere? I mean, I believe in Jesus, but I always wondered how they're supposed to know about him."

"There's a God-shaped vacuum in every man, and men seek to fill that emptiness or reject it for the love of the world around them. You guys aren't the first people to ask that question. I asked the same question myself. Jeremiah 29:13 says, 'And you will seek Me and find Me, when you search for Me with all your heart.' But there is another passage in Romans that explains it better. I have it written down in the front of my Gideon, but it's actually from the NIV."

"What's that?" Striker asked.

"It's the Bible in today's English instead of seventeenth-century English, and, yes, Striker, it says exactly the same thing minus a lot of thees and thous. You're welcome to read it when we get back."

"Let me have it," Swift Eagle said. For a moment I thought I was hallucinating. The chief couldn't have said that.

Chan held his M16 under his arm and reached into his breast pocket with his free hand. He handed the small black Gideon back to Swift Eagle, who opened it immediately. The wonderment on Chan's face was matched by Striker's.

"Romans 1 dash 19 dash 23?"

"That's it. Romans, Chapter 1, verses 19 to 23."

" 'Since what may be known about God is plain to them, because God has made it plain to them.' "

I couldn't believe my ears. He was actually reading out loud. No one will believe this. What am I thinking about? He'd scalp me if I said anything.

" 'For since the creation of the world, God's invisible qualities—his eternal power and divine nature—have been clearly seen, being understood from what has been made, so that men are without excuse.' "

"That's heavy stuff, man," Striker mumbled.

" 'For although they knew God, they neither glorified Him as God nor gave thanks to Him, but their thinking became futile and their foolish hearts were darkened.' "

"I see the lieutenant up ahead," Striker blurted.

"Shut up! I ain't finished!" Swift Eagle barked.

"Sorry, Chief."

" 'Although they claimed to be wise, they became fools and exchanged the glory of the immortal God for images made to look like mortal men and birds and animals and reptiles.' "

No one spoke as we neared the open rice paddy. I peeked back to see the chief's face. He stared straight ahead as he walked, seemingly in deep thought. Striker, struggling with the weight of the dying NVA, looked angry and confused. He didn't ask any more questions. The new information scared him, I thought. As we reached the rice paddy, Striker and Chan laid the prisoner down gently. Chan tried to question him, but he was too weak and drugged up to know what was happening.

"He's a lieutenant. That's all I could get," Chan said.

I felt a tap on the shoulder. I turned to see Sam's pitted face. "I ran out of ace of spades cards. You got any?"

"No, sure don't," I said.

"Ah, crap! I wanted to get 'em all marked." Sam turned and called to Doyle. "Doyle! Got any ace of spades cards?"

"Yeah," Doyle answered.

Sam retrieved the cards and resumed tacking them into the foreheads of the dead NVA soldiers. I stopped him from tacking the dead lieutenant. I don't know why. Final count: twenty-one confirmed. No prisoners.

"Saddle up!"

"Hey, Sudsy, where we going?"

"Dodge City."

DODGE CITY

The last swallow of meatballs and beans always went down in a big lump. It all seemed to be glued together by some foul substance that was undoubtedly supposed to make the food last through another war. The only C-ration food that did taste right was the pound cake, and it was as rare as a pleasant day. It wasn't that C-ration food was beneath me. I grew up on beans and potatoes in West Virginia. For the first twelve years of my life I thought everyone ate that way. Maybe it was because it was time for breakfast, and starting another day on meatballs and beans didn't help my aching back or the big spider bite just under my left eye. But for whatever reason, C-rats just didn't taste good. No flavor. Chan convinced me that by slightly burning the meatballs and beans, then covering them with Tabasco sauce, they began to taste almost like food.

Before the Marine Corps I had never so much as looked at uncooked food in a serious way. I could just barely boil water. Good ol' Mom spared me the indignity of spoiling perfectly good food: She always cooked for me. Chan claimed to be an excellent chef. He would have to prove that if we ever got R&R. I was trying to look serious as he explained the wonders of vichyssoise and the delicacy involved in its preparation when the lieutenant strolled up to our position on the perimeter, chewing, more than smoking, a cigarette that hung out of the corner of his mouth.

"I have to split you guys up. Chan, you're taking over Sanchez's gun." He turned to walk away like he was too busy to talk about it. I couldn't believe my ears.

"Wait a minute, Lieutenant! Why can't somebody else take that gun?" My insubordination surprised me as much as it did him. "We've been together since boot camp!"

"Somebody has to take the other gun, and you two are the only ones left with a machine-gun MOS. I can't put some dumb boot on that gun. Most of these guys can't even take it apart, let alone clean it."

"Has the Marine Corps ever anticipated theoretical need for replacements in this war?" Chan shouted.

"Get a gunner from the rear or another platoon!"

Swift Eagle ambled up next to the lieutenant. He slurped at some strange Indian concoction out of his helmet with a plastic C-ration spoon. Between each bite he stirred in bits of brown plants.

"We'll put you two back together when we get a new gunner," Swift Eagle mumbled with his mouth full.

Lieutenant Campbell nodded his approval. It was settled. I felt like I was losing a brother. It wasn't the kind of thing we talked about. After all, we were supposed to be hard-Corps. Crap, I'd be nineteen in October. It was more than an average friendship, but then, nothing is just average in war.

Chan's parting words came as close to "I'll miss you" as Marine protocol would allow. "Take care of that contagious grin, jarhead. And don't go getting gung-ho without me here to provide guidance. I promised your mother."

"You too, buddy."

Chan walked slowly toward the other side of the perimeter. As soon as I saw Rodgers coming over the crown of the rocky hilltop with his pack and rifle slung over his shoulders, I knew who my new partner was. I tried to hide my disappointment. Rodgers had become dangerously cautious. Red had once warned me about him, and since then I'd seen for myself.

"I'm your new A-gunner." His dejected tone told me he wasn't jumping up and down over the idea either. "Let's get something straight right away, John. I've got seventy-three days left in this armpit, and I don't buy the idea of me being by this gun. I'm short, man. I mean, I'm the shortest salt in the platoon. Next to Jack Ellenwood, I'm the shortest man in Alpha Company. Seventy-three days and I'm getting on that freedom bird and going back to the world in one piece. And I'm not getting killed because of this gun!"

"What makes you think you're the only sucker who wants to go home?" I asked.

"Look, just take it easy on the John Wayne crap, okay?"

"What do you plan on doing when some fool screams 'Guns up'? Should I say, 'Sorry, looks a little dangerous out there for me'? I seem to remember you screaming 'Guns up' a couple of weeks back. Just what did you have planned if I didn't open up?"

He paused and dropped his pack. "You and Chan go overboard sometimes. Even the lieutenant said you guys were crazy. He thought you needed a Section 8."

That one stumped me. I knew the lieutenant thought we were gung-ho, but I didn't think he thought we were nuts.

"I'm still here, ain't I? I've lasted longer than any gunner in the regiment. If I'd've been running around like a fag on ice I'd've been dead the first week in country!"

"You're dumb lucky, and you know it!"

"Maybe, but let's get one thing clear, Rodgers. When you hear 'Guns up,' you better be right on my butt!"

Rodgers sat down, lit a cigarette, and leaned back on his pack. He looked nervous. "I don't know. Maybe you're right." He shot his words out in abrupt spurts. "I might be getting a little edgy. Things change when you're short. Wait till your time is short. You know how many guys I've seen get blown away in the last couple of weeks of their tour?"

"I just hope I get to be short," I said. I leaned back on my own pack. My filthy jungle jacket felt scratchy and stiff with two months' worth of dried body salt. I hated wearing the smelly thing, but unprotected flesh wouldn't last a week in the bush.

"Do you know what's going on back in the world right now?" he asked. "Fags and hippies are becoming Canadians. Jane Fonda is telling the world we kill women and kids. Do you think for one second that rich witch mentioned the thousands of civilians the NVA butchered in Hue? Our own countrymen are sending money and medical supplies to the gooks! Were you on that patrol yesterday?"

"Which one?"

"The one that reconned that arty strike."

"Yeah, I was on it. Charlie got caught cold, too. We found at least fifteen cartridge belts or what was left of 'em. Blood everywhere. Flesh fried onto some of them."

"Any confirmed?"

"No," I said. "But I know where you're heading, and it's true."

"Sudsy told me you guys found a load of bandages stamped gifts from the Friends' Service Committee."

"Yeah, we did."

"I rest my case. Not only are we not even trying to win this war, but our own people are helping the gooks."

"I don't know what we're arguing about. I agree with ya. But you joined the Crotch, man. You weren't drafted. I don't know about you, but I've seen enough to know this much: The NVA ain't the good guys."

"They're bloody butchers. I know that," he said.

"And Jane Fonda's talkin' out her rear end. She's a traitor!"

"I know that, too. I've been here longer than you,

John. What I'm trying to say is, just who's on our side if our own people aren't? The South Vietnamese aren't worth defending."

I hated to admit it, but he was right. I looked east toward the ominous gray mountains. I remembered Red calling the mountains outside Phu Bai a gook R&R center. I turned back to Rodgers.

"Maybe I'm getting a little crazy. I don't know anymore. But I want to shoot these scumbags. If I ain't killing them for America or South Vietnam, I'll just kill 'em for Red or Paunchy or Simmons, or just because they tick me off."

"What's this place done to you, John? I knew you when you first got here, man. You never wanted to kill anybody. You were just a kid. You're not even nineteen yet, are you?"

"I will be on October 12th. Maybe I don't really want to kill. I don't want any of this. I want to go home in one piece, and I don't think I'll make it if I get cautious."

"Let's change the subject," Rodgers said. "We can't change anything anyway." He removed his helmet, then pulled out his wallet, wrapped in clear plastic, from inside the straps of the helmet liner. He removed a folded newspaper clipping from his wallet and handed it to me. I unfolded it. The headline read "Local Man Wounded in Battle of Hue City." Beneath that, framed by the story, was his boot-camp dress-blues picture. I felt total envy. Then he made it worse.

"I've had three different girls send me that clipping. The last one promises me anything I want when I get home."

"That's great! Sometimes I hope I get a Purple Heart just so they'll put it in the paper and remind some of my friends where I am."

I started feeling a little easier about Rodgers. The sun began baking away the morning dew. I grabbed a couple of sticks and threw my poncho over them. It wasn't much of a lean-to, but it kept the sun off my face.

Rodgers looked a little nervous. "Are we going to be here long enough for that?" he asked.

"Yeah," I answered. "Sudsy says we're getting resupplied. Besides, we sure aren't hiding from anyone out here in the open."

Once the poncho was up, I closed my eyes and tried to replace the filth and insects with dreams of strawberry shortcake and fast cars. The popping sound of a helicopter making a steep turn quickly dispatched any hope of catching some Zs.

I opened my eyes. A CH-46 helicopter floated gracefully down to the center of the perimeter. The last mail drop was over two weeks ago. A word from home was becoming vital. The chopper bounced slightly, then settled down. Out of the hatchway leaped a new replacement. He stumbled under the weight of a pack that was far too heavy. He resembled a newborn colt with his legs wobbling in and out. A grenade hung from every available space. He carried at least two canteens too many and enough bandoliers of M16 ammo to supply most of the platoon. But the small stack of mail he clutched in one hand quickly overwhelmed any interest we had in the new boot.

"Is this the gun team?" he asked Rodgers. He held his pack and rifle in his arms and spoke around four letters he held clenched in his teeth.

"This is it," Rodgers said.

The boot dropped his pack. He pulled the letters out of his mouth, revealing that cocky smile that every boot brings to the Nam. He made me feel like an old man. His first words didn't surprise me a bit.

"Are the gooks close? I want to see some combat. My name is Barnes. Orlando, Florida. The lieutenant told me to sit in with you guys for the night." He looked at Rodgers, who was pressing the bridge of his nose and shaking his head. I tried not to laugh. He looked at me, puzzled, knowing he was on the outside of an inside joke. He looked so healthy. That bull neck, like a college football player, that young men coming out of Parris Island always have. Not tired or underweight. No dark rings under the eyes. No conception of fear or fatigue. He had that look that says, "I'm here now, let's get this war over with."

All four letters were for me. Three from the folks and one from a girlfriend named Nancy. Nancy sent me a picture of her in a red bikini. The three of us took turns reading her letter and moaning. The day drifted by rather pleasantly after that. For some reason we didn't move from the small hill all day. A rare treat. A chance to take my boots off and let the jungle rot dry out in the steaming sun. A chance to write a letter. I cleaned the gun oil and grit out of my toothbrush and tried to give my now yellow teeth a good toothpasteless going over. All of this in between a banter of questions from our new boot, Barnes.

"Where's the rest of your gun team?"

"This is it," I said.

"I thought there was supposed to be five guys."

"Yeah, right. And a squad is supposed to be a bare minimum of twelve men, but our biggest squad is seven."

"Well, how many guys are in this platoon, anyway? They told us minimum strength was forty-four men."

"Yeah, I know. Just forget all that crap. This platoon's never been over twenty-two men since I've been here. We have half-strength companies covering areas that need at least a battalion."

"Will we see any gooks today?"

"Don't say that, man!" Rodgers snapped. "You're going to bring us bad luck with that talk." He went back to writing a letter. A deep frown creased his face.

"Don't tell me being short makes you superstitious, too," I prodded. Rodgers ignored me, but the frown re-

Big Red on graduation from Parris Island. This was the photo the author did not recognize in the *Cincinnati Enquirer* years later. Notice in the photo below the change in Red's looks that a few months in the bush caused. "Vietnam made nineteen-year-olds look like thirty-year-olds." (Richard Weaver memorial collection)

Richard "Big Red" Michael Weaver. Three Purple Hearts, Bronze Star with V device, Vietnamese Cross of Gallantry, and several other medals. Red was killed in action at Phu Loc, Thua Thien Province, I Corps Tactical Zone, on May 20, 1968. This photo was taken before moving into the A Shau Valley in 1968. (Richard Weaver memorial collection)

Pvt. Johnnie M. Clark. Boot camp graduation from Parris Island, South Carolina, 1967. Wounded three times in the 1968 Tet Offensive. The Silver Star, three Purple Hearts, the Vietnamese Cross of Gallantry with palm, Vietnam Civil Action Medal, Marine Combat Action Ribbon, and various campaign medals. (Author's collection)

The author and PFC Richard Chan, April Fools' Day, 1968, Phu Bai. A hot miserable dust bowl that felt like R&R compared to the bush. (Author's collection)

PFC Johnnie M. Clark, holding the M-60 machine gun at the Truoi River Bridge, 1968. A new bridge is being constructed in the background by American Seabees. Photo taken just before the long hump into the mountains where we discovered the NVA training replica of the Truoi Bridge. (Author's collection)

First Platoon, Alpha Company, staging at the southern tip of the A Shau Valley for choppers into Elephant Valley. Kneeling, left to right: Doc Michael Turley and Doc Chris Rieger. June 1968. (Photo courtesy of Doc Michael Turley)

Front row, left to right: Lance Corporal Layman holding a can in front of the sleeping author's face, Stew Campbell, Cpl. Bob "Sudsy" Carroll, and Pvt. Abernathy. Lance Corporal Hensley is behind Abernathy. Back row, left to right: Cpl. Fred Huteson, Private First Class Mariani, L/Cpl. Bruce Trebil, and Pvt. Buford Unerstute, the Marine whose heart stopped. (Photo courtesy of Robert Carroll)

Gunny McDermott standing (back to camera) as the platoon is transported up the Truoi River. This is the same way the author was medevaced out later. (Photo courtesy of Sgt. Stacy Watson)

PFC Pat McCrary, An Hoa village, 1969. Feeding the Vietnamese kids as Marines often did. Pat was PFC Barnes in the chapter "Dodge City." He was wounded in the graveyard. (Photo courtesy of Pat McCrary)

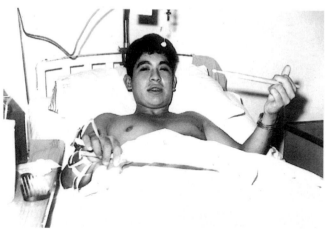

Cpl. Jesus Quintana (Corporal Sanchez in this book) in a stateside naval hospital six weeks after being wounded. He was awarded the Bronze Star with V and two Purple Hearts among other decorations. (Photo courtesy of Cpl. Jesus Quintana)

Cpl. Quintana (Paunchy Villa Sanchez) just four hours before he lost both his legs to a 155mm booby-trapped artillery shell, An Hoa combat base. Four other Marines were killed and the gunny seriously wounded in Dodge City, Arizona Territory. (Photo courtesy of Jesus Quintana)

The author, looking and feeling exhausted, takes a break in the A Shau Valley, 1968. Soon after this photo was taken the author was wounded for the first time by a mortar round. (Author's collection)

PFC Richard Chan poses after capturing an enemy soldier in Quang Nam Province, 1968. (Author's collection)

Gy.Sgt. Mac McDermott fires his 12-gauge shotgun at the enemy along a river in the Thua Thien Province, 1968. Bridge duty was considered easy compared to being in the bush. (Photo courtesy of Sgt. Stacy Watson)

Gunny McDermott of A1/5 gets Marines "saddled up" in An Hoa, August 1968. Note the shotgun and shells, Gunny's calling card. (Photo courtesy of Sergeant Major McDermott)

Sgt. Stacy Watson of A1/5 stands with the flag that was raised over the Citadel by the 5th Marines after the victory of the Battle of Hue City during the Tet Offensive in 1968. Awarded the Presidential Unit Citation. Photo taken before his best friend, Cpl. Frank Burris (Jack Ellenwood in the book), was KIA, August 9, 1968. (Photo courtesy of Sgt. Stacy Watson)

An old French army tank and the three-story bunker that ARVN gunners fired from when the Truoi River Bridge was overrun. The M-24 Chaffee tank was equipped with a 75mm main gun, had a top speed of thirty-five miles per hour, and carried a crew of up to five men. (Author's collection)

"Frenchie" writing a letter home from the Truoi Bridge. It was here that a Marine was pinned under the bridge and an entire Marine gun team killed. (Author's collection)

Eighteen-year-old PFC Johnnie Clark in front of the three-story bunker at the Truoi Bridge, just moments before his first long-term experience in the bush, April 1968. (Author's collection)

mained. I wasn't sure which was worse. A boot ready to shoot at anything or a salt who was scared of his shadow.

Ten days and one hundred fifty zigzagged miles later we found ourselves greeted by an early morning drizzle in a lovely little area called Dodge City. I always wondered what colorful character came up with all these names on the grid map. The name was appropriate. The chief called it a meat grinder. The VC's main effort was shifting to the central province of Quang Nam, with Da Nang as the ultimate target. The lieutenant said two major operations, "Allen Brook" and "Mameluke Thrust," were screening the enemy's avenues of approach to Da Nang. The gooks were calling it the Third Offensive, but it was all part of the Tet Offensive.

A flight of three camouflaged Phantoms flew in formation overhead as we set up a perimeter for an early meal on a small wooded hump on the flat muddy terrain. Rodgers and Barnes started up a game of Back Alley, the Marine Corps's favorite card game. The thunder of bombers sounded close. I pulled out my red bikini picture of Nancy and spent some time drooling and dreaming.

"Wow! I never saw that one!" I looked up to see the freckled face of Sudsy looking over my shoulder and biting his tongue.

"Florida girls, buddy," I said. "Ain't nothin' like 'em. Got any news?"

"Yeah." He sat down and snatched the picture from me. "The whole place is crawling with gooks, man." He spoke with his eyes glued to the picture of Nancy. "The 26th met an NVA battalion at My Loc."

"Where's that? And don't let my picture get wet."

"Three miles northeast of An Hoa," he said.

"That's close."

"They followed 'em across the Thu Bon River into Dodge City. Did you see those Phantoms go over?"

"Yeah. They aren't far away either. Have you heard 'em? They're blastin' somebody."

"Then how come we're just sitting here?" Barnes asked disappointedly.

"Quit saying that, man!" Rodgers snapped. "It's bad luck!"

"What about us?" I asked.

Sudsy handed me back the picture. "You wouldn't believe the crap going on all around right now. The radio's jammed with it."

"What about us?" I asked again.

"Lieutenant Campbell told the gunny that HQ thinks the better part of the 308th NVA Division is roaming around here trying to get to Da Nang."

"Division!" Rodgers shouted.

"What are we doing here with twenty-one men?" I asked.

"Some genius decided that we should thrust through Dodge City."

"Us?" Rodgers shouted. He threw his cards into the mud.

"Well, not by ourselves. We're joining up with the First and Third Platoons. The whole regiment is out there somewhere. We're part of Operation Mameluke Thrust."

My stomach tightened up. I knew better than to think negative. Sometimes negativity sneaks up on a person. Maybe I was just being romantic, but those colorful names popping into my life gave me an eerie sense of impending doom. I'd already heard too much about Dodge City. I let myself slip into the stupidest mental trap of all: I decided this would be the place I'd probably finally get it. I wanted to boot myself in the butt.

It's not my style to think about dyin', I thought. Then why am I sure I'm going to die?

"What's buggin' you?" Sudsy asked. I ignored him and tried to remember what Chan had told me about praying for grace to endure pain or fear. I still didn't know what grace was, but I knew I needed it. God, please give me your grace to endure this chicken attitude I got right now. Amen.

I looked up. Sudsy, Barnes, and Rodgers were looking at me with puzzled expressions.

"What?" I asked.

"You just looked like you saw a ghost," Rodgers said.

"I think I need a cup of coffee," I said, feeling a little better.

"Yeah, me too," Rodgers said. He reached into his pack and tossed me a chunk of C-4 plastique explosive. I pulled an empty C-ration can out of my pack and punched a few holes in it with my K-bar, put the C-4 in, and put a lit match to it. Barnes yelped and dove for cover, landing square in the middle of an old mortar crater filled with mud and rain. It was perfect. We laughed so hard even Barnes had to laugh.

"Barnes, what are you doing sitting in a mud puddle?" We stopped laughing and looked up to see the lieutenant standing over us, rain cascading off his helmet, arms folded, and not smiling.

"They lit that C-4 and I thought it was going to blow up!"

The lieutenant knelt down on one knee beside me. "Think you could give me some help with one of the men, John?" he said, ignoring Barnes and our illegal use of C-4.

It stunned me. The lieutenant needing my help. I was a mere PFC. I felt flattered. So flattered that I committed the ultimate Marine Corps sin. I volunteered.

"Sure, Lieutenant. What do you need?"

"Do you know Private Unerstute?"

"I know who he is, but I don't really know him. The blond guy, right? Kinda goofy-looking?" I remembered Jackson sticking that rubber snake to his rear end.

"Yeah. He's really having a tough time adjusting. He's

scared real bad. He cries incessantly. Sam said he wets his pants on every patrol. I've tried calming him down, but I can't get through."

"Why don't you send him home as unfit for combat?"

"That's the next step, but he's begged me not to do that."

"Why?" Rodgers asked. "I'd take it in a second."

Lieutenant Campbell paused. He looked irritated for a moment with Rodgers butting into our conversation.

"He's an Iowa farm boy, a good kid. He says he has to stick it out. From what I've been able to gather, he's worried more about what his parents think of him than he is about going nuts over here. You couldn't meet a nicer guy, but I'm going to have to dump him before he gets himself or somebody else killed. It's up to you if you want to try to help him. You don't have to."

"Why me? What can I do?"

"He needs to be around someone who can still laugh. I'm hoping your attitude might rub off on him. Talk to him, see if you can get him to relax." Lieutenant Campbell's eyes looked tired. He looked so healthy, so Middle American when I first met him five months ago in Hue City. Day by day he'd grown harder, thinner, and more serious. He didn't look the least bit like a full-faced college kid now.

"Sure, I'll do what I can," I said. He gave me a nod and started to walk away. "Lieutenant?" He turned back around. "Somebody told me you thought Chan and me were Section 8s. Do you really?"

He started chuckling. "Anybody who can laugh through this has to be a little crazy." His look became more serious. "No. The gunny and I were just joking about how you guys are always cracking up. See what you can do about getting that kind of laugh out of Private Unerstute."

"Yes, sir."

A few minutes later PFC Buford Unerstute plodded up

to our muddy position on the side of our small hill. He was thin. He moved slowly, like an old plow horse. A strip of blond hair dipped to his eyebrows from under a helmet that looked too big. His crimson nose was too large for his sunken cheeks. His eyebrows seemed permanently squinched, as if he were straining to see something more clearly. His boots looked at least two sizes too big; in fact, everything he had on looked too big, including his ears.

"I'm sup-po-posed to sit in with you guys." Unerstute's stuttering words fit him perfectly. Dickens couldn't have imagined a shier, humbler, or more instantly likable character.

He reminded me of a basset hound I once loved.

Rodgers looked at him and chuckled. "How did you manage to find utilities that fit that badly?"

Buford shuffled his feet and looked down as he spoke. "I always been odd-sized."

"Pull up some mud and have a seat," I said.

He sat down slowly. He started looking around nervously. He smelled like dried urine.

"How'd you get a fire started?"

"We lit up some C-4," Rodgers said, protecting our coffee from the rain with his helmet.

Buford stiffened. His mouth came open, but no words would form.

"Not you, too?" I said. "How long have you been in the bush?"

"Six weeks."

"Calm down," Rodgers said. "I couldn't stand another swan dive into the mud."

"It takes a few volts to ignite C-4. It's safe to burn," I said, but Buford looked like he was still ready to run. "So you're from Iowa?"

"No. Idaho. Aren't you scared they'll see the fire?" I looked around our small hill at the flat terrain.

"We sure aren't hiding from anybody out here in the

open." I let a quiet moment pass. "Why did you join the Marine Corps?" I asked.

Buford dropped his head and mumbled timidly, "I don't know."

"Unerstute, did the lieutenant tell you where he wants me?" Barnes asked.

"With Swift Eagle's squad. On the other side of the hill. Go straight across."

Barnes picked up his pack and rifle. "See you guys later."

"Tell Swift Eagle I have a can of ham and eggs on the bargaining table," I said.

Barnes waved. With pack and rifle thrown over one shoulder he sloshed away.

"I'm glad that guy's gone," Rodgers mumbled.

"He's okay. Maybe a little boot, but not a bad guy," I said.

"He was bad luck," Rodgers said as he stirred some coffee into the boiling water with the tip of his K-bar.

"Buford, what did you do back in the world?" I asked.

"Just helped out on the farm." He talked as slow as he moved, drawing out each word almost like an old Southerner.

"Did you play ball?"

"No."

"Were you into cars?"

"No. Daddy wouldn't let me have a car. He said I'd just wreck it."

"Women? Sports? Drinking? What'd you do for fun?"

"I never was much good at anything. I liked to farm and take care of the cows and pigs the most. Momma said it was the only thing I was half good at."

"Quit lowering your head when you talk. That's nothing to be ashamed of, liking animals. It sounds to me like your folks were real ego builders. Doesn't it, Rodgers?"

"Sure does."

"Why did you join the Crotch?" I asked.

"Daddy said it'd be a poor day when the country let the likes of me defend the family. They all laughed at me and said I couldn't do it."

"Your folks?" I asked.

"Them and my brothers. So I took off and did it. They ain't written me yet. I'm scared. How come you ain't scared?"

"Bull! I'm as scared as you are," I said.

"No. I seen you and Chan always laughing. How can you do it?"

"Bull crap, Unerstute. Everybody here is scared. People are different in the way they handle things. I get so scared sometimes I just start shaking. When it gets really bad I start reading the Bible. Honest! See, I keep it right here all the time." I pulled my wounded Gideon from my chest pocket, unwrapped the plastic around it, and handed it to Buford.

As he took the little Bible from me, my own words rang clear in my head. It was as if for the very first time I realized what was keeping me on solid ground while others seemed to be floundering. I sure did my share of panicking, I thought, but all I had to do to get squared away was talk to the Man and I got by. Not because I laughed, but because I prayed.

"You got a hole in it."

"Yeah," I said, feeling dumbfounded by my own revelation.

"Yeah. Shrapnel," I explained belatedly.

His mouth fell open. It did that every time he was surprised or shocked, and it looked like he remained in a constant state of shock or surprise.

"We went to church sometimes," he said.

"I went to church all my life from West Virginia to Florida, but I never learned a thing about the Bible. It's the only book in the world that tells the future. Chan says there's ten thousand prophesies in there, and it hasn't missed one yet. You should talk to Chan. He can show you where to look for whatever problem you got and where God tells you how to handle it. And there's all kinds of stuff about fear, man. It's better than doing that!" I pointed to his bloody nubs that were once fingernails. "You should talk to Chan. I'm gonna go get him."

"Wait a second, John," Rodgers said. "You got a leech on the back of your neck." Rodgers bent over a book of matches to protect it from the drizzle. He lit one and touched it to the back of my neck. Buford's mouth fell open again. A large, slimy leech, fat with my blood, fell to the mud. I stomped it with the heel of my boot. It just flattened out and started crawling away.

"You just can't kill those things!" I said.

"Saddle up!" someone called from the CP.

"Did somebody just say those words?" I asked.

"Saddle up! We're movin' out!" Sudsy shouted from the top of the hill. His radio was already strapped on.

"You better chug your coffee," Rodgers said. He handed me a C-ration can of smoking coffee. I took my coffee and chugged it.

"We'll see Chan the first chance we get, okay?" I said to Buford. He nodded yes.

The daily hike was always bad. The weather for these strolls varied from horrible to just awful. For the next three days we thumped foolishly around Dodge City looking for the bad guys. I hoped we wouldn't meet any, at least not until I got Chan back. Rodgers and Unerstute worried me. The nagging feeling that I wouldn't make it through the next firefight hung over me like a vulture. I couldn't shake the feeling that these two would cost me my life. In spite of my own fear, I'd grown to respect Unerstute as much as anyone in Nam just for sticking it out.

In the afternoon of the third day we set up a perimeter on a small ridge on the north side of the Thu Bon River.

As soon as we set in, I went looking for Chan's position. I found him eating pound cake behind a tree stump.

"Where did you get that?" I asked. He raised one eyebrow.

"It's about time you visited." Chan stood up. He offered me a bite of his cake. "You won't believe my A-gunner."

"Same here, buddy. I got two guys that scare me to death." I took a bite and handed it back.

"I have an A-gunner that doesn't know which end to put the bullets in. He's a pig farmer from Missouri. He has positively the worst enunciation of the English language I've ever heard."

"Do you know Unerstute?" I asked.

"Yes. I know who he is."

"He really needs help, Chan. He's scared to death. He shakes all night long. He gets so scared he just wets his pants all the time. Anyway, the lieutenant asked me to try to talk to him to see if I could calm him down. You need to talk to him about the Bible. You know, show him some places he should read."

"Sure. Let's go see him."

"Probably be better if I send him over to you. That way you can talk to him alone."

"Okay." I turned to walk back to Buford.

"Hey, John. Did Sudsy tell you we're meeting up with the First and Third Platoons?" Chan asked.

"Yeah."

"Take care of yourself."

"You too," I said. I gave Chan the thumbs up sign. He returned it. "And keep the bursts short."

"You too. Twenty rounds max," he replied.

"Don't I always?" I said with a chuckle.

"Yeah, right."

An hour later Sudsy showed up looking for Unerstute.
"He's talking to Chan," I said.

"He's moving back to the chief's squad. Tell him to get over there when he gets back."

"Are we getting Barnes back?" I asked.

"No. It's just you two."

"Oh good. I'd hate to get used to too much sleep every night," I growled sarcastically.

"What's up, Suds?" Rodgers asked.

"We're meeting First and Third Platoons on the other side of the river in about an hour."

"Sixty days left, and we go on an operation now." Rodgers looked into the sky as if he were angry with God.

"I wish you'd quit worrying about being short. You're starting to make me nervous," I said. "We better get ready. Here, start cleaning the gun. I'll go get Buford."

I walked around the perimeter. Every man in the platoon seemed to be cleaning a weapon. I found Chan showing Buford something in the Bible. Buford's face looked almost relaxed for a change. The strained lines of stress across his forehead had actually eased away, at least for the moment. He looked up at me as I got closer.

"Did you tell Chan what I told you about my folks?" he asked, as if accusing me.

"No."

"You swear?"

"Yeah," I said. "Why?"

"You swear on the Bible? Both of you?"

"Yes," Chan said. "He never said a word about your folks. It's God. He does things like that."

"What's this all about?" I asked.

"You told me how scared Buford was, so I wanted to show him that one of the bravest men in history was scared to death and wrote this prayer to the Lord. Here, I'll read it.

"The Lord is my light and my salvation;
Whom shall I fear?
The Lord is the defense of my life;

Whom shall I dread?
My adversaries and my enemies, they stumbled and fell
Though a host encamp against me,
My heart will not fear;
Though war arise against me,
In spite of this I shall be confident. . . .
Do not abandon me nor forsake me,
O God of my salvation!
For my father and my mother have forsaken me,
But the Lord will take me up."

Chan closed the Bible and looked up at me. I didn't know what to say. Buford's eyes were misty.

"I don't know, man," I said. "It sure sounds like a setup, but I swear it isn't. I didn't say a word about your folks to Chan. I think you just got the word from the Man."

"Honest, now?" Buford's voice cracked. "You guys wouldn't lie about it, would you?"

"No way," Chan said.

"I don't mean to change the subject, but you've been put back in Swift Eagle's squad, and I think we're moving out soon."

"Okay. We'll be done in a minute," Chan said.

I walked back to Rodgers in a trance. I'd always believed in God, but after all, He'd never said, "Hey, John. Here I am." I felt a little spooked and a lot glad about it. I knew Buford would be okay. Before I could tell Rodgers about it, some fool shouted, "Saddle up!"

We crossed the cool golden Thu Bon River and humped two klicks south. There the terrain flattened out into large fields of brown and green elephant grass and old unworked rice paddies. I turned my collar up and pulled my hands inside my sleeves as the point man led us into the ten-foot-tall grass. A breeze swept across the giant field, making it look as soft as a calm, undulating ocean, but each blade of this wave could cut a man's skin as quickly as a razor, and the slightest cut would be infected within hours.

We finally broke through to a soggy brown clearing. There, in a large perimeter, sat the First and Third Platoons.

Rodgers tapped me on the shoulder and pointed to a mortar team. "Even Weapons Platoon is here. I don't like it."

"Saddle up! Saddle up! Saddle up!" The order ricocheted around the perimeter. We marched straight through the soggy clearing and into another field of elephant grass. The other platoons linked up to our rear. I thought about the mortar men behind us and how glad I was not to be carrying one of those heavy mothers. We crossed another clearing and into a waist-high field of elephant grass.

An occasional island of trees or group of shrubs dotted the landscape. Swift Eagle led his squad left, pulling away from the column and fanning out. Then Corporal James's squad followed. The entire Second Platoon spread out on line, sweeping across the field of saw grass. I held the gun at my hip. No one said a word. I felt anxious. I wanted a drink but I didn't dare reach for a canteen. Two hundred meters ahead a row of tall trees stood out in the flat terrain.

Huge dark rain clouds rolled in from behind the tall trees. Swift Eagle cupped a hand around his mouth, shielding his voice from our front, and called past me to Lieutenant Campbell fifteen meters to my right, "I smell smoke!"

I caught a movement out of the corner of my eye. Someone yelled. Sam fired the blooper. Three uniformed NVA were running away from us forty yards ahead. The sharp, white explosion of a blooper round hit the trailing man square. He flipped forward and landed on his back.

"Guns up! Guns up!"

I ran forward, firing from the hip. The other two NVA

ducked down and disappeared into the elephant grass. I stopped, stood still, and fired the M60 from the shoulder at the area where I'd last seen them. I ceased fire.

"There they are!" Rodgers shouted.

They popped up from the tall grass a good thirty yards closer to the tree line. I let loose another twenty-round burst just as they disappeared again. The entire platoon ran forward.

"Guns up! Guns up!" Lieutenant Campbell screamed as he ran forward. The two NVA were half carrying, half dragging the third, his arms draped over the shoulders of his comrades. They dove behind the tree line.

The lieutenant screamed, "Halt! Guns up!"

I ran forward, with Rodgers close behind. A second later Chan and his A-gunner, the pig farmer, ran up beside us.

"Recon that tree line!" The lieutenant's voice sounded unusually high-pitched. We both opened up, firing from the hip. Pieces of the trees spit in all directions as we raked the area where we had last seen the NVA.

"Cease fire! Move out!" Lieutenant Campbell shouted.

"Quick! Throw in some ammo, Rodgers!" I shouted. Rodgers tore off a belt from around his shoulders. I pulled up the feed cover. He fumbled with the ammo. "Hurry up!" He slapped it in, and I closed the feed cover and started forward again. An M16 opened up to my left.

"Cease fire! Guns up! Guns up!"

We reached the tree line. The NVA were gone. Just on the other side of the trees was a graveyard. Chan opened up. I followed his tracers with my eyes. The NVA were struggling to drag their limp comrade behind a grass hootch fifty yards away at the edge of a thick dark jungle.

"Fire on that hootch!" Lieutenant Campbell shouted.

I ran forward ten yards to the first round grave mound of dirt and opened up. Orange tracers ripped through the wood and grass hootch, streaming into the dark jungle behind it.

"Cease fire!" Lieutenant Campbell shouted from the trees behind me.

"Get back behind the trees!" Rodgers shouted. I turned to see him crouching beside the lieutenant, who was standing. I ran back to the tree cover, gasping for air but too hyped up to calm down and breathe normally.

"Swift Eagle! Take a squad and sweep to that hootch!" Lieutenant Campbell grabbed Sudsy by the shoulder. "Tell First and Third Platoon to move up to the rice paddy one hundred meters to my left! Weapons Platoon too! Chan!"

"Here!" Chan answered as he ran forward.

"You cover Swift Eagle's squad from the left flank! John!"

"Yeah!"

"Take your gun down to that end of the tree line and cover Swift Eagle from the right flank! Hurry!"

"Let's go, Rodgers!"

I ran as fast as I could. Sudsy's transmission rang clear as we went: "Alpha One, Alpha One, this is Alpha Two. We have a shoot-out in Dodge City. . . ." A cold chill sent a violent shiver up my neck.

Others were running in the same direction. They dropped off, taking positions at five- and ten-yard intervals. Daylight was going fast. Huge clouds blotted out what was left of the afternoon sun. We finally reached our end of the tree line, a good seventy yards from the lieutenant's end. Thunder echoed from the sinister clouds. Death felt near, as if it were riding the cold damp wind.

Three riflemen from Corporal James's squad ran by me, scattering into positions on my right flank. A welcome sight. I didn't like being stuck out on the end by myself. I set the gun up behind the last tree and took aim at the hootch on the other side of the graveyard slightly to my left. Rodgers slid in beside me, breathing heavily.

He looked pale. It started raining. Swift Eagle's squad was already twenty meters into the open graveyard and sweeping on line toward the hootch.

"Link up some ammo!" I barked. Rodgers stared into the graveyard.

Without warning the darkening graveyard lit up with the green tracers of enemy machine guns crisscrossing Swift Eagle's squad. One fired from a position twenty meters to the right of the hootch and nearly straight across from me. The other fired from twenty meters on the other side of the hootch. Then a third gun opened up from just to the right of the hootch, raking back and forth and sending tracer rounds whining in every direction. The dark jungle behind the hootch erupted with muzzle flashes. The lead Marine lifted up and flew backward from the blast of two streams of machine-gun tracers hitting him from the right and left. Fifty yards away a helmeted NVA stood up beside the hootch and side-armed a canvas satchel charge into the graveyard. The squad dove behind the oval Vietnamese grave mounds.

Brilliant flashes of light were followed by clouds of smoke and mud. A ChiCom exploded. Then another satchel charge overwhelmed the smallish ChiCom explosion. Then three more ChiComs, one right after another.

Our riflemen couldn't fire, for fear of hitting the pinned-down squad between us and the enemy. I jumped to my feet, ran twenty meters into the open graveyard, and stood on top of one of the round grave mounds. Now I could fire without hitting the squad. Before I pulled the trigger, Chan opened up from the other end of the tree line. His orange tracers pinpointed him. Immediately all three enemy guns shifted their fire from the squad to Chan. Firing from the hip, I opened up on the closest stream of green tracers. The constant recoil of the long burst of fire supported the barrel of the M60 with little

help from me. The incredible weapon was perfectly balanced. I guided my tracers into the nearest enemy machine gun. His green tracers shot up, high into the dark
rainy sky, then ceased. A hit! I knew it. I saw tracers sweeping toward me. My gun stopped. "Ammo!" I screamed
and looked around for Rodgers. He was still behind the
trees. Suddenly my feet kicked out from under me. I was
laying on my face. I felt stunned but I knew I wasn't hit.
A moment later someone pulled me by my feet back behind the mound. Rodgers! I started to thank him but
didn't. It was his fault I was out of ammo.

Bullets thudded into the small mound. More bullets
churned up mud on both sides of us. We huddled against
the grave and each other trying to pull in arms and legs
behind the precious dirt. The graves were made in the
shape of a woman's womb, because the Vietnamese
figure that's where you start so that's where you finish. I
wanted to crawl back in right now.

The firing stopped. We waited a few seconds. I peeked
over the mound. Small clouds of sulphurous gunpowder
hovered above, but no flashes.

"Let's go!" I grabbed the gun and darted for the cover
of the tree line. Rodgers ran past me like I was standing
still. My foot felt odd but I didn't dare look down. We
dove behind the end tree. I checked my right boot.

"Look at that!" I said, and I pointed at the sole. The
heel had a bullet hole clean through.

"Are you hit?"

"No."

"Man, you're lucky you still have a foot!"

The sound of a blooper gun echoed from our right
flank. Two quick explosions cracked behind us like lightning, followed immediately by two more much closer.
Another *bloop*. Ten yards behind us mud and shrapnel
shot out of the ground.

"Incoming!" a voice on our right screamed. "The
gook's got a blooper!"

I turned right with the M60. Three Marines were in my field of fire, already shooting into the bush to our right.

"Ammo!" I shouted at Rodgers, angry that he hadn't already started loading the gun and wishing for Chan.

"Pull back! Pull back!"

"Did you hear that?" Rodgers tugged on my shoulder. The monsoon rain started pelting us like drops of cement. The Marines firing at the blooper vanished in the deluge.

"Pull back!" Someone was pulling at my pack. I looked up. Corporal James shouted down, "Pull back! Pull back to the lieutenant!" The rain pounded loudly into the ground, nearly smothering his shouts.

"We got three men over there!" I shouted back. "Pull back! I'll go get 'em!" He ran toward the three Marines. A few seconds later he reappeared, with the Marines following. Halfway back to the lieutenant the rain eased up enough for me to hear someone shouting.

"Hold it! Do you hear that?" I said. We stopped and stood still. "I heard someone screaming."

"Help us! We got Marines out here! Help! Barnes is hit!" Now the scream echoed from the dark graveyard with frightening clarity. The rain picked up again. I ran to the edge of the tree line with Corporal James.

"I can't see a thing!" James said.

"We got to help 'em!" I said.

"We have to tell the lieutenant! Come on!" He pulled on my arm. I followed him. We ran through the mud as fast as we could. I kept thinking of Barnes, so eager to see war. A vision of the Marine being blown backward by the machine-gun fire flashed through my mind. It had been him. Barnes.

"Lieutenant!" James shouted.

"Here! Over here!" The voice came from the darkness ahead. Now I could see him. The rain was so thick he looked gray.

"Lieutenant! We still have men out there!" James shouted.

"I know. At least three. The rest are all right. Is that everyone from that end?"

"Yes."

"Is Chan okay?" I asked.

"Yes. Follow me. The company is about seventy-five meters this way."

Twenty meters later Swift Eagle emerged from the rain like a ghost. We huddled around him as the lieutenant spoke. "Did you find out who's missing?"

"Barnes, Striker, and Unerstute."

"I can't call in arty with them out there. Let's get back to the rest of the company and see what the CO says."

"We better hurry. The captain already has the mortars set up."

Lieutenant Campbell started running toward the company with the rest of us on his heels.

"Where are you? Barnes is hit bad!" Striker screamed angrily from the graveyard. I couldn't believe he was screaming. He had to know the gooks could hear him as well as us.

"Help! Barnes is hit! He can't move!" His voice sounded panicky. I couldn't stand it. His screams pierced through the driving storm. We had to help.

"Help!" The shout sounded shrill.

I could see men up ahead. Lieutenant Campbell turned back to Swift Eagle. "Show them where the platoon is. I have to see the captain. I'll be there in a minute."

We turned right and followed the chief along a line of Marines lying behind a rice paddy dike that flanked the graveyard. Their helmets were sticking above the dike; their bodies were half under water.

Another forlorn call echoed from the darkness ahead. We finally reached the Second Platoon, all the way at the end of the line of Marines.

"Set up the gun here." Swift Eagle pointed to a spot

between two Marines. I hung the M60 over the dike and sank into the muck behind it.

"Where are we?" I asked.

"The hootch is straight ahead," Swift Eagle said. He turned to lead the other men to their positions.

A loud metallic thump echoed through the crashing rain. A bright flash from an enemy mortar tube lit up their position just behind the grass hootch seventy-five meters straight ahead. I took aim at the flash and waited for another one.

"Hold your fire! Hold your fire!" Lieutenant Campbell ran behind the long row of prone Marines, whispering loud enough to be heard by us but not the enemy. Another thump and flash. For an instant the enemy mortar men were easy targets for the gun. A mortar round exploded one hundred meters to our rear, quickly followed by a second.

"What are we waiting for, Chief?" I whispered. "I got these suckers. They're dead meat. Let me open up!"

"Don't fire!" Lieutenant Campbell ran up behind me. Three more quick flashes and thumps in succession strobe-lighted the enemy mortar men.

"I could hit 'em blindfolded!"

"Shut up! We got Marines between us and them!"

"What are we going to do?" I asked.

He didn't answer. He turned to repeat the order. "Don't anyone fire!"

I turned back to the front. Another series of mortar flashes lit up three separate enemy mortar crews. I could see the mortar men turn away from the tube, covering their ears from the blast.

"I'm gonna open up!" I said aloud.

"Don't!" Rodgers grabbed my shoulder. "You can't!"

"This is chicken, Rodgers! We got guys out there blown away and sitting ducks right in front . . ." A series of mortar blasts behind us drowned me out.

"They think we're back there! If you open up they'll know right where we are!"

"Not if I blow 'em away!" Another series of flashes and the twanging hollow thumps of mortar rounds leaving the tubes reverberated through the air around us. "This sucks of chicken, man!"

"Look!" Rodgers pointed toward another series of flashes from the enemy mortars. Then I saw what he was pointing at. A man silhouetted against the flash, bent over, carrying a rifle and coming our way twenty meters ahead and to our left. I took aim, waiting for another flashing mortar barrage to show me the target. Rodgers aimed his M16. I turned to the Marine on my left to pass the word. He was already aiming. A nightmarish vision of a screaming human-wave assault went through my mind. I shivered. I shook my head to clear the fear and resumed aiming. Another flashing mortar barrage. I tensed, put my finger on the trigger. There, fifteen meters ahead, the silhouetted man.

Suddenly a mortar round exploded close behind us. The light of the explosion revealed the silhouette for a fraction of a second.

"An American helmet!" Rodgers whispered excitedly.

"Don't fire! Marine comin' in!" a voice from the silhouette shouted.

"Over here! Get in here!" someone shouted back.

"Hold your fire! It's a Marine!" another voice called.

The silhouette ran forward, sloshing water as he came. Then he was upon me, stumbling over the paddy dike, kicking my helmet off, and falling face first with a loud splash behind me. He turned and crawled back beside me, bracing himself against the dike.

"John!"

"Striker! Are you okay?"

"Yeah!" He gasped for air and spit out mud. "Barnes!" He gasped again. "Barnes is hit bad. He couldn't move. I had to leave him. We have to go get him!" He spoke quickly, running his words together.

"How 'bout Buford?" I asked. Before he could answer, the lieutenant and Swift Eagle slid in beside us, covering me with mud and water.

"Striker! Who's still out there?" Swift Eagle rattled off the question.

"Barnes! He's hit real bad, but he's still alive. We have to go get him. The gooks are right on top of him, maybe ten yards away."

"Where's Unerstute?"

"I don't know. I couldn't see Buford. As soon as that rain hit I couldn't see a thing!"

"Swift Eagle!" Lieutenant Campbell said. "Go get some volunteers. Striker! Can you lead us to him?"

"I think so. But we gotta be real quiet. The gooks are real close. I could hear 'em talking."

"I'll go, Chief!" I said. My stomach churned. For a moment I wasn't sure I'd actually said that.

"You have to stay with the gun," Lieutenant Campbell said.

"Rodgers can stay with the gun."

"Okay. Follow me. Let's see who else wants to go," Swift Eagle answered without looking at the lieutenant.

"Give me your rifle," I said to Rodgers.

"No," Swift Eagle said. "Just take your .45, so you can help carry Barnes."

I knew I couldn't hit the ground with that lousy .45. Besides, it was probably full of rust. The chief didn't wait for my excuses. He turned and called down the line for volunteers. Ten or more men got up and rushed forward.

"You four. The rest of you go back to your positions. You ready, Striker?"

"Let's go," Striker said.

"Lieutenant," Swift Eagle said as we stepped over the dike. "Make sure these guys know we're out there."

Thirty yards through the flooded paddy, we reached

the more solid ground of the graveyard. Striker seemed to know exactly where he was going. The pounding rain covered the noisy sloshing of our feet, but each step sounded like thunder to me. The faces of the enemy mortar men were clearer with each barrage. Striker stopped ahead.

"Barnes," he whispered lightly. He dropped down and crawled around on hands and knees. "Barnes."

Swift Eagle turned to me and whispered, "You guys go around in a small circle."

We searched for ten minutes. It was obvious that Striker had gotten lost or Barnes had crawled away. We gave up the search and headed back. I thought of Buford. I couldn't imagine what terror he must feel. I knew we were nearing the line of Marines, but I couldn't see anything ahead. A mortar round exploded seventy meters in front of us, silhouetting a long row of friendly American helmets ten meters away.

"Marines comin' in! Hold your fire!" Swift Eagle gave the warning.

"Friendlies coming in!" A voice ahead repeated the warning.

The dike was only a foot tall, just enough to lie behind, and it sure wasn't about to stop any lead, but the first step over it filled my soul with relief.

I found Rodgers and splashed down beside him. He slapped me on the shoulder. "You deserve a medal," he said. He turned his eyes toward the enemy.

"I agree," I said jokingly.

"I mean it," he said, still staring at the mortar flashes. "I told the gunny that you knocked out that gun and took all the fire so the squad could get out of the graveyard."

"What'd he say?"

"He said he's putting you and Chan in for the Silver Star."

"Ah, you're feedin' me—"

"Honest. Chan did the same thing you did on the other end of the tree line."

I couldn't believe it. I loved it. I wanted to write everybody I knew; then memories of last June crept in. The Don Skully Award for the small football player who showed the most courage. Everyone had started congratulating me in front of the entire school. The head coach was the only coach who didn't like me. He said he wanted to make an example out of me, but I'd only missed one practice in three years. If I get a medal, I'll ram it up his nose.

"We're sweeping across at daybreak," a whispered voice came from our right. "Pass it on."

Two hours before daybreak the rain and the mortars stopped. I stared into the blackness until my eyes hurt. The first streaks of morning light brought little comfort. My hands looked like wrinkled paper from being wet for so long.

"We're movin' in!" The word sifted by me and on down the line. We were on our feet, moving forward. I felt like I was in an old war film. On line. Fix bayonets. The sky turned pink and blue. The hootch was clear now in the morning light. I couldn't believe it. We were actually going to storm right over these suckers!

"Fifty-nine days," Rodgers mumbled, more to himself than to me.

Our first steps were slow. Cautious. Forty yards away the pace suddenly quickened. No one spoke. Someone to my right began jogging forward. I started jogging to keep up. Now the whole line was running. Someone let loose a howl. Now everyone was screaming like banshees. A cracking burst of AK fire rung out across the graveyard. Then another. The second burst was a mistake. I could see the muzzle flash from the roof of the hootch. I opened up with a fifty-round burst. At the same time, twenty others fired on the hootch. The sniper's body exploded from the roof, pieces of flesh and cloth flying in all directions.

"Cease fire! Cease fire!" Swift Eagle was finally heard, and the firing stopped. The hootch was burning. Black smoke tunneled one way, then another, in a swirling wind.

"There's a Marine over here!" someone shouted from my right. I glanced over quickly. It looked like Buford lying face down. I looked back to the hootch. Nothing. No firing at all. We swept by the burning hootch and ten yards deep into the thick jungle.

"They pulled out, Lieutenant!" someone shouted.

"We got another body over here! It's a Marine!" another voice called from the left. I ran over to see who it was. Striker stood over a bloody body lying face down. The chief stood next to him looking down.

"Who is it?" I asked.

"Barnes," Striker said. "I don't know how he got over here in front of this gun bunker." Not until then did I notice he was lying in front of a foxhole with dirt and wood built up around it. Hundreds of empty .30-caliber cartridges were scattered about in the mud. His pack was ripped apart. His E-tool had a bullet hole through the shovel end. Striker bent down. He grabbed one shoulder and rolled the body over. Bullets had torn deep creases under each cheekbone, giving him huge dark bruises around each eye. It looked eerie. Dried blood covered another bullet crease under his jaw. Most of the right ear was shot away. I stared at the huge bruises. Suddenly his eyes sprang open. I couldn't speak. I tried to point, like a mute with mouth hanging open. Then a smile spread across his face.

"He's alive!" Striker screamed in disbelief.

"Corpsman!" Swift Eagle shouted.

"How did you get over here?" Striker asked. "Can you talk?"

"The gooks drug me over. They thought I was dead.

They crawled out after me right after you left. One of 'em pulled out a knife and came down on me."

"Calm down. Save your strength," Swift Eagle said dryly.

"I thought it was over for sure. But he just cut my bandoliers off. Then they dragged me up front of their gun. God, I thought for sure you guys were gonna walk right into it! I almost drowned laying there!" He was still perky. I couldn't believe it.

I turned to find Chan. He had to see this. I saw him standing near the burning hootch. I ran over to him.

"John! Come here!" He raised his hand and waved me over. "Look at this." I looked into the burning hootch. A sun-faded tan pith helmet filled with dried blood and gray human brains lay on the dirt floor of the hootch. I bent down and darted inside, grabbed the helmet, and brought it out. Something in Vietnamese was written on the front. I dumped the brains and blood into a puddle and handed the pith helmet to Chan. "What's it say?" I asked.

He studied the writing for a few seconds, then handed the helmet back to me. "It says, 'We're here to stay.' "

"One thing's for sure, this sucker is staying."

"Unerstute's dead," Chan said.

"He shouldn't have been here. I really liked that guy."

"I found no wounds. No blood. Nothing. I suspect heart failure."

"Barnes is still alive. You have to see him!" I led Chan to Barnes. Doc had just finished with a bandage on his leg. It looked like he was losing a lot of blood.

"How's he doing, Doc?" I asked.

"He'll make it." Doc stood up and led us a few feet away. "He probably won't walk again. I don't know why he's still alive. I counted eleven bullet holes from head to toe and some shrapnel holes besides." Doc spoke with his usual boring Boston attitude, as if the wounded were keeping him from something more important.

"That's amazing!" I said.

"What about Buford?" Chan asked.

"All I could find was one tiny little shrapnel wound in his side, but it was so small it was like a pinprick. It couldn't have been what killed him. He died from fright. He had a heart attack out there."

"Correct. I concur."

Doc's face flushed, half with anger and half with embarrassment. He hated being put in his arrogant place. He removed his glasses for cleaning and turned away without a word.

Twenty minutes later a medevac chopper settled down in the muddy paddy. The sun was fully up now, like a blazing ball in the copper sky. I watched as Barnes and Buford were loaded onto the chopper. I wanted Buford alive. I wanted him to go home and spit in his family's face. He could have gone home, but he didn't. I thought of the cowards in Canada.

We started after the NVA, on a force march. The jungle looked dense and black. Their retreat was hurried, and our point man followed it easily. Thirty minutes on their trail led us into a snake-infested jungle swamp. The unmistakable sickening sweet odor of rotting corpses filled the damp, humid air. I found solace in the stench, knowing they were dead gooks. I wanted to shoot more. I wanted them to pay.

We marched on and on. In and out of swamp after swamp. It was nearing evening when we finally climbed out of the swamps and onto solid ground. The terrain in front of us was rolling hills with scattered patches of trees and brush. Without my even realizing it, we had linked up with a huge column of Marines stretching past one hill and over another.

The sun was dying on the horizon. We had to stop soon. I felt like I had to eat something. Cracking rifle fire broke the silence of the march. It was over as quickly as it started.

"Corpsman up!"

Swift Eagle ran by me shouting, "Get in a perimeter!"

"Who's hit?" Rodgers asked. The chief kept running toward the lieutenant. "Who's that they're helping?" Rodgers pointed to three Marines standing over another Marine twenty meters back. For a moment I thought it was Chan.

"I'll go see," I said. I ran back. "Who is it?"

"Ellenwood," Doc answered.

"Jack?"

"Yeah."

"Is he okay?"

"I think so. We need a medevac."

"Let me see my baby!" Jack sounded dazed, like he was in shock. "Let me see my baby!"

"What's he talking about?" Doc asked, his voice beginning to show the strain.

"His baby. I know what he's talking about." Memories of Jack calming me down after my first confirmed kill by showing me pictures of his new baby boy came back to me. "Give me his wallet." Another Marine handed me his helmet. I fumbled for the wallet. "Here it is." I unwrapped the plastic around it, opened it up, and found the color picture of the laughing baby boy. "Here, Jack. Here's your baby." It was too dark to see the photograph clearly, but he calmed down just by holding on to it. I wondered why it had happened to Jack, out of five hundred Marines and with only two weeks left.

Our night ended in a perimeter waiting for a medevac that didn't come.

The next morning started with the humming noise of thirty to fifty helicopters flying in formation in the eastern sky.

"Good grief! What's all that?" Rodgers asked.

"I don't know," I said. "Hey, Swift Eagle! What's going on over there?"

Swift Eagle looked up from his can of congealed lima beans and ham fat. He gazed stoically at the huge formation. "I think it's the 101st Airborne. They get a noon meal. Hot, too!"

"What? Are you kidding?"

"John." I turned to see Doc. The arrogance replaced by a solemn face looking down at me. "Jack's dead."

"Dead? How? He wasn't hit that bad!"

"He had a stomach wound we didn't find till this morning. He could have made it, but we couldn't get a medevac chopper." Doc spoke as though he was pleading for understanding. "There just weren't any choppers."

I followed the flight of the Army armada of helicopters until my vision blurred. Then I cried.

MERCY KILLING?

The lieutenant put Chan and me back together. I was thankful for that, almost as thankful as Rodgers was to get away from the gun.

"Saddle up!" The gruff voice sounded far away. I felt numb over Jack's death. Not sad. I was too tired of it all to be sad. I felt anger, too. Anger at our incompetent corpsman who didn't find a stomach wound. Anger at the Army for darkening the sky with helicopters bringing hot meals to Army units that were already too soft while my friend bled to death for lack of a single medevac chopper. But most of all, anger at the gooks.

"Here's your pack," Chan said. I watched the medevac chopper fade into the hot morning sun. "You knew him better than I did, but that was one decent man." Chan nudged me with my pack. "You all right?"

I felt myself sighing. "I wonder if I'll be sane when I get home." Chan didn't answer. I put my pack on. The straps dug into my sore shoulders. It felt heavier than usual, or maybe I was just weaker. I threw the M60 over my shoulder and nestled the hot metal into the little saddle of callus and muscle between my neck and shoulder bone. The never-ending hump started again. I kept hearing Jack ask for his baby. Push it out. Think clear. I wonder how far I'll walk before it's over? Fifteen miles a day times thirteen months equals three-ninety-five times fifteen equals . . . "Chan?"

"Yeah."

"What's three-ninety-five times fifteen?"

"Five thousand, nine hundred, and twenty-five."

"What? How could you figure that so fast?"

"You're trying to figure how many miles we'll hump at fifteen klicks a day for thirteen months, right?"

"Wise-turd."

"How you feel?" Chan asked quietly so no one else in the column would hear. I knew he really cared. I was lucky to have such a friend. Mom always said I made friends easily. I used to think that was good. I wasn't sure anymore. Maybe I shouldn't make any more friends.

"I'm okay," I said, though I wasn't. Nothing felt right. I liked Jack. I liked his wife and I liked his fat baby. I wanted to see that fat baby. I wanted him to know his dad died like a hero. He should have. He didn't. He died walking along in a war, a war that our leaders didn't care about winning but that I still did, and I still didn't know why I felt alone.

"What happened to the rest of the battalion?" I asked.

"They kept going when Jack got hit. Alpha stayed put."

By noon the treeless, rolling hills turned into a thick jungle. First Platoon dove into the dense bush while Second and Third continued on, just skirting around it. The captain pointed at a narrow path leading into the jungle. Lieutenant Campbell motioned Second Platoon toward the path. Striker took the point and Second Platoon filed down, leaving Third Platoon alone.

The jungle felt so vibrant, so noisy compared to the rocky, rolling terrain we'd just left. Screeching birds filled the tops of each tree. The temperature dropped twenty degrees almost immediately. Bright sun rays danced off thousands of plants in a million shades of green. Strangling vines spiraled up a million branches tangled together forever in a struggle to see the sun.

The column stopped. No one spoke as each man dropped instinctively to one knee. A whisper started at the front of the column. Each helmet turned, repeating the call.

"Guns up!"

"Guns up!"

"Guns up!"

I stood and struggled past the first two men in front of me. Then the others moved away, and I ran forward. Adrenaline started pumping. I kept hearing Jack's voice. "Let me see my baby!" I could feel Chan behind me. The path veered right around a huge red thornbush.

"Get down!" The whisper was enough. I dropped quickly to the left side of the path, landing next to Lieutenant Campbell. He pointed to a hootch of bamboo and dried brown leaves twenty meters up the path. Fifteen feet to the left of the hootch was a large mound of dirt ten feet long and four feet high. Striker lay to the right of the path ten meters closer, flat on his stomach and aiming at the hootch. The hootch sat in a tiny clearing, engulfed by a bright circle of shimmering sunlight that shone through the thick canopy of overhanging branches.

Lieutenant Campbell rose to a crouch, ran forward to Striker, dropped to one knee just behind him, and motioned Chan and me forward. I started to stand. Chan grabbed my pack and pulled me back down. Then I saw why. Two helmetless, khaki-clad NVA soldiers, each carrying a small bowl of rice, came out of the hootch with AKs slung over their shoulders. One stuffed rice into his mouth with his hands as he spoke. The other started laughing. They walked toward the dirt mound. The laughing NVA reached it first. He lifted a bamboo trapdoor and propped it open with a stick. They both crouched over, then stepped down and in. Lieutenant Campbell looked back and motioned us forward with his right hand as he silently mouthed the words "Guns up."

We stood to a crouch and ran forward. My gear felt clumsy. Chan's rifle butt collided with his bandolier of magazines. We made too much noise. How could they not hear us? I dropped to my stomach beside Lieutenant Campbell to the right of the path. Chan knelt on one knee just beside me. He broke a belt of ammo from around his shoulder and linked it to the fifty-round strip belt already in the gun.

"Okay, that's three," Lieutenant Campbell whispered. "Right?" Striker turned his head to answer. His big face flushed red around the huge black mole between his bushy eyebrows.

"Yeah, I count three, Lieutenant," he said, his eyes darting as he spoke. He turned back to the bunker with a jerk of his neck.

Lieutenant Campbell looked back at Chan. "Swift Eagle up!"

Chan turned and whispered the word back to Sudsy. "Swift Eagle up!"

Sudsy turned and repeated the order. A few seconds later Swift Eagle peeked around the giant red thornbush where the path veered right. He ran forward without a sound, like a cat on soft paws. He knelt down beside the lieutenant.

"Take your squad and flank that hootch on the left," Lieutenant Campbell said quickly. "Tell Murphy's squad to flank the right. Hurry. There's at least three in the bunker. Send Corporal James's squad up. We'll assault the bunker in five minutes, along with the gun team. Striker will go in with us."

Swift Eagle didn't say a word. He turned and ran back down the path. Ten seconds later Corporal James's squad of six men moved up behind Chan and me. To the right and left of the hootch thin shafts of the hot noon sun broke through the overhanging canopy like a thousand brilliant golden threads. The damp jungle was drying out. The faint odor of fish broke through the musty air.

The five-minute wait stretched into a dream about a trip home and lying on the beach in Saint Petersburg then building a tri-level tree house in Charleston. Jack's baby. A sudden chill shook me. I wiped away the stinging drops of salt from my eyes. A drink of grape Kool-Aid, that's what I needed. Absentmindedly I reached for my canteen.

"Let's leapfrog up!" Lieutenant Campbell said. I stared into his wide-open dark brown eyes. He stared at my hand as I fidgeted with the snap on my canvas canteen pouch. What am I doing? I thought. I put both hands on the gun.

"Let's go, Chan," I heard myself saying. My heart started pounding.

My feet moved forward as I crouched with the gun on my right hip. I heard Chan's boots behind me. I jogged past Striker, who was prone and aiming at the bunker. The screeching birds stopped. I flattened out to the right side of the path just before it entered the circle of sunlight, twenty yards from the hootch. I tried to bury myself in a thick bush. I crawled under and partially through it until the barrel of the M60 protruded through. The flash suppressor touched the circle of sunlight.

Suddenly something clammy dropped heavily around my neck. I froze. One of the NVA came out of the bunker. I could see his face, wrinkled around the eyes, not the usual kid in uniform. I aimed. Something cool touched my right ear, followed by a soft, paralyzing hiss.

Snake! God! It slithered slowly around my shoulder until one tiny eye stared into mine. Then it stretched itself away from my face as if to get an overall view, his tongue shooting out almost rhythmically. I stopped breathing. Through the leaves of the bush a blurred image of the NVA soldier moved toward the hootch just behind the scaly, gray, flat head waving back and forth hypnotically five inches from my nose. The NVA entered the bamboo hootch. The snake began to entwine itself around my neck. Huge drops of sweat rolled from under my helmet and down my face. The snake's eye seemed to

follow the drops to my chin. Suddenly the weight of another snake fell on my back. It started squirming down
my left leg to the back of my knee. It stopped. It began
hissing.

A second NVA came out of the bunker. At the same
moment the snake in front of my chin followed the drops
of sweat from my chin to the ground as they splashed
into the beginnings of a tiny puddle. I felt my eyes darting back and forth from the slow-walking NVA soldier
to the flat hissing head of the gray snake. The NVA
stopped. He turned his head, slightly cocking his right
ear, in search of the sound. He looked my way. Oh God!
He hears the hissing, I thought. He took a step, then
leaned toward me, his slanted eyes squinting to see what
the hissing sounds were. I tightened my grip on the gun,
slipped my finger around the trigger, and tried aiming
without moving. The snake tightened its grip on my
neck. The NVA unshouldered his AK47.

"Nguyen," a voice from the hootch called. *"Nguyen!"*
The NVA soldier turned. He shouldered his weapon,
gave one last look, and walked into the hootch. I heard
movement behind me. Something pushed my leg. The
weight of the snake on the back of my knee disappeared,
followed by the clump of something landing in the brush
to my right. Chan! Thank God! Took him long enough!
The snake around my neck loosened its grip. It slithered
slowly away from my face. Finally I felt the tail end drop
from my neck and I breathed. A hand touched my calf.

"You okay?" Chan whispered. I gave him a thumbs
up. The rustle of men moving forward sounded too loud.
Suddenly two NVA ran from the hootch firing. M16s
erupted all around me. The khaki-clad North Vietnamese dove for cover behind the bunker. I opened up
with a twenty-round burst. No return fire. Chan threw a
grenade.

"Frag!" he shouted. "Outgoing!" The apple-shaped
grenade bounced off the bunker, landing between the

hootch and the bunker. I closed my eyes. Two seconds . . . three. Four. Five! Dud! A dud!

"Guns up!"

I crawled back out of the bush, stood to a crouch, and walked forward, firing from the hip, first at the bunker, then sweeping tracers through the bamboo hootch. The hootch caught fire. Flames spread quickly. A moment later the entire hootch burned out of control. I moved into the small clearing of sunlight, running to the right until I had a straight shot into the bunker door. A muzzle flash spit from the darkness inside the bunker. I hit the ground. Chan opened up semi-automatic. I shot a long stream of tracers through the door. The flash ceased. Suddenly a ChiCom grenade flew from the bunker, landing ten feet to my right.

"Frag! Incoming!" I screamed as I shot another twenty-round burst into the bunker. I covered my helmet with my arms and nosed my face into the damp earth. No explosion. I started firing again.

"Cease fire!" Lieutenant Campbell shouted. A jungle breeze shifted smoke pouring from the flaming hootch into my face.

Chan grabbed my arm. "Let's move!"

We stood, ran right, and flattened to the ground again. Short, stocky Corporal James ran up to the dirt bunker, being careful to stay out of the line of fire. He leaned against a wall, put his rifle between his legs, and pulled the pin on a grenade. He let the spoon fly, held for a count of two, stepped out, tossed the frag through the door, then jumped back. I opened fire on the bunker door to keep anyone from throwing the grenade back out. Out of the bunker the grenade flew anyway. James hit the dirt just as the frag exploded, sending shrapnel slapping through the leafy jungle.

"James!" Lieutenant Campbell shouted. "Catch!"

James looked up from the dirt. Lieutenant Campbell threw him another grenade. James pulled the pin, let the

spoon fly, and held for another count of two. He threw
the frag in. Harder this time, like an angry pitcher. He
dove back against the bunker. I opened up again. Orange
tracers streamed into the dark hole. An explosion shook
dirt from the outside of the bunker. A cloud of smoke
poured from the open door. The bamboo door fell shut
as the stick holding it collapsed from the explosion.
James moved forward. He cautiously lifted the bamboo
hatch and started to prop it up with a stick. A ChiCom
grenade flew out the open door, glancing off Corporal
James's shoulder and bouncing to eight feet in front of
Chan and me. James dove back, letting the bunker door
slam. We buried our faces in the dirt. I tried to crawl
under my helmet with my hands and waited. Nothing.

"James!" Lieutenant Campbell called again. "Catch!"
He tossed him another grenade.

James caught it, then dropped it. He picked it up, pulled
the pin, moved back to the bamboo door, grabbed it with
his left hand, let the spoon fly, counted two, lifted the
door, and threw in the frag. He jumped back away from
the door. An explosion rocked the bunker again. The
door blew open in a cloud of smoke, then slammed shut.

Lieutenant Campbell moved forward, with Sudsy
right behind him. Sudsy reached over his shoulder and
pulled the antenna higher as he ran. The squad circled
the bunker. I still couldn't see the chief's squad or Murphy's squad. I stood up. Chan got to his feet and quickly
linked up another belt of ammo. We moved forward
cautiously.

Lieutenant Campbell looked around at the squad,
then shouted, "Fire in the hole!" He pulled the pin on another frag. James lifted the hatch out and up. Lieutenant
Campbell threw in the frag. James let the door fall shut
as they both stepped to the side. The bunker shook from
the muffled explosion. The door flew open again in a
cloud of smoke, then fell shut.

"Let's get a body count." The lieutenant spoke quickly

as he pointed a thumb at the door of the bunker. James opened the hatch, propped it up with the stick, crouched over, and stepped down and in. A moment later he dragged the tattered body of an NVA out. His left arm and leg dangled loosely, only held on by a couple of tendons. James pulled him a few feet from the bunker. The smell of gunpowder filled the air.

James stepped into the bunker again. A moment later he dragged another bloody corpse out by the feet. The body was riddled with shrapnel holes, and the head was cracked open from the concussion. James laid him beside the other. "That's it," James said with obvious disappointment.

"Can't be!" Striker blurted out. "I saw three of 'em go in there!"

"Are you sure?" the lieutenant asked.

"Positive!" Striker looked mad that they doubted him. He moved forward, leaned his rifle against the bunker, and stepped down into the hole. "Here he is!" Striker shouted from inside. "They hid him under the floorboards!" Striker came out rear end first, dragging the body of another NVA.

"Hey! It's a woman!" James said.

"She's still alive!" Sudsy said.

"How could anyone live through that?" James said in disbelief.

"She ain't very alive," Striker said, bending over her, checking the wounds.

"Oh, bad! Look," Lieutenant Campbell said as he pulled away her tattered shirt. "Her whole stomach's gone."

"Yeah, no chance," Doc said from behind me.

"Come here and get a closer look, Doc," Lieutenant Campbell said.

Doc moved forward. He bent over her and shook his head. "She'll never make it. I don't know why she's alive now. Look at all the blood coming out of her ears."

"Did you hear that?" Striker said. "Her stomach just made an awful sound, like a drain opening. She's really suffering!"

Someone stepped forward with an M16, pointed it at her chest, and fired a single shot. The body jumped from impact. No one spoke. We stared. Her nostrils moved, sucking in to get oxygen. "Good God."

The word struck something in me. I wondered if she believed in God.

He fired a second shot. Again the body jumped from impact. We waited. Her nostrils flared again. Then her mouth came open.

"She's still alive!" Doc shouted. He removed his glasses and wiped sweat from his face. "Somebody shoot her with a .45."

I wondered if she'd ever heard the name of the Lord, even as my hand reached down to my side.

Chan looked concerned. I wasn't sure why. He handed me a C-ration can full of smoking hot chocolate. "How you feeling?" he asked.

"Fine. How 'bout you?"

"No complaints anyone cares about."

I looked around the perimeter. It didn't look right. The rise of the small rocky hill hid the other side of the perimeter from view. I couldn't remember coming here. "I must be turning into a real space-cadet!"

"Why?"

"I don't know, really. I don't even remember setting up in this place."

"You remember the mercy killing?"

"What mercy killing?" I asked. Chan looked puzzled. I thought for a minute without speaking. "Oh, yeah. The woman in the bunker."

"Are you all right?"

"Yeah. Other than being in the Corps, I'm just fine." The dying yellow face of the woman in front of the bunker flashed vividly through my mind. "No. I'm not all that good right now. How do you talk to God when you just murdered someone?"

Chan looked down for a moment. He reached into his pocket and pulled out his little black Gideon. He held it and closed his eyes for a silent prayer, then started thumbing through it. Suddenly he stopped and laid his Bible on his lap, then looked me in the eyes. "Johnnie, God has used war to judge the nations from the very beginning. He will use war to judge the world even in the last days. David wasn't condemned for killing Goliath and then cutting off his head. He was used by God to fight evil as a witness to Israel and the world."

"Chan, I killed that girl. For all I know she might have lived long enough to have accepted Christ before she died." I'd finally said it. That thought hadn't left my mind since I'd pulled the trigger.

"Doesn't hold up, Johnnie. I mean you can feel that way if you choose, but it's just not true. It's not Biblical. He's a just God. He doesn't let anyone die without the opportunity to accept Christ. And I don't mean just through missionaries. She chose either to accept, reject, or ignore the truth during her life. The Holy Spirit was a witness to her. The world around her was witness of good and evil. And nature is obvious evidence of God's existence. She had a choice just like everyone on this planet. If she wanted to know God, He would never have allowed her to die without finding Him."

"It all sounds real good, Chan, but I just can't buy it all that easy. I mean, what about little babies that die? That crap sure isn't true for them."

"God tells us in the Book of David that babies would be with him. They're under the age of accountability. When David's baby boy died, we're told that David would be with his baby in heaven."

"What about crazy people? You know, mental retards

and stuff like that? They can't accept Christ, they get screwed right from the start."

"Don't be ignorant. There's a purpose to everything and everyone. Besides, we're told that they are taken care of too, in the Book of Job."

I was ticked off. I didn't say anything else for a while, and he didn't either. A couple of minutes later I realized I didn't feel so sick inside anymore. After a couple more minutes I couldn't help seeing that he was right again. I hated always losing arguments to this little turd, even if it was for my own good. I decided to talk.

"You know our discussions can become a real pain sometimes."

He gave me his "I told you so" closed mouth and Snoopy grin before he answered, "Well, I told your mother—"

"Oh, God! Not again!"

"—that I would take care—"

"Why in the world did I ever let my folks come to Parris Island graduation?"

THE WOMAN

Seven months in the bush brought on many changes. A lot of friends back in the world stopped writing, including a brother and sister. Most never wrote to begin with. I would never have imagined that a simple letter could be so important, except maybe for old people. I remember reading about Vietnam in the paper. It had never seemed like it was really happening. But now, for me, Vietnam was no longer some bizarre fantasy war on Walter Cronkite. The jungle, with all its death and fatigue, was the only thing that was real. Flushing toilets, cars, and knives and forks didn't exist. Civilization was the fantasy.

I felt ready for a cage. I had to have R&R soon. If not, certain parts of my anatomy might never operate properly again. Female water buffaloes were looking better all the time. No one bothered explaining why Chan and I had gone so long without an R&R. Men who were boot to us had already gone and come back. We guessed they were waiting for more gunners to show up before they trusted the gun to a rifleman. We did a lot of guessing. Like we tried to guess why we were still PFCs after so many months in combat. I had more than one friend in the Army. Three to be exact. All three were sergeants after six months, and they were still stateside.

"There's a freeze on all promotions in the Fifth Marines," Lieutenant Campbell said. He pulled the bolt out of his M16 and peered through the barrel.

"What the crap does that mean?" I asked.

"I don't know. Ask your congressman."

"I know what that means," Chan said. "They want to keep us at eleven cents an hour."

"Your R&R came through," the lieutenant said matter-of-factly.

"Where?" I asked, trying not to scream.

"I'm not sure. Go ask Sudsy." We turned to find Sudsy.

"Wait." Gunny looked left and shot a jawful of tobacco juice at a long column of giant red ants marching by five feet to the left of the CP. I always envied the four of them—Gunny, Lieutenant Campbell, Sudsy, and Doc—sitting in the command post in the center of the perimeter, able to sleep all night if they wanted to.

"Nice shot, Gunny," I said.

He leaned back on one elbow and crossed his calloused bare feet. "I got a can of meatballs 'n' beans. You got any dry writing paper?"

"I think so. Let me go check supplies," I said.

"I'll locate Sudsy," Chan said. "Where is Sudsy, Lieutenant?"

"I think he went on the water detail."

Chan walked away.

"How 'bout throwing in a pack of coffee, Gunny?" I asked.

"Yeah, sure. You wouldn't have any new socks stuffed away somewhere, would ya?"

"We already traded them," I said.

"For what?"

"A toothbrush, peaches, and pound cake."

"Ah! Couldn't top that anyway."

"How 'bout a book, Gunny?"

"How did you get a book?"

"Traded a pack of Salems to a black gunner in Third Platoon back at An Hoa."

"What is it?"

"A who-done-it."

"How much?"

"I'll loan it to you for a pack of hot chocolate."

"It's a deal."

"I found him!" Chan jogged up to me with a huge silly grin pasted all over his Chinese face.

"If I didn't know better, I'd swear you found a woman instead of Sudsy. That grin's immoral."

"Australia! And would you try to think of something besides women and boom-booming all the time!"

"Round-eyed women! When?"

"One week, but try to control yourself."

"I won't even know how to act around people."

"Australia. I was there in forty-four." Gunny leaned back farther, as if the memory soothed an old wound. "The women love Marines in Australia." He straightened up, realizing he'd grabbed the full attention of all of us and looking a little embarrassed. "Leastwise they did in forty-four." He cleared his throat then spit another shot at the ant column.

"I'll bring that paper back over in a minute, Gunny," I said.

"Don't forget the book."

I gave him a thumbs up as Chan and I headed for our position on the perimeter.

"The last girl I saw looked like a reject from Dachau. Remember? That girl on Truoi Bridge and the kid who sold that horrible candy," I said as Chan booted a stone in soccer fashion.

"Oh yes, he tried to market his sister to you."

"Right. Boom-boom five dollar."

"Seems like years ago, doesn't it?"

"God, it really does. I feel like I've been here most of my life."

"I know what you mean," Chan said as we reached the gun. "I tried to explain to my girl just how long one single day is over here. It's futile. No one can understand."

"That's weird," I said. "I tried to tell Polly—"

"Which one is that?"

"The one in Missouri. I tried to explain how old I'm getting or just how the time is different. It sounds like bull to them. Remember the last time we got mail call?"

"Just barely," Chan said. "My mother informed me of the Tet Offensive. As if I were unaware of it," Chan said sarcastically.

"I got that letter from Polly. She's been going to school in Missouri. Well, she went home on a break and met three friends of mine and hers, and the jerks thought I was away at college."

"Isn't everybody?" Chan smirked.

"When she told 'em where I was, one of these jerks said I was probably having a great time because they had two uncles who had gone back to Vietnam twice because the pay was so good."

"Navy and Air Force, right?" Chan asked.

"Right on the nose."

"Let's just think about R&R."

"Saddle up!" Swift Eagle's voice carried across the perimeter. Just hearing those two words made me tired, but this time even they couldn't erase my thought of R&R. My spirits were up too high. I couldn't help thinking what an odd pair Chan and I were. While he was majoring in medicine and minoring in ministry in college, I was majoring in football and minoring in drinking and women in high school. Somehow, for God's own obscure reasons, we'd become closer than blood brothers. Now we'd really get to party together.

The hump started again. I nestled the gun on my right shoulder. The thick callus that had developed from the side of my neck to my shoulder bone from the constant weight and rubbing of the gun seemed to be getting thicker. I'll probably be permanently lopsided when this war is over, I thought. Humpback of the Fifth Marines.

Hours passed. Our direction did not change. A straight shot toward the pale gray mountains along the

Laotian border. As we inched closer the mountains grew greener and greener, until no other color existed. We crossed a small stream. My feet were wet again. The jungle rot on my feet sent streams of pain up my leg until I didn't think I could go any farther. But I did.

More hours passed. We finally reached the ominous mountains and started up a small trail that looked too well used. Dense green, unfriendly foliage bordered each side of the steep trail. Striker started grumbling about staying on the trail. I didn't like him behind me. He grumbled about everything. This time he was right, though I felt like belting him for mumbling out loud when we couldn't see a foot to either side of us. Staying on a trail like this was a great way to get ambushed. We all knew it.

The trail got steeper and steeper until grabbing branches to pull myself forward was the only way to negotiate the incline. We followed the path over the mountain, then down the other side, where it ran into a mountain stream. On the left a small brown hill stuck out like a short bald brother of the steep, green, tree-covered mountains around it. It overlooked the open area between the two large mountains where the path crossed the stream.

We wasted no time getting up that little hill. The gunny placed Chan and me where the field of fire was clear. I set the gun down on a slightly pitched slope. The gunny spat a stream of tobacco out the side of his mouth and looked me straight in the eye. "I'm telling everybody to hold their fire till you open up. Make sure you get as many as you can in the open before firing."

"No sweat," I said. Chan gave the gunny a thumbs up.

The gunny returned the sign and rushed off to check another position.

"Think we're in Laos?" I asked.

"We've been in Laos for the last hour," Chan said.

"How do you know? I didn't see any road signs," I said sarcastically.

"Quite elementary. Differences in vegetation and so on." Having finished his usual line of bull, Chan pretended to be busy checking his rifle.

"How do you know where we are?" I asked again.

"I asked Swift Eagle."

"Did you really?"

"Yes. He said this is where Delta Company ran into it two weeks ago."

"You mean hand-to-hand?"

"That's what the chief said. He said Delta's gunny sergeant was up for the Medal of Honor."

"Oh yeah?"

"After he ran out of ammo he killed six NVA with his K-bar."

"I wish you hadn't said anything about that hand-to-hand crap." I pulled out my .45. The blue-black metal was rust brown. I pushed the clip release button. Nothing happened.

Chan started laughing. "You'd be better off with a bayonet," he chuckled.

"This is ridiculous! I oiled this miserable piece of junk a few days ago."

Sudsy ran at us, crouching along the slope of the hill. He looked naked without his radio strapped to his back. He dropped to one knee beside us.

"Lieutenant says dig in." He paused, gasping for air. "He wants you to open up first when they cross the stream." He inhaled again and raced off for the next position.

Chan rolled his eyes back and looked toward heaven.

"Did he say dig in?"

"Yep, he sure did," I answered.

"I find that depressing."

"Don't worry about it. We can't dig in. We threw our E-tools away. Remember?"

"Was that us?"

"Something about them being too heavy. We never stay in one place long enough to dig in anyway."

"Ah, yes," he said. " 'Salts don't carry unneeded weight.' It's all coming back to me now. Must have been your idea."

"I move that we ignore the order as usual."

"You guys are really crazy! Aren't you scared?" I didn't recognize the high-pitched voice, but whoever it belonged to was serious. Chan looked as surprised as I felt. We rolled over onto our sides and looked behind us to see the totally distraught face of a thin young Marine boot. I didn't know his name yet. He had joined us two days before. He shook like a cold, wet puppy. He flattened out on his stomach like he was under fire.

"Who are you?"

"My n-n-name is Arvis. Arvis Hendry." I wasn't sure if he stuttered or if he was just that nervous.

"Calm down, Arvis," I said.

"What are you doing here?" Chan asked.

"Corporal Swift Eagle told me to bring the two crazy gunners an E-tool." He felt behind him without lifting his head from the ground until he found the E-tool. "Here." He handed it to us, jumped to a crouching posture, and ran back to his position.

The scene in front of us looked like a Salem cigarette commercial. Chirping birds overwhelmed the distant thunder of artillery, for a pleasant change. A rare, wood-scented breeze sifted between the mountains to our front, rustling the leaves like a fall day. It cooled my sweaty body down to an almost human level. War was out of place here. I wanted to take off my rotting boots and go barefoot in the softly flowing stream below. I couldn't help thinking the only thing missing from the tranquil setting was two lovers on a picnic.

Something moved through the vegetation below. A big bird lifted off into the blue sky squawking. Suddenly an

NVA soldier emerged from the cover of the trees. He wore the usual green pith helmet. It looked greener than most. Brand new, I guessed. Fresh troops from the North. My heart started pounding. He paused at the stream and looked both ways like a kid crossing a busy street. He carried his AK47 with both hands. Something was missing. No pack!

Finally he crossed the stream. Two more pith helmets appeared. My heart joined my Adam's apple. Chan tensed up. I tightened my grip on the gun. I put the lead man in my gun sight. Someone started digging into the rocky earth behind me. The man in my sight turned. He stared straight into my eyes.

I heard my teeth grinding. The noise didn't matter. It was too late. I squeezed. The first orange tracers seemed to go right through the lead man, like he was made of papier-mâché. The first burst blew him back, arms flailing like a mannequin thrown into the air. I kept firing and firing.

"Cease fire! Cease fire!" Chan was shaking my shoulder. I felt like he was waking me from a hazy dream. My lip hurt. Blood. A generous piece of my lip was wedged between my teeth.

"Guns up! Let's get a body count!"

"Got some ammo?" I asked Chan.

"We're ready."

I stumbled down the hill, following Corporal James's squad, plus a couple of extra men for support. We reached the stream. One man lay half in and half out of the water. His right arm and part of his shoulder had been torn from his corpse and were lying on the legs of another body three feet away. Crimson, pulsing blood colored the crystal water of the stream.

"Good shootin', John. He looks like Swiss cheese," Sam said.

I tried to ignore Sam. The bloody scene reminded me of the movie I saw on my last date back in the world,

Bonnie and Clyde. The second NVA lay face down, still breathing. A bloody trail led into the brush, revealing where the third had somehow managed to crawl away. Hot, dank air had replaced the earlier breeze. It was as though the tranquility had been killed too. An eerie impression came over me that it might never return.

Corporal James nudged Striker with his M16 and pointed at the trail of blood.

"See how far he got, and be careful. It gets pretty dark in there. Take Jones with you."

A painful groan brought our attention to the NVA still alive. He lay on his stomach. Then he shuddered in pain. Corporal James cautiously rolled him over with his foot while pointing an M16 at his head. No weapon. Everything looked safe. James knelt on one knee and removed the pith helmet. Long shimmering black hair tumbled across the face of an exceptionally beautiful Vietnamese woman. It stunned me. The last thing in the world I expected to see was a beautiful woman.

"Wow! How old do you think she is?" somebody said.

"Twenty at the most," said Corporal James.

"I bet she's half French."

"Yeah. She's too fine to be all gook."

Chan and I were speechless; we appeared to be the only ones who were. All I could do was stare. A flawless complexion matched her beautiful features. Her striking eyes, more rounded than the usual, gave hint of a Eurasian background. She wore the same khaki uniform that most NVA did, and the same Ho Chi Minh sandals, made from American tire tread. I wanted to throw up. I knew I'd probably just killed one of the most beautiful women I had ever seen.

No one took their eyes off her. The closest thing to a female any of us had seen in months were two women who had popped out of a hut on a search-and-destroy mission. Village women looked haggard or hawk-faced.

Most were toothless and weather-beaten from years in the paddies. This woman was a flower in the desert.

We gathered around her in a semicircle. Her khaki shirt, which was quickly sopping up her dark red blood, had two holes just above the belt line. The semicircle of Marines moved a step closer. The moment felt dark, primitive. We stared hypnotically. She clutched her stomach in pain, looked up at us, and said something in Vietnamese. She repeated it again, her eyes squeezed shut. Then she said it again, this time with her eyes opened, steaming with defiance. I recognized only one word: Marines.

Corporal James broke the trance. "Chan, what's she saying?"

"She says Marines are murderers and animals."

Sam dropped his blooper gun. His eyes bulged. His coarse, dirty, furrowed skin matched his strange personality perfectly. He suddenly looked very old. In an instant, before anyone could stop him, he fell to his knees and ripped the woman's trousers down her thighs in one violent motion. I was stunned. No one moved. By the time we reacted, Sam had ripped her bloody shirt up over her head. I lunged forward with two others, grabbed Sam by the shoulders, and threw him onto his back. He gasped, out of breath and panting.

The woman started cursing us. Large glittering tears trickled down her face. Chan yelled, "Corpsman up!" then knelt beside her. He quickly tore her shirt in half and tried to stop the bleeding by tying the two pieces around her waist.

"How bad is it, Chan?" I asked.

"Looks like three hits by the gun."

"Can she make it?"

"I don't know. Looks like one round went through her back and out her side. It's the most serious."

The huge hole in her side gushed blood each time she cursed us. Sam jumped to his feet.

"Why don't we all get her before she bleeds to death!" Sam shouted.

"Yeah, why not?" someone added.

"That would be a mistake," Chan snapped at Sam, then stared at him, almost daring him to respond.

For a helpless moment it looked like a fight. I knew Sam was just crazy enough to grab his weapon. I took two steps back and put the M60 on my hip. Sam paid no attention to Chan or me. He kept a fixed stare on the naked girl. I could hear my teeth grinding.

"This guy in Delta told me they ambushed a chick up near the rock pile." Sam's speech had become slow and deliberate. "They took her clothes off and stuffed flares up her to keep it warm while his whole squad . . ." Sam's coarse laugh overwhelmed him until he couldn't finish his sick story.

Striker and Jones appeared from the brush. They stared at the woman without speaking.

"Well, where's the gook?" James barked.

"Couldn't find him," Striker replied, eyes glued on the naked girl. "He's in bad shape, though. There's blood everywhere. Hey! What's this? We gonna gang bang her?"

"Keep it cool. She's probably dying," James said.

"Oh, well," Striker grumbled. "Ain't enough of her anyway." Striker looked at Chan, then down, as if he was embarrassed or maybe just regretting his choice of words.

Still, no one took their eyes off the girl for more than a moment. Sweat dripped off my eyebrows. Corporal James lit up a cigarette. He carefully placed the precious matches back in his helmet. One boot rested comfortably on the shoulderless corpse. He exhaled a long, disconsolate stream of smoke. His rifle resting on his hip, held by one hand on the stock, reminded me of a hunter posing over a fallen deer.

"How 'bout it, Chan?" the corporal said. "Is she gonna live?"

"She might if we get her medevaced real soon."

"I don't know, Chan. She looks like she's lost a lot of blood."

"She has, but it doesn't look like anything vital was hit."

"I'll go see what the lieutenant says." Corporal James dropped his cigarette into the stream and started back up the hill.

"Don't bother with the lieutenant," Sam said. "Just ask Swift Eagle."

A half hour later a medevac chopper appeared overhead and lowered a basket for the wounded woman. Chan and the corpsman had managed to slow the bleeding considerably by that time. They delicately strapped her into the swinging basket and gave the chopper gunner a thumbs up. The hovering helicopter swung left, as if blown by a powerful gust of wind. The whirling rotors smacked against the tallest treetops, then the chopper swung right, seemingly out of control. For one horrible instant it looked like the heroic effort into Laos would end in disaster. Finally under control, the medevac gained altitude and disappeared over the mountaintops.

A wave of pride swept through me. It wasn't the first time I'd seen Marines risk their own lives to save a wounded enemy, but this time I felt wonderful. I wasn't sure why. Maybe because she was young and beautiful. Maybe because she thought Marines were animals. Or maybe because I was the Marine who shot her. Whatever the reason, I felt proud of being an American.

We saddled up right away. We all knew every gook in Laos knew exactly where we were after the medevac. I was glad to be leaving Laos. By the time we reached the valley, only the glow of the sun was still visible on the horizon. Our pace quickened as we crossed the first rice paddy. Huge black clouds rolled across the darkening sky, bringing a light drizzle and poor visibility.

By the time we reached hard ground on the other side of the paddy, the light drizzle had turned into a deluge. The column halted. My back ached. My legs begged for rest. I felt physically and emotionally drained. The gun weighed a ton, and my pack straps felt like they were nearing bone. I closed my eyes. . . . Sometime later I found myself being led by Chan to our position for the night. It looked like a perimeter, but I wasn't sure.

I didn't like our field of fire but felt too tired to complain. It looked like bushes in front of us, or was the rain just getting heavier? "Who cares?"

"What?" Chan asked.

"I was talking to myself," I whispered.

"If you are able to communicate with yourself, then you should take the first watch. I can't stay awake."

"I'll try, but my eyelids feel like lead."

Chan didn't answer or bother removing his pack; he fell into an instant coma. I took off my helmet, hoping the cold rain might wake me up. It didn't. I put it back on. I felt my eyes closing again. I tried to think of home, but I felt too miserable to think of anything pleasant. More rain. God, I hated this country. At least the rain kept the mosquitoes off me for a night.

Man, I thought, I'm getting awful skinny. I'll probably make it through the bloody war and die of some disease. I don't want to get old anyway. Drinking legal might have been nice. My friends will think I died a hero. I'll probably die of jungle rot. Probably have to be a closed casket. I'll never get to wear those darn dress blues. Chan says I'm making eleven cents an hour with combat pay and overseas pay. Who the crap can afford dress blues?

An hour passed. The rain lightened from a downpour to a pour. Something sizzled bright colors, like a sparkler moving in circles. Stay awake, I thought. I have to stay awake. The sparkler exploded into the mud on my right. "Incoming!"

Another B-40 rocket sizzled overhead, exploding twenty meters behind us.

"Guns up!"

I opened up with the M60.

"There's a flash!" Chan was shouting and pointing. "Ten meters left!"

My tracers zeroed in on the last flash.

"Cease fire!" Chan said.

"Do you see anything?"

"No."

"Ow! Chan! Something just hit me in the helmet! Felt like a brick!"

A numbing explosion blasted me forward. A frag had hit my helmet and bounced to the ground nearby. The flash stayed on my eyes. "I'm hit! God, I'm really hit this time! My back's burning!" I rolled left. "It's the barrel! Chan!"

"Johnnie! Are you okay?"

"God, I'm glad to hear you! Yeah. No. I don't know. There's a lot of warm stuff running down my leg, and it ain't rain." Another rocket exploded to our right, throwing mud around us. "Can you see?"

"Not yet."

"Are you hit too?"

"Yes," Chan said. "Listen."

"I don't hear anything."

"Neither do I."

"Think we should call for Doc?"

"Can you see yet?" Chan asked.

"No."

"They might be on top of us."

"Have you got your rifle?"

"Yes."

"I think I'm bleeding from the groin, too!"

"Bad?"

"No. I don't think so. Chan, feel my legs. Are they okay?" Chan moved closer. He hit my boot. I felt it. "God. Thank you."

"They're bleeding but still there."

"See if you can get the gun ready, I'll call the doc."

I oriented myself and pulled the M60 to me. She felt like solid mud, but nothing was out of place. I still saw spots. Memories of being timed taking the gun apart and putting it back together blindfolded came back to me. The only sound around us was the pounding rain.

"The gun's ready. I don't know what good it'll do. I can't see or hear."

"Corpsman!" Chan's call scared me. A moment later the call was echoed by the position on our left.

I tensed. I tried to straighten my left leg. It hurt. A sense of total helplessness swept over me. Then panic. "I'll never run again!" I blurted.

"What?"

"I can't play ball!"

"Hold it, you're okay."

"Am I crippled?"

"If you'd avoid catching frags with your fat head I wouldn't be lying here bleeding and having this absurd conversation!"

The exact words I needed. My panic subsided. I found myself giggling and feeling ashamed. I'd always wondered how I would react if I got hit. Now I knew, and my pride hurt more than my knee. Heavy boots splashed into a puddle of mud behind us. My night vision was still a useless series of yellow spots from the blast.

"I can't believe it. Hit you right in the head!" Chan started giggling. "Oh, it hurts to laugh!" He laughed again, trying to smother the sound with his hand.

As always, the laugh was contagious. I started giggling and crying at the same time.

"If one of you isn't wounded, you soon will be!" The

threatening whisper belonged to Corporal Swift Eagle. Another pair of feet hustled up behind us.

"Who's hit?"

"Is that Doc?" Chan asked.

"Yeah."

"We're both hit. Check John first."

"Then what's funny?" Swift Eagle growled.

"The frag . . ." Chan started to giggle.

"It hit me in . . ." I started snickering. I couldn't talk.

"Let's get 'em back to CP," Swift Eagle said. "Grab an arm."

"Think they're in shock?" Doc asked.

"No. They're both too crazy to be in shock."

The chief pulled me up like he was either mad or in a hurry. I came up on my right leg. "Can you walk?"

"No." The laugh was over. I started to straighten my left leg but the pain said no. I forced the leg to straighten. "I think I can hobble."

"Need help?"

"Yeah, Lieutenant. Grab an arm and leg. We'll carry him back to CP."

"Can you get Chan, Doc?"

"Yeah, right behind ya."

In the center of the perimeter was a small grass hootch. They carried me inside. I could hear Sudsy calling for a medevac.

"How ya doing, son?" a familiar voice asked from the darkness.

"Is that you, Gunny?"

"Yeah."

"I don't know. My knee hurts."

"How bad? Is it shrapnel?"

"It's not too bad," Doc said. "Looks like some time in Da Nang."

"I didn't know you guys found a hootch," I said.

"You and Chan will be sleeping in a real bed tomorrow night," Doc said. "Maybe tonight."

"No way. Can't get a medevac," Sudsy said.

"Chan, you in much pain?" Doc asked.

"Yes." Chan sounded weak.

"How bad is he, Doc?" I asked. Doc lit a match and quickly moved it all around Chan looking for wounds.

"A few shrapnel holes, but he'll be okay. Gunny, hold a match over my pouch for a second." Gunny lit a match, and Doc fingered through his pouch until he found what he wanted. "Okay, got it."

I sat up to get a look at my leg. My trousers were covered with red mud. "Wow! I've lost a lot of blood!"

A moment later Doc stuck something in my leg.

"This is morphine. You won't feel anything soon. . . ."

"What's all the bouncing?" I opened my eyes, then shut them. The sun was bright. Someone had my legs. I opened my eyes again, squinting to see what was happening.

"I hear a chopper."

"You sure do, girene."

"Swift Eagle?"

"I'm here, Johnnie. You're in for a good time in Da Nang, buddy. Your taxi's here."

I focused in on the chief's voice. His mud-spattered face showed no emotion, as usual, but I sensed friendship in his tone. It felt good.

"Don't catch any of those rare diseases in Da Nang, now." The lieutenant's voice surprised me. He was helping Swift Eagle carry me to the chopper. First-class service, I thought. "See if you can bring back some dry writing paper."

"Sure will, Lieutenant."

"Hurry up!" I couldn't see who was shouting. The wind from the chopper rotors blew water into my face. "Hurry up! Get him on!" It was the door gunner. They lifted me in. Swift Eagle shouted something, but the noisy engine drowned out his words.

"Where's Chan?" I shouted.

The chief gave me a thumbs up. The door gunner dragged me away from the open hatch. I couldn't understand the speed at which things were taking place around me.

"Go!" he screamed.

The rickety H-34 helicopter sounded like it might not get off the ground. Once it did, it climbed quickly, circling as it gained altitude. For an instant I could see the guys below. They were moving out again. I felt guilty for leaving them.

"Sit back, dummy, before you roll out."

"Chan! I was wondering where you were."

An odd sucking sound followed by a loud smack against the chopper wall on my right made me cringe. The gunner started firing at muzzle flashes below. A loud metallic thud came from the cockpit.

"Woooooo-we!" the pilot shouted. "Thank you, Uncle Sam, for this steel plate I got my butt on!"

A moment later we were out of range. The door gunner slid back toward Chan and me. "Are you okay?" His bushy mustache made him look like a walrus.

"Yes, but your aircraft has a new hole in it," Chan said.

"That's par for the course. We picked up a medevac in Dodge City about a month ago and got hit thirty-seven times in an old bucket just like this one. We still made it home."

"No one got hit?" I asked.

"Yeah, the copilot, but he lived."

"We've spent time in Dodge City, only in the mud. We're gunners. Wouldn't want to change places, would ya?"

I knew the answer, but I wanted to see if these fly-boys had proper respect for the grunts.

"Ain't no way, dude! I've been down there once too often already."

"You were a grunt?" Chan asked.

"For one week. With the Ninth."

"How'd you get out of the bush? I heard you have

to have three Purple Hearts to transfer from gunner to chopper gunner," I said.

"Yeah. That's what I heard too, but I had a good buddy who was an office pogue in the rear, and he wrote me up a duty change."

"Are you feedin' me some bull?" I said.

"Nope. It's the truth." He held up his right hand as if he were swearing in.

Chan and I looked at each other in disgust.

"Can your friend do it again?" I asked.

He shook his head. "Rotated home."

"Is there actually a movie theater in Da Nang?" Chan asked.

"Sure is. On Freedom Hill. Got cold beer, too."

"I bet you guys get beer every night, don't you?" I asked.

"Yep. We even have our own little refrigerator."

"It feels like we're going down. Are we at Da Nang already?" I asked.

"No. We're picking up some KIAs on Hill 188. See it?" He pointed at a muddy hilltop surrounded by barbed wire. It stuck out like a brown-cratered thumb in a sea of green.

The chopper settled into the muck of the mountain with a squish instead of the customary bounce. Four solemn-looking, helmetless Marines hustled toward us from a nearby sandbag bunker. They were shirtless and splattered from head to toe with dried mud. They carried a dead Marine wrapped in a poncho liner. Ten yards from us they sank into green muck up to their knees. When they reached the open hatch, they heaved the corpse in. It landed at my feet. The expressionless face just stared. Chan and the door gunner dragged the stiff, heavy corpse away from the hatch. Two more shirtless Marines came toward us carrying another dead man wrapped in a poncho spotted with dried blood. They heaved the corpse in and stood staring with the same blank faces. Then huge tears started streaming uncontrollably down the cheeks of one of the young men. I'd never seen anyone cry such huge tears without a sound or the slightest change of expression.

The chopper lifted off grudgingly from the sucking mud. Not a word was uttered by anyone. Wind swirling through the open hatch lifted the poncho nearest me, revealing a blond-haired, handsome boy.

"Look at his face, Chan."

"Yes. He was a good-looking guy." Chan leaned back with a sigh. "I wish we'd try to win this war."

"I wonder why we don't. I mean the real reason."

"We'll probably never know."

"Did you hear what old MacArthur said?" I asked.

"When?"

"My mom wrote in her last letter that he was appalled at what the government was doing to the American fighting man. He said he could take the First Marine Division, sweep to Hanoi, and end the war in three weeks."

"You know he's right." Chan sighed. "And I know and the gooks know, but I'm beginning to think we'll never do it."

"My leg is starting to hurt pretty bad."

"Mine too. The morphine is wearing off."

"I'm a PFC, and I could have told the morons that after one month," I said.

"Told them what?"

"That we could end the war in three weeks if we went to Hanoi."

"If we don't do something offensive, we're going to look just like the chicken French."

"How long has it been since you two slept in a bed?" the door gunner shouted from his position near the open hatch.

"I don't even remember!" I answered.

"I do!" Chan said. "At least seven months!"

"Well, get ready for a real bed!"

"Welcome to Da Nang!" the pilot shouted from the cockpit.

We came down on a portable landing pad about fifty yards from a group of gray Quonset huts. NAS was painted in large red letters on the roof and side of the nearest building. I could see people running from hut to hut. Others ran toward us carrying stretchers. Another medevac chopper lifted off to our left. It wasn't one hundred feet off the ground before another landed in its place. A drab green truck pulled up beside us. Two corpsmen jumped out, opened the back doors of the truck, then rushed over to us.

"Give us the stiffs!" a tall young corpsman shouted at the door gunner.

Two other corpsmen ran up to the open hatch. "Wounded first! Who's hit the worst?"

"After you," Chan said with a motion of his hand.

"Where am I going?" I asked as I struggled onto a stretcher.

"Your friendly Naval Aid Station," a corpsman answered.

A minute later they dumped me onto an operating table and rushed off again. Chan was close behind. Two corpsmen laid him on a table beside me. He looked like he had just gotten off a roller coaster the hard way. Fifteen tables lined the wall to my front with muddy Marines, all of them bleeding. Tubes ran in and out of each man. Plastic bags of blood and glucose and God knows what else drained over each bed.

Doctors shouted for instruments while others shouted for thread or bandages. The large room was a pandemonium of noise. No one seemed to be in charge. Bright lights glared off white walls. Even the doctors were dressed in blood-spattered white, with only their eyes showing. Medical personnel rushed about, colliding and shoving each other out of the way.

The pain was getting worse. A whiff of ether smacked

my nostrils. Normally, the smell of hospitals made me sick, but it had been so long since I smelled anything but the stench of the jungle and unwashed bodies that I found the antiseptic aroma strangely comforting.

I felt like a caveman. The electric lights fascinated me. The air felt abnormally cool. Maybe the loss of blood, I thought. Air conditioning! "Chan! It's air conditioning!"

"Where are you hit, Marine?"

I looked to my left to see the harried face of a young corpsman.

"My legs."

He reached for a large pair of scissors and started cutting up one leg of my trousers to the hip. A grenade fell out of one of the huge trouser pockets and bounced between the corpsman's feet. He turned pale. Then he lost control.

"You jarheaded moron! What are you doing with a grenade in here!"

His panicky scream startled everyone around us into silence. He was still too stiff with panic to pick up the grenade from between his feet.

"Haven't you heard, Squid?" I said with as threatening a tone as I could muster. "There's a war going on out there, and frags are tools of my trade." The frightened corpsman squatted slowly, delicately picked up the grenade with a forefinger and thumb, and ran out of the room holding it at arm's length.

The wounded around me were getting quite a chuckle, especially Chan, and I must say I was feeling rather pleased with myself until a doctor appeared from nowhere and shoved a pill in my mouth.

"This is Darvon, Marine. It will help relieve the pain a little. I can't give you anything else for now. We're out of nearly everything. We have to save what's left for the more seriously wounded."

He turned to the frightened corpsman, who had by now reluctantly disposed of my grenade.

"Cut his boots off and dig the shrapnel out."

The most serious wound was just under my left knee. The doctor was pointing to that spot when he said the word "dig."

A moment later three very large characters, all dressed in white, waltzed up to my table and proceeded to hold me down by my hands and feet. Things were beginning to look very grim again. I wanted to resist being held down, but six months of C-rations and humping fifteen to twenty miles a day had turned me into a walking skeleton. I was too weak to put up a struggle.

It felt like he was digging for clams. I screamed until someone gave me a towel to bite. He finally ceased the torture, stepped back from the table, and made the most ludicrous statement a man in his position could possibly make.

"Well." He paused, looking into the now gaping hole in my left leg, scratching his head like Stan Laurel, and sounding like a female impersonator. "I guess it's too deep to dig out."

My head dropped back to the table. I kept waiting to hear the Hallelujah Chorus from Handel's *Messiah*. The pain felt worse now than when I got hit. It convinced me that these fools were using me for on-the-job training.

The brunt of the Tet Offensive was over, but the combat was still heavier than at any other time in the history of the war. That fact became more alarming to me after they sewed me up, cleaned me, and wheeled me into a long Quonset hut filled to the limit with wounded Marines.

I fought back a loud sigh at the touch of clean white sheets. It felt so clean, cleaner than anything I could remember. I drifted into a deep sleep.

"How are you feeling, Marine?"

The soft voice sounded too pleasant to be anything but a dream.

"Wake up. Time for medicine."

I opened my eyes slowly for fear of chasing away my sensuous illusion. Huge round blue eyes seemed to be staring back at me through a thick fog. What was that smell? Lilac, I thought. Benita George used to wear lilac, or was that Jody Abbott? Oh, what a body. Benita was blond. I blinked my eyes. Either some of the fog had cleared or I had perfected dreaming. Bleached-blond hair surrounding large white teeth. I blinked again. Huge, healthy, positively American breasts. Couldn't be.

I slowly raised my right hand toward the lovely vision. I gave one breast two light pats. Hm. Firm dream, I thought. She smiled.

"I think you'll live, Marine." She reached for a tray beside the bed and hoisted out of it a bayonet, disguised as a needle. "Roll over."

I felt like a beached whale. I quickly nodded off and into a world full of large, friendly blondes.

"PFC Clark?"

That is not a dream, that is a nightmare, I thought. I opened my eyes. A stern-faced major in dress greens looked down at me.

"Yes, sir."

"I am presenting you with the Purple Heart medal on behalf of the United States Marine Corps." A young Red Cross girl handed him a purple box, then focused in on me with a camera. He opened the box and showed me the medal. "Would you like me to pin it on?" he asked.

I looked down to discover I was wearing blue pajamas. "No, I'll just lay the box by me."

"As you wish. This young lady is here to take a picture if you want. We suggest that you have the photo taken to send to your folks back home and let them know you're okay. Marines will come to their door with a telegram informing your next of kin that you have been wounded in hostile action in Quang Ngai Province." He turned and practically marched to the next bed.

"Smile," she said, and I didn't. "That will be one dollar." She tore the Polaroid picture from the camera and handed it to me like a traffic cop.

"But I don't have any money. We don't get paid in the bush. I don't even know where my wallet is."

"Your belongings are in the medical bag hanging on the side of your bed. You will receive a one-hundred-dollar Military Payment Certificate today. I'll come back later for the dollar."

She never got her dollar, and I never got my hundred. Twenty-four hours later I was flying south toward an Air Force hospital in Cam Rahn Bay aboard a C-130. Vietnam looked so pretty from the air, a giant green quilt with each square piece a different shade of green. I envied pilots.

The giant snub-nosed plane bulged with wounded Marines. I couldn't see Chan, but I figured he'd be aboard. I dozed off again and didn't wake until we bounced down at Cam Rahn airstrip. The engines whined to a stop. As we were unloaded from the plane, I noticed a strange silence. No artillery! We had landed so far away from the war there wasn't even the sound of artillery.

The Air Force hospital at Cam Rahn looked more like a cheap housing district in the U.S. But the Waldorf wouldn't have looked any better to me. Paved roads led us to the hospital, and I thought I actually saw streetlights. Sidewalks and well-kept hedges linked all the little one-story buildings together. Army and Air Force people walked about, carrying soft drinks instead of M16s and towels instead of packs. Everyone looked clean.

They wheeled me into a hospital ward. The wonders continued to unfold. Cold air-conditioned air slapped me in the face. Television sets mounted above some of the beds just about took my breath away. Telephones rang, and women nurses strolled in and out of the building. "I don't believe this!"

"Can you believe this?" a familiar voice said.

I looked right. Chan lay in the bed next to me.

"Chan! I've been wondering where you were."

Before he could answer another voice interrupted.

"Just like downtown, ain't it, dude?"

The voice was slow, deep, and monotonous, with a faintly nasal intonation. The face looked like a New York Italian's. Definitely a New York something.

"It's unreal!" I said. "I can't even hear artillery."

"You guys are Marines, no doubt. Da Nang must be overflowing again."

"Yeah, it is. Are you a Marine?"

"No way, man. I just broke my arm playing volleyball down at the beach. I'm Air Force."

"Volleyball?" I asked in disbelief.

"Beach?" Chan echoed my disbelief.

"Sure," he said. "What do they do to you clowns anyway? Where have you been, another planet?"

"Yeah. It's called the bush." I rolled toward Chan, hoping to end the conversation.

"Hey listen, man. I wanna quiz ya about the war when I get back from the latrine, okay?"

I ignored him. "How you feeling, Chan?"

"A lot better now that she's here."

His eyes led me to a beautiful red-headed Red Cross girl doing her best to maneuver a cart full of books and magazines through the swinging doors of our ward. She pushed the cart to the foot of my bed and stopped.

"Hi, fellas." She smiled. "See anything you'd like?"

My heartbeat picked up a couple of extra thumps. All we could do was stare. I felt like a country boy visiting the big city. Before either of us gained our composure, she dropped a pencil. The pencil bounced between our beds. She seemed to pay no attention to the pencil; she grabbed two magazines, walked between our beds, and handed one to each of us. She then turned around and bent over from the waist to retrieve the pencil.

Though normally Chan's manner conformed to an accepted standard of propriety and good taste exceeding that of most Marines, with the combination of combat fatigue, pain, short dress, long legs, exquisite rear end, and generous view, the strain was too much. He succumbed and leaned so far out of his bed that his head banged into mine, which coincidentally had drifted into approximately the same area. Naturally, she turned around in time to see us gawking.

Chan winced slightly, closed his eyes, and grimaced as if in great pain. I had never seen him more embarrassed. I decided to come to our weak but nonetheless hopeless defense.

"We've been in the bush a long time, ma'am, and you're our first mini-skirt."

"I would like to apologize . . ." Chan began.

"You haven't seen a mini-skirt before?" she asked unbelievingly.

"They were coming in just as we were going out," Chan said.

Chan spoke the painful truth, undoubtedly the single most atrocious crime against good timing I had personally committed.

"You have to be Marines." Her smile let us know she understood.

"Are you wounded badly?"

"No, just shrapnel," Chan answered.

"Speak for yourself," I said. "Mine hurts!"

"I suppose you've been on R&R by now?"

"No," we said in unison.

She looked pleased with our answer. She looked around secretively before continuing.

"If you two want more than a look, it'll cost you fifty each. Make up your minds. I'll be back later."

With that she pushed her little cart away, leaving me thoroughly jolted.

"That's a shame," Chan said quietly, as much to himself as to me.

"What is?"

"That a beautiful young lady, who very likely began her adventure as a Red Cross girl in Vietnam with humanitarian and patriotic ideals, has become no more than a prostitute." He looked at me seriously. "I think we should pray for her." He stared at me, then broke into a smile. "You look like I just stole your candy."

He was right, that's the way I felt.

"Look, Chan"—I suddenly felt angry with him, but I wasn't sure why—"I don't want to pray." I stopped myself from going on with some angry comment on how I just wanted to lust in peace.

"Sorry," he said. He knew how I was feeling.

I was almost happy to see two solemn-looking characters dressed in white appear at the foot of my bed with a wheelchair. A half-dozen examinations later, a bespectacled physician informed me that I had managed to catch four or possibly five strange little jungle diseases ranging from a touch of malaria to worms.

"According to your records, you've lost forty-two pounds."

That hurt. I hated losing weight. I hadn't realized how skinny I'd become. One of the strange ironies of war was how all the trivial concerns, like worrying about my physique, had not entered my mind once in seven months. In a bizarre kind of way it felt good to forget all the trifles.

A few shots later I was wheeled back to bed.

"I reconned the area in a wheelchair I confiscated," Chan said as the two medics lifted me into bed. "You won't believe who is occupying a bed in the ward at the end of the hall!"

"Who?"

"Staff Sergeant R. C. Jones!"

"Senior Drill Instructor R. C. Jones? I don't believe it."

"Hello, men." I knew that baritone voice. That voice had given me nightmares. It was true. There he stood, big as life, hanging on to crutches for balance.

"Sergeant Jones? What are you doing here?" I hesitated ending the question without a "sir." There was a time when I swore I'd nail this sucker if I ever met him off Parris Island.

"They can only refuse a transfer so many times. I had to get into this war. Been with the Ninth for about three months now. My gunner got killed and I had to jump on the M60. Got about fifty rounds off, and next thing I knew I was on a medevac. Thank God I made it over here before the mother was over!"

I knew he really meant what he was saying.

"If we don't try winning, it may never be over," Chan put in.

"That's the bloody truth," Jones replied. "Chan told me you two were put up for the Silver Star. That's bleedin' wonderful! You came out of PI Marines. Do you remember that fat-body that got the hernia in the squad bay?" His eyes got angry.

Chan and I exchanged glances. We remembered all too well chunky Private Peoples. Our three DIs made him do sit-ups, push-ups, and leg lifts in front of the platoon until he ruptured himself. Then they cursed him all the way to the ambulance, promising to drive his fat body out of the Marine Corps.

"Yeah, I remember him," I said.

Jones let loose a chorus of curses before telling us why the uproar. "The little girl wrote his congressman and started another investigation."

"Is that right?" Chan said, trying to act surprised.

"Do you remember that pantywaist that climbed up the water tower and threatened to jump? Maybe that wasn't your platoon."

"No, it *was* ours," I said.

I remembered it like it was yesterday. One more character who should never have joined the Corps. He panicked when he climbed the tower. All the DIs in the battalion marched their platoons to the tower and made them stand in formation around it. Then each DI threatened him with various tortures if he didn't jump. It was only about fifty feet, and he probably would have lived. He finally came down.

"That twerp got himself killed his third day in country, up at the rock pile. I tried to drum him out but he made it." Sergeant Jones's voice trailed off. In spite of his harsh language, he couldn't hide his obvious regret over the boy's death.

Before we ended our reunion I hit the sergeant up for a small loan. When he heard the reason, he acted happy to give it to me.

With loan in hand, nothing stood between me and the Red Cross girl. Chan confiscated another wheelchair, and I wheeled it to the head for a quick cleaning before the big date. Thirty minutes later Chan came after me.

"What are you doing?" he asked.

"How long has it been since you flushed a commode?"

"You mean you've been in here flushing that commode?"

"Man, it's been a long time since I've seen that apparatus."

Chan started laughing. Then he laughed harder. He leaned back, clapping his hands and losing temporary control of his chair. It rolled right, banging Chan's newly stitched leg into a hard porcelain sink. Dark red blood soaked through his blue pajamas.

Ten stitches and thirty minutes later Chan was back in bed beside me and groaning to the tune of taps vibrating through the hospital over a tinny-sounding intercom.

I requisitioned a pair of crutches from a patient who was not aware of his generosity. I was ready. Chan was asleep before taps finished. My palms started sweating like they did before hitting a hot LZ. I knew she wouldn't show up; it was too good, too much to hope for.

The fluorescent lights weren't even cool when she appeared in the doorway at the end of our row of beds. When she sauntered toward me, carefully placing one foot precisely in front of the other to give her hips a smooth, sensual sway, the sweat left my palms and went to my forehead. She still wore her short gray Red Cross dress and carried something under one arm.

I grabbed my crutches and slid out of bed as quietly as a cripple can. I started to giggle but managed to swallow it. She led me out of the one-story ward with no difficulty and across a small asphalt parking lot where I felt sure everyone in Cam Rahn Bay could hear me plodding across the asphalt. She guided me to a row of trucks with big red crosses on the hoods. We made our way to one that was conveniently open and unoccupied. Once inside the back of the truck, she lit a small candle and produced a six-pack of American beer from the brown paper bag she had tucked under her arm.

The night looked to be proceeding along quite nicely. The war was an old dream. Her name was Linda. She came from Dallas, was twenty-two years old, unmarried, and physically luscious. Her ambition centered around making enough money to buy a house.

"I only need about twenty-five more guys," she said with a bright, perky smile that came closer to a cheerleader's than a harlot's.

"A house! Can you make that much?" I asked naively.

"Oh sure," she said matter-of-factly, her sky-blue eyes springing open wide with information. "The girl I replaced made forty thousand bucks in eleven months."

I stupidly tried to divide fifty into forty thousand on ten fingers. Not enough fingers. I felt a bit upset, realizing she hadn't been swept away by my charm, or at least my good looks.

She stood to remove her gray Red Cross dress,

stooping slightly to avoid bumping her head. I felt myself melting faster than the candle. Her dress fell lazily to the floor of the ambulance.

The flickering candle gave off just enough light to drive me crazy, revealing a tight, muscular body. Her beautiful shoulder-length red hair waved naturally around a face that could have been doing soap commercials. She had the complexion of one of those people who probably couldn't even spell the word "pimple." She pushed a long red twirl of hair away from her slightly upturned nose and smiled enticingly. I fell immediately in love—or in lust. Definitely in something. I tried unbuttoning my shirt, but I couldn't get my eyes off her long enough to find the buttons. For no sane reason the thought that this might be the last beautiful girl I'd ever see drifted into my mind.

The clang of an emergency bell erased my trip down paranoia lane, replacing it with a brand-new fear, the fear of getting caught. Heavy boots hustled across the asphalt, getting louder and closer. Someone opened the cab door of our truck. The truck rocked with the weight of a large man jumping into the driver's seat. I froze.

"Maybe he won't open up the back," I whispered.

The starter whined. The driver stomped the gas pedal and cursed.

My lovely and naked accomplice was perfectly calm. I was ready to panic. She leaned back comfortably, observing me the way a psychiatrist might study a patient.

The engine whined again. How could she be so cool? I thought, rather angry at the idea.

Voices outside the truck made me hold my breath. The engine whined again. I didn't think the candle could be seen from outside, but out of nervousness I started to blow it out anyway.

"No," she whispered with her hand covering the candle. "Just relax." I didn't. The engine whined once more. The driver cursed. She put her finger up to her thick red lips, reached into the bag that had held the beer, and pulled out a round black object.

In the flickering light the object didn't look familiar. The engine whined. The driver cursed again. The truck rocked, then the door of the cab slammed shut. Boots stomped toward another truck. A door opened and closed. An engine started on the first try. I squinted to see the black object more clearly.

"Oh no!" I said. "It isn't!" I said covering my mouth to keep from laughing out loud.

"Yes, it is," she said. "A slightly used U.S. Army distributor cap." I tried to smother the noise, but it was no use. I laughed until I cried. "You're a real redhead. I mean, everything matches. I mean I haven't been with a girl in a long time. In the jungle, the war, ya know . . ."

"We'll take care of that. . . ."

"Besides jungle rot, various worms, and what may be a touch of malaria, PFC"—the stern-faced doctor looked down at his chart with a slight hint of disgust—"you now also have gonorrhea." I slumped against my pillow. I looked at Chan. His bed was cranked to a sitting position. He pretended to be reading a magazine, with his Snoopy grin plastered across his contented face. He said nothing.

Every morning during every humiliating, painful penicillin shot, he grinned and said nothing. Oh, one day he hummed and said nothing.

We spent over a month in the hospital. For over a month Chan held his tongue in check, not once succumbing to the temptation of "I told you so." He drove me crazy.

SOMETHING IS SMOKING AT
FIRE BASE ALPHA

Chan healed up first and was sent back to the bush. A week later the ax of health fell on me. The flight back to Da Nang gave me too much time to think. By the time we landed, my dread of going back to the bush was close to plain old fear. A few minutes after landing, a beer-bellied sergeant with a deep Southern accent pointed me toward a row of six big deuce-and-a-halfs with the engines already rumbling.

"That's a convoy of Seventh Marines." He clenched the remains of what looked like a week-old cigar between his teeth. "They're goin' to An Hoa. Tell 'em you're hitchin' a ride."

"What about a weapon? I don't have a weapon." Two Phantom fighters roared down the airstrip and shot into the sky.

"What?" he shouted.

"I don't have a weapon!" I shouted back.

"Pick one up at An Hoa." He shrugged his shoulders. "It's only twenty-five miles."

"I know how far it is. There's a war going on out there, Sergeant."

"You got a whole company in those trucks. I'm sure they'll take real good care of you."

For the smallest part of a moment I tried to assess my chances of not going to the brig if I decked this fat jerk. No chance. The trucks honked their horns, then began moving. I gave up trying to reason with the idiot and ran for the trucks. As the first two started picking up speed, clouds of dust and dirt rolled from under the big wheels. By the time I reached the tailgate of the third truck in line, I was no longer hospital clean. Two Marines held out the butt of their M16s. I grabbed hold and put a right boot on the edge of the tailgate. They hoisted me in. I spit out a mouthful of dirt. "Thanks."

"Are you a boot?" a voice asked. I turned and saw a big black Marine with corporal stripes drawn on the front of his camouflaged helmet cover. A toothpick hung out of one side of his mouth, and a scrungy-looking beard covered his face. For an instant I felt insulted. Then I realized I had on new boots and new utilities.

"Where did you get that NVA pack?" he asked.

"I'm not a boot. I'm just coming back from Cam Rahn Bay."

"You get hit?"

"Yeah."

"Scoot over and give the man a seat." He nudged the man beside him. His voice sounded friendlier.

I fell forward as the truck hit a small canyon in the road, landing where I was supposed to sit. A whiff of body odor from the men around me nearly brought tears to my eyes. These guys were grunts all right. I had never noticed how bad we smelled. Funny how bad odors don't affect you when you're part of the problem.

"Where's your weapon?" the corporal asked.

"They didn't issue me one. They told me to wait till I get to An Hoa."

"Boy, you're somebody's fool!" he said, then laughed.

"Are we going through Dogpatch?" I asked.

"Yeah."

The already insufferable odor was getting worse. I stood up to get a look at Dogpatch. Actually I just wanted some fresh dusty air. Dogpatch was a group of plywood shacks and bamboo hootches along the side of the potted dirt road between Da Nang and Hill 327.

There was nothing special about it except the name. It made a good reference point, since most Marines had been through it at one time or another.

Tall bamboo fence poles with three strands of rusty wire lined both sides of the road most of the way to keep the water buffalo away. Strangely enough, all the people were missing. Normally the kids would be shouting for handouts as we drove by. We rumbled by a shack on the left with a tin roof and sun-faded red cloth hanging where a door should have been. Between the house and the dusty road stood a piece of sturdy American chain-link fence stretched between two solid cement poles. A boyish face peeked from behind the red cloth. Fears of an ambush flashed through my mind. I looked ahead to the lead truck, instinctively feeling for my weapon, then fighting off a surge of panic.

Suddenly the cab of the lead truck lifted into the air, bringing the truck onto its back wheels like a horse rearing for a fight. One Marine flew from the truck and landed on the road. Two more fell over the tailgate and into the road and were almost run over by the second truck in the convoy. A deadening explosion followed. The convoy stopped. An orange and red ball of fire shot past the cab of the wounded truck and billowed into the blue air, then quickly evaporated into dark black clouds. The cab of the wounded truck crashed back to earth with a flat thud. Men scrambled out of the idling trucks. Everyone was shouting and pointing and running for the edge of the road to look for cover. I found mine beside the black corporal and regretted not punching the fat sergeant.

The corporal looked at me and laughed. "Somebody's fool."

The ambush never came. It was just a land mine. Every morning sweepers cleared the road of mines and every night the VC laid more. This one had been laid after the sweep, and the villagers in Dogpatch knew about it.

Twenty minutes later a bulldozer from Da Nang pushed the smoking truck off the road and we started for An Hoa again. The only casualty was the driver. He had lost both legs. I couldn't help wanting to do things the Korean way. If they got ambushed or caught sniper rounds from a village in Vietnam, they leveled the village. But then, they were fighting a war, and we were fighting a police action.

The rest of the trip went by uneventfully. In forty minutes we reached An Hoa. I bid farewell to the Seventh Marines and started walking toward the Fifth Marines HQ. Nothing had changed. It was hot, and artillery kept it noisy. A layer of dust an inch thick covered everything, and it smelled like the inside of the New York sewer system. The tubes were the worst offender. They were open urinals, and at 115 degrees, they were always upwind. But compared to the bush, An Hoa was still a slice of heaven. For a minute or two I debated the pros and cons of reporting in, but I was too cowardly to go AWOL, so I finally forced myself into the Fifth Marines headquarters, a big dusty tent surrounded by sandbags.

I pulled open a screen flap and peeked in. A regimental clerk pounded away on a big IBM typewriter.

"Excuse me, Corporal."

He stopped typing and looked at me like I was bothering him. "What do you want?" he barked.

I don't like this guy, I thought. What is this pogue doing sitting here camouflaged from head to foot behind a typewriter? "Real cute camouflage, Corporal. Know where a grunt might find some?"

"You better have a reason for being here, PFC."

I stepped up and inside the tent. It had a wood floor that was raised a foot off the ground. Half of the tent looked like the colonel's sleeping quarters, separated by a camouflaged screen. To the right of the typewriter was a long table covered with maps. A large posterboard that looked like a graph hung on the wall behind the table.

On top of the graph in large red letters someone had neatly printed SCOREBOARD. I handed the corporal my release from the hospital and orders to return to duty.

"Alpha Company, First Battalion, Fifth Marines," I said.

"You picked a bad time to come back, wise guy," he snickered. For an instant I thought about punching him. Then I remembered Tijuana and the brig. I decided to be forgiving.

"It's always bad out there, Corporal. What's up?"

"We just sent out three gunships for the Second Platoon. They hit something big over in the Arizona Territory."

"Any medevacs?"

"Not yet." He dragged the words out as though he were bored. "We got resupplies going out in a couple of minutes." He stood up from the typewriter and walked to the other side of the tent. He sat down in front of a large radio and called the airstrip. "Charlie-Tango this is Fi-yiv-Romeo H.Q. . . . Over. . . . Hold Chop-Wun for Alpha Two. We got a rider. . . . Over."

While he talked to the airstrip I couldn't resist the pull of an unfinished letter beside his typewriter. It practically reached up and begged me to read it, so I did.

Dearest Susan,
    Each day and night the war takes its toll upon me. I've lain in this muddy trench for two days now, waiting for the enemy to attack . . .

"Get away from that typewriter!" the corporal shouted from his radio. His face was as red as a sun-burned drunk. I started laughing at his face as much as at the letter.

"I bet this is why you pogues need the camouflage."

"You better watch your mouth, PFC. Your next meal might be in the brig. Your chopper is waiting. Dispersing is next door. Tell them I said to issue you a weapon, and beat feet over to the chopper pad. And for your information, I'm writing a book about the war!" He looked nervous. He turned back to his radio and picked up a pen. He started to write with the wrong end.

"Be careful, Corporal. You'll get ink on your camouflage." I walked out of the tent utterly pleased with my last comment and unable to restrain my laughter.

I picked up an M16 at dispersing and headed for the airstrip. The smile didn't leave my face until the chopper left the ground. Five minutes later the safety of An Hoa was a brown dot on a green horizon. The sun was starting to drop. I could see the pilot and copilot leaning toward each other, shouting back and forth over the noise of the engine, then looking back at me. The copilot unbuckled himself from his cockpit seat and came my way. He bent down on one knee in front of me, removed his dark sunglasses, and shouted, "Your unit is under fire! We've been called off! We're dropping you off at Fire Base Alpha!"

"Why?" I shouted over the roaring engine.

"Another chopper will pick you up tomorrow! We aren't going back to An Hoa!" He stood up and made his way back to the cockpit. Almost immediately the CH-46 helicopter started downward. I stuck my face against a glass portal. We circled downward toward a large, muddy hill, the top of which had been bulldozed flat. It bristled with artillery barrels sticking above a network of sandbag bunkers. Concertina wire around the hill looked to be thirty to forty yards thick. We set down on a big square piece of corrugated steel matting. The copilot gave me a thumbs up and I jumped out. I nearly fell on my face. I'd forgotten how heavy a full pack, canteens, flak jacket, rifle, and ammo could be. The CH-46 lifted off, its giant rotors blew me forward as I tried to hold my helmet on. After it had pulled away, a cool breeze hit me, the kind of breeze we never felt in the stifling jungle below.

I felt ridiculously conspicuous standing on the landing pad with no idea of what I was supposed to do. A helmeted head popped up out of an underground bunker twenty-five meters to my left with two huge antennas sticking out of the top of it. He waved me over. In the center of the compound stood a flagpole. A yellowish South Vietnamese flag with three horizontal red stripes hung limp beneath Old Glory. Beside the flagpole, resting atop a fifteen-foot post, sat a large wooden birdhouse. Under it, a big, bearded Paul Bunyan of a Marine wearing nothing but cut-off trousers sat in a lawn chair, throwing seeds to a group of brightly colored birds and drinking a beer. Judging from his golden tan, this wasn't the first time he'd done this.

As I neared the man who had waved, I realized he had a lieutenant's bar painted black on his helmet. I wasn't sure whether to salute or not. I decided that they probably considered this a combat area. No salute.

"You're just here for the night, right?"

"Yes, sir."

"See that bunker over there? The one closest to that big bearded guy?" he pointed.

"Yes, sir."

"Go over there and tell the men lying in it that you'll be bunkin' there tonight." He turned and disappeared into his sandbag cave. I looked around to see if anyone else was aboveground besides me and the bird feeder. There wasn't a soul visible. Must not be too worried about getting hit, I thought. I walked over to the bird feeder. He turned toward me as I got close, revealing blue eyes surrounded by a network of bright red blood vessels. I hadn't seen eyes that bloodshot since Tijuana.

"Yeah, bro, what do you need?" His voice seemed to come from his stomach.

"The lieutenant told me to bunk in here for the night."

"Where ya coming from?"

"Cam Rahn Bay," I answered.

"You get hit?" His eyes looked fully open for the first time. He sat up in his chair.

"Yeah. About a month and a half ago."

"Come on in, man. I'll introduce you to the guys." He stood up slowly, as if the motion weren't easy. "What's your MOS?"

"0331."

"Machine gunner? God, that's awful! Come on in."

I followed him down four sandbagged steps. We bent through a narrow doorway and into a twelve-by-twelve-foot sandbag room with cots against all four walls. A fat candle flickering from a small wooden shelf provided the only light besides the shafts of the setting sun streaking through the doorway. A thin, mustached, and shirtless Marine rested comfortably on a camouflaged poncho liner draped over his cot, studying the foldout in a *Playboy* magazine with the intensity of a student facing finals.

On another cot, against the opposite wall, lay another prone Marine, this one face down and snoring peacefully under a bushy head of blond hair. Vintage *Playboy* foldouts sixty-six through sixty-seven covered the wall behind the snorer.

"We got company for the night, comrades," the bird feeder announced. The snorer kept snoring. The reader looked up, nodded once, and went back to reading. "Don't pay attention to these two, Gunner. We had a little blowout last night."

"Little!" the reader said with a tired chuckle. "We got stoned out of our minds!"

"That's your cot. What's your name?" the bird feeder asked. "I'm Bill."

"Better known as Wild Man," the reader said. "I'm Joe Constantine."

"Better known as Surfin' Joe," Wild Man countered.

"And this is Banger Berkeley Adams. He claims to have banged every girl in Berkeley, California," Surfin' Joe said.

"We're all from California. Where you from?" Wild Man asked.

"I'm John Clark." I suddenly felt that my name was terribly insufficient, too close to John Doe. "I'm from Florida."

"Far out!" Surfin' Joe exclaimed. "You ever catch any waves at Daytona?"

"Here, have a hit." Wild Man handed me a smoking hand-rolled cigarette.

"No thanks. I don't smoke."

"This ain't no cigarette, Marine." He held it closer. I took it from him.

"What is it?" I asked.

"It's a joint, man. You know, weed." I knew that if I looked as ignorant as I felt right now I was one sorry sight.

"Look, I don't know anything about this stuff. I've never even seen it before except in a movie once they showed us in school. Showed people going crazy and crashing—"

"That was a bunch of bull!" Wild Man blurted out. Then he started laughing.

"We used to bring joints into those movies and pass them around while the lights were out," Surfin' Joe said. Then he started laughing too.

"You've never seen grass before?" Wild Man asked in disbelief.

"I thought Florida was cool!" Surfin' Joe said.

So these were the infamous California Marines, I thought. My DI always said there were more fags and freaks in California than the rest of the planet combined.

"I thought you guys would get some great weed out in the bush," Wild Man said.

"Are you serious?" I said. "Haven't you guys ever been in the bush? You sit around smoking grass out there and you'd die. If the gooks don't kill you then your own men probably would."

"Well, this ain't exactly downtown Saigon," Joe said sarcastically.

"This is R&R to the grunts, and you know it," Wild Man snapped at Joe. "You feel like trading places with him?"

"Fat chance, bro!" Joe said. He chuckled and turned to me. "What are you doing here, anyway?"

"I'm coming back from Cam Rahn Bay."

"You get hit?" Joe asked with renewed interest.

"Yeah," I said, trying to hide my bulging pride. "My unit was under fire so the chopper dropped me off here till tomorrow."

"Who are you with?" Joe asked.

"Alpha, One-Five."

"Really!" Wild Man said. "We fire for you guys sometimes."

"One-Five!" Joe said. "That's Staff Sergeant Morey's outfit! Do you know ol' Morey?"

"Yeah. Not real well though. He's in Third Platoon most of the time, but sometimes he comes with us, and sometimes my gun team goes with them."

"He's a great guy. He was ranking staff in my unit at ITR," Joe said. "Did you know that guy is on his third war?"

"Yeah, I know. We get on him every time we see him."

"Why?"

"That guy's been through Iwo Jima, Guadalcanal, and Chosin Reservoir as a grunt and never got a scratch. Not even a piece of shrapnel. So we got a running joke about him disappearing when the shooting starts. It's all in fun, though."

"Does he still have that droopy mustache that curls around the corners of his mouth?"

"Yep. That's him. Always looks pale," I said.

"Even in the bush?" Joe exclaimed.

"Yep."

"Look, if you're staying here all night, you might as well get loaded with us. You won't be stoned tomorrow." Wild Man said. He relit the joint.

"But I don't even smoke cigarettes. I can't inhale smoke."

"It's easy," Wild Man said as he passed the joint to Joe.

"Yeah, watch. Just take a big hit into your lungs like this." Joe inhaled until his cheeks looked flush. "Then hold it down for as long as you can." He sat up on the cot. Tiny puffs of smoke floated out of his mouth with each word. He passed it to me. I took hold of it with my forefinger and thumb. Something popped inside, breaking off the crimson ash. I stomped it out on the hard dirt floor.

"What was that?" I asked.

"Just a seed," Wild Man said. "Here." He lit a match and held it out. I put the joint to my mouth and leaned forward. The first puff told me why they called it weed. It tasted like burning weed. My throat closed to keep the smoke out of my lungs, but I forced it down. It came right back up, followed by a month's worth of coughs that brought tears to my eyes.

"That's okay. Everybody does that until they get used to it," Joe said.

"Since this is your first time . . ." Wild Man said with a huge grin surrounded by hair. He reached under his cot and pulled out a cigar box. He opened it and pulled out a ten-inch-long, burnt-orange cigar with the circumference of a fifty-cent piece. Joe started laughing at the sight of it. "You ever heard of a Ban-San Bomber?" Wild Man asked.

I shook my head and coughed again. Wild Man held the huge cigar up and marveled at its beauty. Joe held out his hand. "Here. Let me smell it." Wild Man handed him the cigar and Joe ran it by his nose twice. "Far out, man. Here. You do the honors." Joe handed me the cigar.

"If we're going to do the Bomber, let's do it right, man. Let's have some sounds!" Wild Man said. He pointed under the still-sleeping Berkeley Banger's cot. It looked like an expensive radio, I thought.

"Where do you get stuff like that in Nam?" I asked.

"You don't, man," Joe answered. "Banger got that in Bangkok on R&R."

"You ever get to listen to AFR, man?" Wild Man asked.

"What?"

"Armed Forces Radio."

"You can't have a radio in the bush," I said.

"Yeah, of course. Stupid question," Wild Man acknowledged. "Well, go on. Light up."

"And this is Specialist 4 Robert Townsend, the enlisted man's DJ in sunny Saigon! This is for Seaman First Class Frank Soper aboard the *Sanctuary*: The Doors, Jim Morrison, and 'Riders on the Storm.' "

"Talk about skatin' duty. Can you imagine coming over here and being a disc jockey or sitting on a ship the whole time?" Joe asked, not really expecting an answer.

I took the first puff off the Ban-San Bomber. It tasted like the tailpipe of somebody's truck. Wild Man handed me an unopened fifth of OFC Canadian whiskey. "Take a shot and swallow that smoke." I handed the Bomber to Joe and started coughing up smoke again. "Go ahead, take a swallow."

I opened up the bottle and downed three big gulps. When the burning subsided, I decided I felt pretty good. Joe and Wild Man kept staring at me with funny little grins on their faces, as if they knew something I didn't. Joe passed the Bomber to Wild Man. He took a long, slow puff, his hairy, barrel-shaped chest expanding farther and farther as he filled it with smoke. When he couldn't take any more, he handed it to me again. I was determined to keep the smoke down this time just to see what would happen. I inhaled more slowly, fighting back a cough all the way to my lungs.

"That's it, that's it. Now quick take a shot of whiskey." Wild Man handed me the bottle. I handed Joe the Bomber. I gulped. "Now hold it in. Don't let that smoke out!" My eyes bulged from the strain. It felt like the smoke was leaking from my ears. That tailpipe must have had wheels attached to it, I thought. I coughed. A cloud of white smoke shot out of my lungs. My eyes watered. The air became dense and resinous. I followed a column of smoke through the door and into the dark sky. I felt a nudge.

"Here."

Wild Man handed me the half-empty whiskey bottle.

"Aren't you worried about getting caught?" I asked. "What if the lieutenant comes rolling in here?"

"He knows better. I'll kick his butt if he comes in here," Wild Man said.

"I don't see what's so great about this stuff. I don't feel a thing."

Joe and Wild Man started laughing again. This time I laughed with them. Wild Man inhaled another long drag off the Bomber and handed it to me. "Here." He forced the word out while trying to hold the smoke in. "You ain't no Marine if you don't keep it down this time."

I took the Bomber and sucked in as much smoke as I could. I started feeling dizzy. I exhaled the smoke slowly, trying not to cough. Finally the smoke emptied from my lungs. I felt deflated.

"Did you guys notice that it's dark outside?" I said.

Wild Man laughed triumphantly. Joe quickly followed, bursting into a loud cackle. " 'I don't see what's so great about this stuff,' " Joe said mockingly, then started laughing again.

"Fire in the hole!" A shout from outside echoed

through the bunker. Suddenly one of the big guns fired. "Man your guns!" another voice shouted. Boots running, getting closer. "Man your guns!" Wild Man put the Bomber out, grabbed his helmet from a nail on the wall, and darted through the door. The snoring blonde awoke with a startled jump, shook his head, grabbed his helmet from under his cot, and ran out. Joe got up slowly, tightened the laces on one boot, leisurely pulled a green T-shirt on, and casually walked out the door.

"Hey! Are we getting hit?" I shouted at Joe.

He peeked back in. "No. It's just a fire mission. Sit tight. Have another toke off the Bomber. We'll be right back." He turned and disappeared up the steps. I leaned back on my cot. My head felt a little off center. Funny. I'd only heard one round. Probably a spotter round. My rifle, I thought. Why am I holding my rifle? I leaned the rifle against the end of my cot.

"For the MPs of Saigon . . . Donovan."

"Sunshine came softly through my window today. . . ."

I love that song, I thought. Reminds me of Barbara Windham, what a perfect face. . . . I think I'll drink to that.

"We're back!" Wild Man's hoarse voice interrupted Donovan. Joe came in behind Wild Man. He threw his helmet on the ground.

"Light up that Bomber!" Joe shouted.

"Yeah, give me a hit off that thing," Banger Berkeley added as he came in behind Joe. He plopped down on his cot, grabbed the bottle off the floor, and took a swig. Wild Man lit up the Bomber and passed it to me.

"What happened?" I asked.

"Sounded like the gooks were either too close to call in artillery or else they took off," Joe said. "Pass me the whiskey."

I inhaled another huge amount of smoke, this time without coughing, and passed the Bomber to Berkeley

Banger. He wasn't good-lookin' enough to be the stud he claimed to be. A long nose and thin lips. Downright ugly. Wild Man nudged me again. "Here." He handed me the whiskey. "You ain't no Marine if you can't chug it to the OFC on the label."

I did.

The rest of the night blurred by. Pieces of the night floated through my brain in between the pounding of the world's most horrible headache. Darts flew at the big nose of a picture of Lyndon Johnson, then I was dangling from the barrel of a giant cannon and falling into space.

"You got a chopper coming, Marine! Get up!"

I opened my left eye. It hurt. Sun. It can't be! It's daylight! The sunlight forced the eye closed again.

"Get up. You got a taxi comin' in!"

I opened my right eye, hoping that it wouldn't corroborate my left. Sunlight! Oh, no! A blurry face stood over me with the barrel of a .155 hanging over his head.

"Are you okay?" the face asked.

"No."

"What's wrong?"

"I feel like I should be hugging a commode."

"Get up! You got a chopper coming in to pick you up."

"No, thanks, I'll just wait here."

"Speak up! I can't hear you."

"I can't make it today. Sorry."

"Hey, Jack! Come over here and give me a hand with this guy!"

I could feel someone picking me up. I tried to open my eyes, but it hurt. My mouth was cotton. My teeth hurt. My legs hurt. My ears hurt. "What's that noise? Turn it off."

"You'll have to pull him in. This guy is really blasted."

"Hey! Man! He puked all over my boot!"

"Here's his rifle and pack."

I was going up. So was my stomach.

"Man, you look green!" I opened my eyes. The door gunner was talking to me.

"I feel green. I think I'm going to throw up."

"Here, hang out the hatch. I'll hold your feet."

I rolled toward the hatch, took my helmet off, and stuck my head out. The wind smashed against my ears. The ground swirled. I puked. And puked. And puked.

WELCOME BACK

"Can you get off okay?" The young face covered with dark flight glasses seemed honestly concerned. "I sure hope you ain't no boot." My head stopped spinning, but I felt weak all the way down to the ankles. "Can you get off?"

"Do I have a choice?"

"There it is, bro."

We dropped down faster than usual. My stomach came up. I wanted to throw up, but there was nothing left inside. This chopper was in too big a hurry. I knew what that meant. I wonder if God's going to let me die drunk.

"Is it a hot LZ?" I asked.

"I think so. You better lock and load, bro." He let loose a five-round burst at the ground below. My head pounded with each shot.

"What are you firing at?"

"Just making sure she doesn't jam!" he shouted.

"We're goin' in!" a voice from the cockpit shouted. My stomach tightened. I didn't feel drunk anymore. Just like, back in the world, I could always sober up when I saw those flashing red lights. The gunner started firing. We dropped like the dip on a roller coaster, then steadied up, hovering ten feet above the ground. Small white puffs of smoke spit from a group of long-leafed banana trees. The door gunner fired back.

"Get out!"

I jumped through the hatch. The chopper started up before I hit the hard ground. My stomach rumbled. I belched up more whiskey and spit it out. Twenty-five meters to my front an M60 peppered the banana trees. Fifty meters to my rear another M60 opened up. Cracking AK rounds wailed overhead. Marines shouted back and forth behind me. I belched up another mouthful of whiskey and puke. I couldn't believe this was happening to me. I flattened to the ground. I'll never drink again, I swore. Oh, God, I hope you let me drink again.

"Find some cover, fool!" I looked around to see who was shouting. The gunny's head peeked up from a fox-hole twenty meters to my right.

"Gunny! It's me! I'm back!"

"Chan's over there!" He pointed to the gun straight ahead of me, then ducked back down as AK fire ripped across the open perimeter. Thank God, I thought. Chan's okay.

"In the tree! There's a gook in the tree!" a voice screamed at the top of his lungs behind me and to the left. I turned to look back in time to see five Marines on their knees firing up into a tall, thin-trunked tree with a cluster of branches at the top. A rifle fell from the top of the tree, followed by the limp body of a man, which bounced off two limbs and thudded to the dry earth in a splash of dust.

"Chan! It's me! John! I'm comin' over! Give me some fire!" I jumped to my feet and ran zigzagging toward the sputtering M60. Chan sent a spread of tracers up and down the line of banana trees. Tiny clouds of dust kicked up around me as the gooks spotted a moving target. Chan fired from behind a fallen banana tree. Five yards from Chan I dove the rest of the way. The landing sent another shock wave through my stomach. I belched up a couple more shots of whiskey.

"Nice timing! You got any ammo?" Chan spoke without looking at me. "The tree line's full of gooks."

Then he turned. "I don't believe it. You're finally getting a mustache."

"Where's your A-gunner?" I asked.

"Dead."

"Who?"

"A boot. Arvis Hendry, remember? He's back at the CP. We couldn't get the body out."

I remembered the scared boot.

"I don't have any ammo," I said.

"We're almost out. Look!" He pointed at a uniformed NVA running from the cover of one tree to another one closer to us. "We're about to get overrun!"

"What's going on?"

"We're surrounded!" Chan shouted. "Why did that chopper drop you in here?"

"I don't know. He didn't even know it was a hot LZ!"

"Look at this! We have one belt of ammo left!" Panic was beginning to creep into Chan's voice. "Third Platoon's already lost four men back there that I know of."

"Third Platoon! Is the whole company here?"

"No. Just the Second and Third. We're in real trouble, buddy." Chan's eyes sobered me with a serious stare.

"I'm going after some ammo. Somebody back there has some."

"Wait." Chan grabbed my arm. "Let the CP know you're coming."

"Hey, Gunny!" I screamed as loud as I could. The chaotic firing around the perimeter drowned me out. I turned to Chan. "He'll never hear me over all this. I'm going for it. Gunny should know who has gun ammo." I swallowed back a small belch.

"Be fast!"

"Like the wind!" I clutched my rifle, crawled around to face the CP, trying to stay below the level of the fallen tree. I lodged one foot against the tree to get a good push off, took another deep breath, and screamed, "Why am I doing this?" The first five steps felt like a man running underwater with broken legs. I wished for tennis shoes and asked God to protect me. Then I realized my flak jacket was on Fire Base Alpha. The whine of a bullet zinged past my left ear. I dodged right, then left, then right again. I thought about what horrible marksmen the gooks normally were. Their only chance of hitting me was if I dodged into one of their misses. I stopped dodging and ran straight for the CP. I could hear the gunny shouting to get down. I dove into his shallow foxhole, landing on top of him. I tried to burrow down but my butt was sticking out in the open.

"I need ammo for the gun!"

"Welcome home!"

"Move over! My butt's sticking out!" Gunny moved but there still wasn't room. "I need gun ammo!"

"Third Platoon might have some!" Bullets thudded into the ground with frightening force, kicking dirt into my face.

"Okay!" I jumped to a crouch and ran for the Third Platoon. They looked to be spread into a half-moon shape covering the north and east. Halfway there I shouted ahead, "I need gun ammo!"

"Get down, you idiot!"

"Over here!" An arm waved from a shallow foxhole. I dove in beside the foxhole. My body strained to get under my helmet.

"M60 ammo!" I said as I tried to catch my breath without looking up.

"Here! Get out of here with it! You're drawing fire!" He handed me two belts of ammo and ducked down.

I grabbed it and jumped up. My feet wouldn't move fast enough.

"Comin' by, Gunny!" I shouted ahead. The gunny waved. I veered by his foxhole.

The lieutenant peeked up from another hole. "Keep your head down up there! We got air strikes coming in!"

I kept running and weaving. "Show the Phantoms where the gooks are!" the lieutenant shouted. I didn't look back.

"Comin' in, Chan!" I dove in beside him. Pieces of fallen tree flew into the air from a barrage of AK fire. A small gray snake slithered from under the tree five feet to my right and wiggled away. I wanted to be that small. I wanted to follow him. "Chan, we got air strikes comin'. I got two belts."

"When?"

"Sounded soon! Want to trade places? I just don't feel right with this little peashooter."

Chan looked at me seriously, then broke into a smile. "I wondered when you would want this thing back. Yes, might as well. You're useless as an A-gunner anyway." We changed positions, staying under cover of the tree. The gun felt good, like an old girlfriend. I fired a ten-round burst at a muzzle flash in the tree line thirty meters away. Three Phantoms roared overhead at treetop level. Flames shot from the tail of the camouflaged Phantoms as they hit their afterburners and climbed straight up, rolled over, and banked gracefully back around. I opened up on the tree line, spraying tracers back and forth to mark the bomb run.

"He rocked his wings!" Chan shouted.

"Burn, suckers, burn!"

Like lightning, a sleek Phantom dropped from the blue sky over the banana trees low enough for me to see the pilot's face. Two long cylindrical bombs floated softly away from the screaming jet, tumbling lazily end over end until they crashed to the earth. The napalm spread like a violent wave coming ashore, engulfing everything in fire. Clouds of orange and red flame swallowed the line of trees. My face burned. I jerked my head down behind the tree. My eyebrows and mustache were smoking. "Chan!"

"Good grief! It singed the hair off your face!"

"How bad is it?" I was scared to touch my skin. The

acrid stench of the singed mustache hair brought up another mouthful of whiskey.

"Looks like a sunburn." Chan peeked over the tree. "Look!" A man screaming in agony ran from the flaming banana trees on fire from head to toe. I took aim, but I didn't fire.

"Put him out of his misery!"

"I don't want to waste the ammo!" I barked angrily.

A few seconds later he collapsed. I could feel Chan staring at me. I hesitated to look him in the eye. I knew he would be shocked. It shocked me, too. I turned to see Chan's face. He was looking at the fire.

"I'm sorry," I said.

"Don't be. You were right."

A single Phantom swept over the tree line. At least three AKs opened up on the low-flying jet.

"How could anybody live through that?" I asked.

Another Phantom streaked across the tree line, strafing it with .20-millimeter cannons. Then a third Phantom swept low over the trees, releasing two more napalm bombs. The hungry flames rolled over the area, eating everything they touched. We ducked down from the blast of heat. Still, it made me gasp for air. Once the wave had passed, I peeked over our tree. Another burning man ran from the scorching tree line. I pulled the M60 butt to my shoulder and walked a quick stream of tracers into him. He dropped to the ground in a smoldering heap.

The Phantoms made strafing passes all around our scattered perimeter, then disappeared high into the blue sky. The right flank lit up with heavy small-arms fire, popping and cracking like a string of firecrackers. Suddenly it stopped. All was quiet now except for the crackling flames to our front.

"Choppers! We got choppers comin' in! Give 'em cover!" someone shouted from the center of the perimeter.

Red smoke swirled like crimson fog from the CP. Two Huey gunships banked sharply around the perimeter. I fired a short stream of tracers at the smoking tree line. The Hueys circled twice, firing M60s. A green and black CH-46 helicopter drifted down to the center of the perimeter. A large nylon net bulging with boxes of ammo and C-rations swung heavily suspended by a long, taut cable under the double-rotored chopper. Cracking AKs opened up from the surrounding bush. The CH-46 hovered over the red smoke, preparing to drop the sorely needed supplies. The chopper swung in an erratic circle. I could see the pilot bend over and the copilot leaning over him frantically struggling to right the craft.

An enemy machine gun opened up on our right flank. Green tracers flying high across the perimeter zeroed in on the spinning helicopter. At the same time another volley of AK fire opened up from the left flank.

"Guns up! Guns up! Guns up!" The calls came from the right flank. I grabbed the gun. Chan grabbed the ammo. We jumped to our feet and darted toward the right of the perimeter. A blooper gun opened up on the bush ahead. It was Sam. The entire perimeter was in the open. I could see prone Marines spread on line firing into the bush on the flank.

"Guns up!"

We ran toward the voice. I could see Swift Eagle, flat on his stomach, pointing at the flash of an enemy gun one hundred meters straight ahead. The engine of the crippled chopper began palpitating. I dove to the right of Swift Eagle; an instant later Chan belly-flopped to my right and began feeding the gun. I opened up on the enemy gun flash. Orange tracers glanced off a bump in the terrain. I stood up, firing the M60 from the shoulder like a rifle. "Get down!" someone shouted from the left. My orange tracers spiraled in on the enemy flash. The flash stopped as a pith helmet flew into the air, then floated to the ground like a Frisbee. I hit the ground. Sand and rocks kicked up around me from incoming AK fire.

An enemy rocket shot out of thick brush seventy-five meters to our front. It climbed slowly at first, spiraling toward the wounded chopper, then gaining speed like a shooting star. It sizzled overhead. I followed it with my eyes as it zeroed in on the sputtering helicopter. I held my breath and cringed, but the rocket sizzled just under the front landing wheel of the CH-46, arced two hundred meters past the opposite side of the perimeter, and exploded in a tree, breaking it in half. Another machine gun opened up on the helicopter from the other side of the perimeter. A Huey gunship, rockets firing, dove at the enemy gun. The Huey pulled up at the last possible moment. The enemy gun went silent.

The CH-46 started smoking. Flames shot from the back rotor. Then it fell, straight down, the updraft of wind shooting the flames high above it. It crashed to the ground, crumbling over the large net full of supplies. The flames spread quickly. The door gunner crawled from the burning wreckage, his back aflame and screaming in agony, his face red with blood. I could feel the heat of the burning helicopter on my already scorched face. Marines from the CP ran to the aid of the burning crewmen. One Marine shoveled dirt onto the burning door gunner with his bare hands. Another butt-stroked the already broken Plexiglas cockpit in a frantic effort to free the pilot and copilot.

"Get your eyes on the enemy! You've seen choppers go down before!" Corporal Swift Eagle stormed up and down the line of Marines, all of whom were still stunned and staring at the fallen chopper. It seemed a perfect time for the enemy to charge. Swift Eagle knew it. We were vulnerable. "I'll kick butt on the next Marine that looks back! You better know I mean it!" A flight of three Phantoms ripped overhead at treetop level, blazing a barrage of .20-millimeter cannon fire. They climbed high, banked back around, and swept over the enemy line with three more napalm bombs. I ducked from the wave of heat, trying to save what was left of my mustache.

The Phantoms banked back around and napalmed the opposite side. I could hear the sucking explosions, but I didn't turn. Black smoke fogged over the perimeter. A penetrating odor like burning gasoline filled my lungs until I coughed.

The firing stopped. Only the crackling sound of dried leaves and trees burning remained. A horrible scream came from the CP, the kind of scream you can feel in your spine. Still, no one looked back.

Ten minutes later a voice from the CP called out, "Medevac coming in!"

An old H-34D drifted high over the burning treetops until it hovered directly above the blazing wreckage in the center of the perimeter. It dropped quickly, landing twenty meters from the CH-46. I clutched the M60, waiting for the cracks of AK fire. It drew no enemy fire. I knew it was over. Three Huey gunships circled the perimeter, ready to give cover to the medevac. Two minutes later the medevac lifted off. Still no enemy fire. I felt as though I'd stepped out of a drunken nightmare. I puked again. My mouth tasted dry with whiskey.

"Welcome home, John!"

I turned to see Sam standing behind me. His pitted face and rotten teeth looked as ugly as ever, but I was glad to see him, glad he wasn't dead.

"How you been, Sam?" A thick cloud of black smoke covered us just as I spoke. It smelled like burning plastic. I tried to spit it out, but the taste of carbon stuck to my taste buds.

"Chan told us you guys had a great time in the hospital." Sam spit a shot of tobacco to his left and knelt down on one knee, leaning slightly on his M79. "Did you hear about Swift Eagle?"

"No."

"I think his old man died. He can go home to take care

of his mom if he wants, or at least go back for the funeral or whatever it is that Indians do."

My stomach tightened. Swift Eagle! I couldn't imagine being out here without him. "When's he going?" I suddenly wished more than ever that my wound had sent me home.

"He ain't! That crazy Indian loves it out here, I guess."

"You're kidding!" I said, selfishly pleased. If anyone deserved to go home, he sure did.

"Saddle up! Second Platoon! Saddle Up!" Gunny shouted from CP. A minute later another CH-46 floated through the smoke to the center of the perimeter, dropped off supplies, and took off without wasting a second. As Second Platoon filed by, Corporal James, Swift Eagle, Gunny, and Lieutenant Campbell tossed each man his share of food and ammo. Twenty minutes later we found ourselves marching north through the still-smoldering trees and brush. Everything looked black and charred, even the dirt. I couldn't believe I was humping in the bush again. I felt depressed. We marched by the body of a dead NVA. He didn't look burned at all. His eyes and mouth were wide open, like he'd been hit by an electric shock.

"Napalm," Chan mumbled behind me.

"Sucked the air right out of him, didn't it?" I said. "I wonder why we aren't getting a body count?"

"Third Platoon is staying for that." Chan nudged me with his rifle. "Look at that." I turned to see what he was looking at. Twenty meters to our right a large, charred, four-legged animal leaned stiffly against a smoking tree trunk. "It isn't a water buffalo."

"Is it a tiger?" I asked.

"I don't know."

Fifty yards farther we left the burnt area. The point man hacked a trail through the thick brush with a machete. I could feel the salt, grit, and sand on the back of my neck. I yearned for the cleanliness of the hospital.

Soon I'd smell like everybody else again. Just as well, I thought. The gnats seemed to like me a little more than usual. Probably not used to anything clean. Clean, what a laugh. I hadn't had a bath in three days. Back in the world, I used to take a couple of showers a day.

We broke through the thick brush and into a long valley of tall elephant grass.

"Sure miss ol' Smilin' Jackson," I said with a quick glance back at Chan.

"Yes. Me too."

"I was thinking about him the other day. You know he never led us into one single ambush," I said.

"He's probably back home now. That character was supposed to write us."

"It's funny how nobody ever writes back once they get back to the world."

"Paunchy wrote us."

"Really!" I said. I looked back at Chan. "He's alive?"

"Yes. I'll tell you about it when we set in."

I felt like I'd just gotten my second wind. I had prayed for Sanchez to make it, but I never thought he would. He just looked too pale when we put him on that medevac. I wasn't sure he'd even want to live without his legs. I knew I wouldn't.

Three hours later dusk crept over the landscape.

We crossed an overgrown rice paddy field, then followed a well-used trail that led past a sparsely wooded area. Our tiny column turned left into the woods for about twenty meters. We circled into a perimeter. A large, strong hand grabbed me by the arm. I turned to see Swift Eagle leading me back toward the trail.

"This edge of the perimeter will cover the trail," he whispered. He pointed Chan and me to a spot behind a thicket five meters away. Then he patted me on the helmet. "I'm glad you're back."

"Thanks, Chief," I said. He turned, walked to the CP

in the center of the perimeter, and bent down on one knee beside Lieutenant Campbell.

"Darn!" Chan whispered.

"What?"

"Watch it. This bush is full of thorns."

I moved two rocks out of the way, leaned back, and tried to make myself comfortable. "I'd almost forgotten just how miserable it is to sleep in the dirt."

"The hospital bed is but a faded memory," Chan said.

"What about Sanchez's letter?"

"It was truly inspiring. He's in the Philadelphia Naval Hospital."

"How's he getting along? Did he say anything about his legs?" I asked.

"He's taking it like a Marine. I almost cried when I read that letter to the chief's squad. He said he can do just about everything except swim with his new legs."

"God, that's great—" Chan slapped his hand over my mouth as he ducked lower behind the thicket. He stared toward the trail. I peeked around the bush. There, five meters away, a pith helmet silhouetted against a light gray sky moved cautiously along the trail. I strained to see the shadowy figure more clearly. The scent of fish filled the air as he plodded by. I wanted to fire, but I knew that would be stupid. Sixty seconds passed. Total silence.

Another pith helmet. This one moving fast. Not quite running, but walking fast. Another helmet. Then another silhouetted against the darkening sky, along with the sound of many sandals and the rustle of canvas web gear. The clank of a canteen. Men breathing hard from a long, fast march. They filed by rapidly. My mouth felt too dry to swallow. I aimed the gun at the trail through the thinnest part of the thicket. They continued filing by. I tried counting. Sixty-six, sixty-seven, sixty-eight, sixty-nine, seventy. They kept rushing by. Thank God I didn't open up! This might be a whole battalion.

"Don't fire," Chan whispered, squeezing the blood out of my arm with his grip. I wanted to tell him I had no intention of firing, but my mouth felt too dry to whisper. Salty sweat began dripping into my eyes. They burned.

Then the last pair of Ho Chi Minh sandals hustled away. Quiet. I looked at Chan. "Maybe we should have opened up."

"No way!"

"Alpha One. Alpha One. . . . This is Alpha Two. . . . Over." Sudsy's voice was low but clearly heard around the perimeter.

"Alpha One, we need a fire mission at YC 8485NINER4. Reinforced company of NVA regulars. Do you copy?"

"YC 8,4,8,5, NINER, 4. We copy Alpha Two."

"Alpha Two, Alpha Two . . . this is Fire Base Alpha preparing to fire white-peter round."

"Fire Base Alpha . . . Alpha Two. We copy. Fire when ready."

"Firing smoke."

"Here comes a spotter round," I mumbled. "Chan."

"Yeah," he whispered.

"You wouldn't believe these guys at Fire Base Alpha. They just sit around and get loaded."

The faint whistle of a faraway artillery round getting closer brought us up to our knees, straining to see where it would land. The white-phosphorus round would send up a mushroom cloud of white smoke. From there the explosive rounds would be zeroed in on the target. The whistle grew louder. Louder. "That's too close!" Chan said. The whistle got shrill.

"Get down!" a voice from the CP shouted. A low, muffled explosion erupted from the CP. I looked back as a huge mushroom cloud of thick white smoke billowed high into the night air directly over the perimeter. Agonizing screams from the CP filled the air. Three small fires lit up the CP. Men scrambled around. I could see someone rolling in the dirt, his back afire, screaming. The sulphurous-smelling smoke spread over the area like a white fog.

"Alpha one, Alpha one, this is Alpha two, over!" Sudsy's words ran together in his excitement.

"Alpha two, this is Alpha one, over."

"Alpha one, that spotter round hit the center of our perimeter! Lieutenant's been hit, he's burned, we need a medevac! Tell those idiots, cease fire! Repeat! Cease fire! Tell Fire Base Alpha they are hitting Marines! Repeat, Marines!"

HAPPY BIRTHDAY, BABY-SAN

The chopper lifted off grudgingly, coming back to earth once, then twice, before finally lumbering into the hot blue sky. Chan strolled back to our position. His face looked tired.

"How is he?" I asked, gulping down a mouth full of Halazone water.

"He'll be okay." Chan fingered the fifteen straight black hairs that he fancied made a mustache. "He has some pretty bad burns though. He might go home." He slumped down beside me, leaned back, and pulled his helmet over his eyes.

I handed him the canteen with a nudge. "How come that chopper had so much trouble getting off?"

"It had six stiffs on board."

"From Alpha?"

"No. Delta Company really hit it last night. The door gunner said they made contact with a battalion."

"Battalion! What are we doing out here running around in six-man squads while the gooks send in fresh battalions?"

"Interesting question." Chan sat up and pushed his helmet back. "It's obvious, actually. They don't want public opinion down on them for sending any more troops over. They're trying to fight divisions of NVA with regiments of Marines." He leaned back, looking pleased, as if he'd just won a debate.

"They got to be running out of people soon. We're killin' these suckers at ten to one."

"They'll send in the women and children first."

"Heard any more about the peace talks?" I asked.

"Yes. They can't decide what shape the table should be."

Just then Striker jogged over to us. He dropped to one knee beside Chan.

"We got a new lieutenant," he said.

"I hope he's not some gung-ho moron," I said. "What's his name?"

"Lampe," Striker answered. He looked at Chan. "He's got a cross on, painted black."

"Is that right?"

"Yeah. Does that mean he's a Christian?"

Chan looked up, then looked at me. His eyebrows went up, as if Striker had struck a chord.

"No. Not necessarily." He pulled a can of beef and rocks out of his pack, grimaced, and shoved it back in.

"What's he got it on for?" Striker asked.

Chan stopped searching his pack and gave Striker a fixed stare. "Are you really interested, or are you feeding me a line of bull?"

Striker looked around nonchalantly, tilted his head back, then shrugged his shoulders, "Yeah. Sorta." He picked a blade of grass and chewed on it nervously. "How do you do it? I mean, what do you do if you want to be one? Put it in writing or something?"

Chan pulled a piece of writing paper out of his pack. He looked at me. "Let me have our pen." I pulled our battered Bic out of a side pocket in my NVA pack and handed it to him. "You got the Gideon they gave you?"

"No. I threw it away," Striker mumbled.

"Here." Chan handed him his tiny Gideon. "Look up these verses." Chan spoke as he wrote. "Look those up and we'll talk about it." Chan handed him the paper. Striker snatched it and shoved it into his breast pocket as if he didn't want anyone to see.

"Yeah," he said, nodding his head as if he were nervous. "Okay."

"Striker," I said. He turned back. "Who's the dude who rates camouflage?"

"He's a forward observer. Joe Elbon. An old buddy of mine from ITR. Calls in the big stuff." He turned and walked back to his position. For the first time since I'd met him, Striker didn't seem like such a jerk.

The hump started again, through jungle, fields, hills, and ravines.

I wondered about our new lieutenant. It felt as if he had decided to take a tour of the countryside with no specific direction in mind. I pitied the poor suckers with Columbus, sailing and sailing for the end of the earth.

We climbed up an embankment so steep that huge ancient oak trees lay about, fallen because their roots could no longer take the angle. We reached the top and worked our way down the other side, which slid into a wide rocky ravine. Now I could see the point man. It was Striker. I missed Jackson. The winding ravine looked like a dried up riverbed, but during the monsoon anything can be a river. Striker disappeared around a bend up ahead, then he darted back again and flattened against a rock wall. He waved his hand to get down. The small column dropped like dominoes to one knee. Heads began to turn and whisper. I already knew.

"Guns up!"

"Guns up!"

We were up and moving forward before the word reached us. I unwrapped the fifty-round rip belt from the stock as I ran forward.

Lieutenant Lampe knelt beside Striker and Sudsy. I dropped to one knee in front of them. Chan came in beside me. I removed my helmet and peeked around the bend. A network of dirt bunkers stretched out for twenty-five yards at the mouth of the ravine. Brush was scattered about to camouflage the bunker system from the air. Three grass huts sat huddled together in a group of tall trees just beyond the bunkers. At least twenty NVA soldiers milled about near the grass hootches. I could see many more moving deeper in the trees and bush behind the hootches. To the right, down a grassy slope was a small, fast-moving river. A long line of small wooden sampans were tied to the water's edge. They banged against one another as the swift current rushed toward us. I pulled my head back and took a long worried breath.

"That ain't no platoon." I looked at Chan. He leaned out slowly to look around the bend. He flattened back against the ravine wall.

"At least a regiment."

"I counted twenty-one sampans," Striker said.

I could feel sweat cooling off my body. Each head turned to the new lieutenant. Each mind thought the same thing: Is he stupid enough to try something with seventeen men? Suddenly the rattle of leaves above us replaced all our thoughts. I looked up. Swift Eagle slid down into the ravine.

"We got about twenty sampans tied up at the foot of the slope, Lieutenant, and at least that many pulled up into the trees on the opposite side of the river. I guess two companies, maybe a battalion."

Lieutenant Lampe looked scared, but not panicky. He looked like you'd expect a Marine lieutenant to look— six feet tall, about one hundred eighty, white-sidewall haircut, pug nose, clean-shaven, acne scars under his ears and down his neck. He was an Annapolis grad, judging from his class ring, which he shouldn't have brought into the bush. He put his head down for a moment as if to clear his mind or remember some useless bit of guide-book information. He looked up, squeezed his pug nose between thumb and forefinger, then turned to the chief. "Let's pull back." He turned to Sudsy. "Stick close."

"Right on your butt, Lieutenant," Sudsy answered.

Corporal Swift Eagle waved the platoon back. Fifty meters down the ravine we split into two columns along both walls. Swift Eagle pointed at Sam, then pointed up to the bush on Sam's left. "I want an LP ten meters out." Sam moved to the wall, and Corporal James gave him a boost up by the seat of the pants. Swift Eagle pointed at Striker, then to the bush flanking the other side of the ravine. Striker's big black mole lowered an inch from the frown, but he moved without a word.

"I want the gun here," Swift Eagle said, pointing to three large round rocks five meters in front of him. I flipped down the bipod and flattened out behind the gun with Chan at my right.

Lieutenant Lampe snatched the field phone from Sudsy, dropped to one knee, and flattened out a grid map, holding down each corner with a stone. "Alpha One . . . Alpha One . . . This is Alpha Two. Over."

"Roger, Alpha Two . . . This is Alpha One. Over."

"Alpha One, we've hit the big time at coordinates Alpha Tango Tango Hotel Foxtrot Lima Lima." The communication went back and forth in code. Then there was a "roger."

"Pull back!" The chief suddenly sounded excited. Couldn't be that, I thought. Striker hustled over the edge of the ravine wall, sliding down fast. He landed on his feet and ran straight to Swift Eagle, moving past the new lieutenant and the new FO, Corporal Elbon.

"Chief! We got gooks on the flank! Lots of 'em!" Striker looked into Swift Eagle's face, still ignoring the new lieutenant. Striker spoke quickly and too low for me to hear it all. Swift Eagle rushed over to the lieutenant.

"We got a lot of gooks on our flank, Lieutenant. They're moving around."

"Let's get out of here!"

Swift Eagle didn't wait for a point man. He led the way himself, with the lieutenant and the FO close behind. The column moved out quickly, leaving Chan and me to bring up the rear. I hated being on the rear. I could feel myself moving faster and faster, as if I were being chased. I tried to walk backward, but the loose rocks underfoot were hard enough to walk on going forward. One hundred meters down the ravine the column stopped. Swift Eagle hustled from the front of the column, slowing for an instant in front of each man to stare into his face, then rushing to the next face until he reached Chan and me.

"Did anyone call in Sam?" he asked. His eyebrows pinched together. He looked worried.

"You mean he's still back there?" I asked. He didn't answer. He turned back to the column.

"Pass the word up. We left Sam. My squad up. We're going back for him."

Lieutenant Lampe jogged up beside Swift Eagle. "What's up, Chief?"

"We left Sam the Blooper Man back there."

The lieutenant's round face grew long. He put his head down for a moment and squeezed his pug nose between his forefinger and thumb. He exhaled heavily through his nose and looked up.

"Okay, how many men in your squad?"

"Five without Sam."

"Take them and the gun team, too. We'll set up a perimeter here. Make it fast, Chief. We're running out of light."

Things were happening too fast. I hadn't realized how late in the day it was. That made the situation more critical. A man lost or left alone in the jungle was rarely ever seen again.

The walk back down the ravine felt ominous. I wondered how many times we could make this trip into an area with that many gooks without making contact. I wouldn't have put any money on our chances of tiptoeing in and out more than once.

I expected to see the enemy around each bend. I held the gun on my hip. Boyhood imaginings of holding off hundreds of Germans and Japs with a machine gun shot through my mind. Seven seconds. Seven seconds. What kind of fool figured out a gunner only lasted seven seconds after a firefight began? Why would they tell us the truth about something like that? Keep your burst short. Keep your burst short. Twenty rounds. Twenty rounds. Twenty rounds.

Swift Eagle stopped. Another bend in the ravine blocked our vision. We flattened against the wall as Swift Eagle poked his head around. He motioned us forward. The way was straight for twenty meters, then curved left around a huge round rock. Swift Eagle peeked around and under the rock, then jerked his head back as if he'd been stung. He looked back at us and mouthed the word I dreaded, "Gooks!" He looked left, then right. We scrambled up the embankment like scared children, stumbling and sliding back down, then clawing up again until at the same instant we organized. We helped chunky Doyle up and over. He put his rifle out and pulled the next man up, repeating the process until we were out of the ravine. Quickly we moved away. Ten meters through thick brush we reached the edge of the swiftly moving jungle river. It looked to be twenty meters wide, and deeper than I had thought. We listened for movement.

Branches cracked underfoot to our front. My heart stopped. I couldn't feel myself breathing. Vietnamese voices drifted through the air from across the river. We all turned at once. Suddenly the sound of many men forcing their way through tangled brush to our left yanked our heads back around to a new danger on our side of the river. Swift Eagle slid noiselessly into the dark water like a snake. We followed. The cold covered me with goose bumps. The current pulled my legs downstream. I struggled to hold on to an overhanging branch with one hand and the gun with the other. The weight of my pack pulled me under as my limb sagged. I kicked my boots around in search of something solid, but the current swept them from under me. I couldn't hold my breath any longer. Panic seized me. I started to drop the gun and reach for the branch with both hands. A strong hand grabbed me by the back of the collar of my jungle jacket, then switched the grip to my flak jacket and pulled me up. I gasped for air as quietly as I could, swallowing coughs until my eyes bulged.

We clung to the river's edge, our helmets and weapons barely visible in the overhanging saw grass and water weeds. Something moved in the water near my right cheek. The red and black head of a snake rippled by my face, the long body weaving tiny waves of water up my nose. I shivered. Two Vietnamese laughed from the far bank. They were hidden by thick brush and leafy vines that lined the river on that side like a ten-foot green wall.

Through the saw grass and weeds the tops of small trees ten meters away moved as enemy soldiers fought their way through the thick pockets of brush. I knew we couldn't fight from this position. The thought of being a prisoner flashed through my mind. The voice of a Vietnamese called from farther away. My grip was slipping from the limb. The shaking treetops started moving away from us, back toward the ravine.

We let a minute pass. All seemed quiet. Swift Eagle pulled himself from the water first. Chan dragged himself to solid ground. I tossed the gun to him and used the limb to pull myself out. We moved as quietly as we could. At the edge of the ravine we stopped to listen. Still quiet. Swift Eagle started to move down into the ravine again. Suddenly the sound of someone moving through the brush to our right stopped my breathing. I jerked the gun around. An American helmet poked through the brush.

"Sam!" I held my enthusiasm to a whisper. Sam's face was flushed with anger and fear.

"You left me back there!"

"It was my fault, Sam," Swift Eagle said.

"What am I supposed to say? It's okay, man, don't worry about it?" For a moment it looked like Sam was going to swing. He stared hard at the chief's expressionless face.

"Let's get out of here," Chan said, breaking the tension.

"Yeah. Come on," Doyle said nervously.

The chief turned away. "Move out." We slid back down to the ravine.

The walk back to the platoon felt like a frightening dream that didn't want to end. Lieutenant Lampe's face already showed the strain of command. He barely controlled a dangerously loud laugh at the sight of Sam. He quickly regained his composure and looked around for the gunny, who stood right behind him. They exchanged a couple of words I couldn't hear, then turned and passed the word. "Saddle up!"

We moved back down to the mouth of the winding ravine at a quick-time pace. The yellow sun was turning orange as it dropped. No more than fifteen minutes of daylight left, I thought. We climbed to the top of a small barren hill. Lieutenant Lampe relayed a message to Alpha One, then turned the show over to Corporal Elbon, the new forward observer.

Soon the faint whistle of a big 1.55 spotter round could be heard overhead, pushing air out of its way. A moment later a white mushroom cloud peeked above the treetops in the distance.

"Right on! Fire for effect! Repeat. Fire for effect!" Corporal Elbon's voice carried across the tiny perimeter. Soon the whistles of 1.55s filled the air above us. Loud cracks followed by thunderous explosions lit up the darkening jungle at the other end of the ravine. A chorus of faraway screams sifted through the artillery explosions.

"Fire for effect! Keep firing! Fire for effect!" Elbon shouted from the center of the perimeter.

"Saddle up!" Gunny shouted.

"Fire for effect!" Elbon repeated.

An artillery round landed at the foot of our small hill. I jumped.

"Short round," Chan said calmly.

A minute later the column moved down the mountain with 1.55s still whistling overhead. An hour later we set up a perimeter on the bank of a river and spent the night fighting off mosquitoes. By morning I felt like a victim of Dracula. The sight of green smoke made me forget my swollen, mosquito-bitten face.

"Saddle up!" someone shouted from the CP. "Choppers!"

"It would appear we're going for a ride, Baby-san," Chan said.

The chopper ride back to An Hoa took no time at all. I wondered if the pilots could ever imagine just how miserable the same distance on foot was. We spent the night in a tent near the tubes. Our tent smelled like the inside of a urinal. I guess they didn't want us to get too comfortable. The whole company had been brought in. A bad sign.

The next morning started with a predawn company formation. Some jerk pogue camouflaged from head to toe passed out gas masks to everyone. Another bad sign. I couldn't imagine fighting in the darn things. There was no peripheral vision and very little frontal. We tried the gas masks on while some skinny captain told us we'd be landing in a hot LZ that would be hit with tear gas first. We marched to a long row of waiting assault choppers and began filing on, one squad at a time. I still couldn't believe it. Some of the men were getting openly hostile about the idea, screaming out loud that they wouldn't fight in masks. Two black riflemen in Third Platoon threw their masks in the dirt and refused to enter the chopper next to the one Chan and I were filing into. Sergeant Mooney of Third Platoon ran toward the two with his M16 rifle ready. Just then the ramp hatch of our chopper closed. A few seconds later we were airborne.

My heart pounded blood into my face until it felt flush. Chan helped me strap the gas mask on tightly, then I helped him. His eyes told me he couldn't believe this either. The supposedly clear plastic I was to see through was yellowed, scratched, and battered. It would be a miracle to spot a charging battalion at five meters. After a twenty-minute ride we started circling. I could see two more choppers circling behind us, then three, then five. Finally we began circling down. Chan held out his hand. I shook it. We gave each other a thumbs up.

The chopper hit the ground with a slight bounce. The hatch fell open. We ran out. We found ourselves in an open field. Pockets of smoke hid whole areas like a fog. I could taste the bitter tear gas through my mask. Other choppers were landing and taking off around the field, their rotors blowing the gas in all directions like giant fans. Marines ran toward a tree line to our left. I could barely see other figures running in another direction. AKs opened up on the left from the tree line. M16s opened up on our right. I couldn't see what was going on. My scratchy yellow vision frustrated me. I started to rip it off, then wondered for an instant if it was really tear gas. AKs started firing from behind me. Gas or bullets, what's the difference! I ripped the mask off, threw it to the ground, and cursed the Marine Corps as I ran toward the tree line. I could feel a strong wind hitting me in the face as I ran. My eyes burned. I began coughing. I spotted a smokeless area to my right. I ran for it, holding my breath until I reached it, then gasping for the clean air between biting coughs. Mucus poured from my nose and water from my eyes.

"Second Platoon!" someone shouted from the fog. "Second Platoon! Over here!" The voice sounded close.

"First Platoon! Mount up! Over here!"

"Hey!" Someone grabbed my shoulder. "This First Platoon?"

I turned to see who was talking to me. It was a black Marine, his eyes swollen, watering, and red. He started coughing.

"I'm Second Platoon. I think I heard First Platoon over there." I pointed to our left. He headed that way.

"Second Platoon! Over here!" A strong wind scattered the gas into thin gray pockets. I could see the voice now. It was good ol' freckle-faced Sudsy. Most of the platoon huddled nearby. Not one man still wearing a mask.

By the time all the platoons were organized into units again the gooks could have played a couple of hands of poker and still had time to dig a tunnel out of our poorly planned trap. Somebody in Third Platoon killed a gook in a tree, and First Platoon got two prisoners who were too stoned to notice the gas or the assaulting Marines. Second Platoon blew up two tunnels. Total: one confirmed; two POWs.

The walk back to An Hoa was the usual pain in the butt. Then it got worse. Sixteen inches of rain worse. Not that I counted the inches, but that's what they told us on Armed Forces Radio when we finally reached An Hoa. They called it the northeast monsoon. We called it everything else. We spent the night at An Hoa. Even the constant blast of the big 1.55s couldn't keep me from feeling cozy in a back corner of the big tent. Hearing the pounding rain and not being in it felt wonderful. Sudsy and Doyle played cards by candlelight in one corner of the tent.

"Let us prepare coffee." Chan tossed me a small piece of C-4 from the cot on my left.

"Yeah. Good idea, Chan," I said. Suddenly the flap door of the tent blew open, spraying water over the row of cots. Sam jumped up and tied it shut again. Another series of 1.55s exploded toward their targets.

"In Florida we'd call this a hurricane," I said.

"Man! They're sure lettin' loose tonight."

The voice came from the cot on the other side of Chan. It was Corporal Elbon, the new FO.

"Want some coffee?" I asked.

"Yeah. That sounds good."

He moved over and sat beside me on my cot, facing Chan. He was brisk and serious and overly handsome, like one of those unsmiling models for *Gentleman's Quarterly*.

"What are you doing traveling with a grunt unit?" Chan asked.

"I've done it a few times. Usually for big operations. Sometimes they send us out just to keep us on our toes. Don't they mind if you guys cook with C-4?" Joe looked slightly concerned as I put a match to the C-4 inside our C-ration can-stove.

"We don't ask," I said.

The flap of the tent jerked open again. This time a Marine carrying a thick-barreled sniper rifle in his left hand rushed in with water pouring off his camouflaged poncho. He seemed to be protecting something with his right hand.

"Is Joe Elbon in here?" a husky voice asked.

"Yeah," Joe answered. "Back here."

The dripping Marine moved toward us slowly, his boots squishing water with each step. He squinted to see us in the dimly lit tent.

"Joe?"

"Back here," Joe repeated.

"It's me. Harpo." He pulled a tiny sad-faced black-and-white-spotted puppy from under his poncho.

"I got Killer with me."

He held the tiny sad-faced puppy out with one hand. Joe jumped to his feet, his serious face gone and gushing with happiness. He took the puppy and started kissing his little black dot of a nose. The puppy seemed to cheer up, too. He started licking Joe all over the face. He chirped what was supposed to be a bark.

"Thanks, Harpo," Joe said between licks. "How'd you know I was here?"

Harpo pulled off his poncho, revealing a totally shaved head, and sat on the end of Chan's cot with his sniper rifle between his legs. His rifle had the fattest barrel and biggest scope on it I'd ever seen.

"That was easy to find out. Everybody's in."

"Why?" Joe asked.

"Thuong Duc special forces camp is getting hit or overrun or something."

"You mean we're saving the Green Berets again?" I asked.

"That's what it looks like," Harpo said.

Chan looked up from stirring our coffee. "Wait till the chief hears about this," he said.

"What are you doing in here, Joe?" Harpo asked. "Why aren't you in the CP tent?"

Joe looked like he wanted to avoid the question. He glanced down and mumbled something none of us could hear.

"Speak up," Harpo said.

"There's a guy in the CP I hate. No big deal. How 'bout you, Harpo? Got any more confirmed with that cannon?"

"Who do you hate in the CP?" I asked.

"I'd rather not talk about it," Joe said. His tone was serious. He flushed and gazed down at his hands, trying unsuccessfully to conceal a seething anger. I decided to be nosy another day.

"Chan, did you see that?" I pointed at Harpo's rifle.

"Yes. I've never seen a barrel with that thick of a bore."

"I just got a fourteen-hundred meter confirmed two days ago," Harpo boasted proudly. He pointed to the last notch in a row of small cuts on the rifle butt.

"Fourteen hundred meters?" Chan asked. "Really?"

"Yeah! My partner found 'em with a small telescope. Then I found them in the rifle scope. Three gooks sitting around a small fire eating rice, with AKs lying next to 'em. It took three shots to get one."

"Three shots? Why didn't they take off?" I asked.

"I was so far away that either they didn't hear the shot or they didn't pay any attention to it. None of 'em even looked my way on the first two misses. I had to walk up to the one I was aiming at. The first two shots were short. They all stopped eating and pointed at the ground where my rounds kicked up dirt, but they didn't know what it was. They just kept squatting there holding bowls. Then the third shot blew this one right off his haunches." Harpo laughed. "The other two dropped their bowls and beat feet out of there."

"Mind if I look at your rifle?" Chan asked.

"No, go ahead." Harpo handed it to Chan, who handled it as if it were something precious.

"This rifle probably cost two or three thousand dollars," Chan said.

"At least," Harpo agreed.

"Have you heard anything else about this operation?" I asked.

"I know the Seventh Marines and some ARVN regiment are already there. Scuttlebutt says they found a whole division of NVA."

"That's why they've kept me with you guys," Joe said, as if the mystery was over.

"I'm sure it is, Joe," Harpo said. "They've been using Puff and B-52 strikes."

"That explains it," Joe said. "I was wondering why I hadn't been reassigned. I don't usually stay with a grunt outfit this long."

"If you're the one who calls in the Phantoms and Puff, ol' buddy, you ain't goin' nowhere," I said. I gave Joe a slap on the back.

"It's a double-edged sword, John." Chan's teeth gleamed in an ironic smile. "FOs don't come along unless they know you're going to need the big stuff."

"He's right," Joe agreed.

"I wish you guys luck tomorrow," Harpo said. "I got a feeling you're in for a big time. You remember Jonsey?"

"Yeah," Joe said. "Where did you see him?"

"His recon team came through two days ago. They sat in on a hill above the Vu Gia River near Thuong Duc for eight days, barely moving a muscle the whole time. On the eighth day a whole company came strolling by in daylight. They called in air and artillery and got a bunch of 'em. Then, the very next day, another full company walked into the killing zone. They said they counted two hundred four dead and they didn't lose a man. There must be a ton of gooks in that area!"

"Think he was exaggerating?" Chan asked.

"No. His buddies said the same thing." Harpo stood up. "I have to get going. What are you going to do about your baby?" Harpo gave the droopy-eyed puppy one last pat.

"I don't know," Joe said. "Take care." Joe stood up. They shook hands, then Harpo slapped Joe on the back and gave him a quick strong hug. He rushed out of the tent and into the dark storm. Joe stood for a few moments, then sat down with a faraway look.

"How long have you guys known each other?" I asked.

"Since I was born," Joe said. "That's my brother."

The flap door of the tent burst open just as a loud crack of lightning shot an eerie blue light across An Hoa. Sudsy stepped inside our tent. Water cascaded off his poncho as he pulled the hood back.

"Is Corporal Elbon in here?" Sudsy squinted to see faces in the dim light.

"Yeah, over here," Joe said.

"They want you at the CP. We're movin' out."

The tent erupted in shouting and cursing. Someone threw a helmet at Sudsy. He pulled his poncho hood over his head and ran out. I couldn't believe it. I wanted more than anything to sleep out of the rain. I had my heart set on it. Joe put Killer in his pack, snatched up his gear, and stood up.

"Good luck."

"You too, Joe," I said.

"See you in the mud," Chan said.

Joe gave us a thumbs up, then turned and maneuvered through the tent full of angry Marines.

Ten minutes later we stood in formation in the blinding storm. Corporal James went by each man in the platoon counting out loud. When he finished he ran back to the lieutenant.

"Left face!"

The shout could hardly be heard over the pounding rain. The hump was on again. I was already tired. A vicious sheet of driving rain staggered the column like a hurt boxer as we reached the barbed-wire gate to exit An Hoa. Three hours later the rain subsided. By the time the first streaks of sunlight outlined the steep mountains ahead, I was half dry and half asleep. The low roar of a flight of Phantoms opened my eyes a little wider. The sound of bombs hitting the earth like giant drums echoed from the mountains. We crossed at a shallow point on the wide Vu Gia River. We reached the other side, crawled up the river bank and onto a winding dirt road that paralleled the river. A streaking Phantom ripped overhead with black smoke trailing behind.

"Hey! That Phantom's hit!" Doyle exclaimed, but no one paid any attention. I could hear small-arms fire. It sounded about a mile away.

"Take five!"

"Take five!"

"Take five!"

"Smoke 'em if you got 'em."

Swift Eagle sent three men into the bush on the right flank of the road as the rest of the column collapsed on both sides of the road. Some men quickly dug for C-rations while others just fell back and closed their eyes. I threw oil on the M60 with my toothbrush and watched Sam, Doyle, and Corporal James start up a tired-looking game of Back Alley. Sam claimed the men of Alpha had bought him a Corvette playing cards. I wondered if it was true. I knew a lot of money changed hands. No one seemed to treat MPC like real money. It looked like Vietnamese Monopoly money. It was colorful and about the same size. No one cared. They couldn't spend it any other way. Chubby Doyle pushed his Coke-bottle-lensed glasses farther up on his pug nose and looked up from his cards.

"Hey, what's the date? It's October, isn't it?"

"No," I said. "Is it?"

"Yes," Chan said. "It is October 9, 1968," he said in a businesslike, matter-of-fact tone.

"Really!" I said. "October 12 is my birthday. I almost missed it. I thought it was September."

"Do you hear that?" Sam asked. The rumbling engine of something big suddenly sounded very close.

"That's a tank," Corporal James said tentatively, as if he wasn't sure. He stood up and looked down the road.

"That does sound like a tank," Chan said.

"Sounds like more than one," Doyle mumbled. He and James looked toward the rear of our resting column. I wanted to look too, but I felt too tired to stand.

"Here they come," Doyle said.

"This looks big," James said.

Sam stood up and lit a cigarette. "I don't know," he said dryly. "Tanks are useless crap in this war. I don't know why they even bother bringing them out."

Chan stood up, then put out a hand to lift me up too. I let him. Sam was right. So far tanks had proved useless, but there was still something inspiring about seeing these giant steel monsters churning toward combat. I felt a chill. Death felt close.

"Saddle up!"

We split into two columns, one on each side of the road. Three huge tanks rumbled by us. Their width dwarfed the narrow dirt road. The ground vibrated with their power. A tanker with goggles sat exposed in the turret of each tank. Each man gave us the thumbs up as they passed. The rumbling monsters rounded a bend up ahead and disappeared from sight. Small-arms fire sounded closer as we marched. Our pace quickened. Every tired eye looked up as a Huey gunship dove from the clean blue sky, firing rockets and M60s at a target about a thousand meters ahead. We rounded a slight bend in the road and found a company's worth of Marines resting against an embankment on the right side of the road. They were ragged and dirty, and some of them were bloody. I could hear shouting at the head of the column, then we started running forward and past the company of weary Marines. The column stopped.

"Get to the side of the road!" someone shouted from the front of the column. We moved to the right side of the road, leaned against the embankment, and stared at the wide river in front of us. A giant engine cranked up then revved up its power. The tanks were getting ready up ahead.

"Second Platoon up!"

We ran forward. I could see the captain standing in the shade of a huge oak tree, motioning us to him with frantic waves. He stood behind one of the tanks. As we ran forward we passed three corpsmen working on five wounded Marines lying on the side of the road.

"All right! Listen up!" The captain's red mustache seemed to flair out with excitement as he shouted over the rumbling diesels. "See that hill on the other side of that stream?"

I took a couple of steps to look around the tanks. Just

past them and out of the shade of the huge oak was a clearing two hundred meters square. The dirt road went through it. On the other side a tributary feeding into the wide river cut the road in half. The remains of a blown-up wooden bridge protruded from the center of the tributary. Across the tributary and to the right of the road was a steep, bald hill.

"We hit a semicircle of fortified positions on the hills around that clearing. Second Battalion sent E Company up that hill. They had to pull back. We're going to take that hill. We have tanks now, and they will provide cover fire."

A sleek new Cobra helicopter gunship swept overhead with mini-guns blazing. It strafed the bald hill then banked straight up, made a roll like a World War II fighter plane, and nose-dived straight down at the top of the hill. He fired six rockets, then leveled off, just missing the rocks and debris from the flashing explosions.

"Are you listening? This isn't a fireworks display, Marines!" The captain's anger pulled our attention from the hill. His face was red. "Some of you are going to get hit going up that hill, and I want you to know what you're doing. Do not stop to help the wounded. The corpsmen will follow up and take care of them. Don't stop for anything. Now, E Company says that little stream you have to cross looks deep. They didn't get that far, so we don't know for sure, but find a shallow spot to cross, and be quick. There are two hills to our right flank that you can't see from here. They're at the far right of the clearing, and the gooks have fortified positions on both of them, so you may take fire from the right flank when you cross the clearing."

Captain Nelson stepped away from the tank and pointed at the hill. "All right. When you cross the stream don't go straight up the hill on this side facing us now because you will come under fire from the right flank. Go up the hill on the side facing the river and the road."

He paused, then turned and looked at us, staring for one instant into the eyes of each man in the platoon. "As soon as you enter that clearing you'll come under fire. There's an ARVN regiment on the other side of the river that should take care of our left flank."

"Hey! Wow! Far out, man! We're going to be on TV!" someone shouted.

Captain Nelson's face tightened with anger. I turned to see who said it, inwardly already knowing. Sam was pointing at two pudgy-looking men. One had a portable TV camera on his shoulder. The other carried a black box. They wore camouflaged baseball hats instead of helmets, and beautiful new lightweight Army flak jackets instead of the clunky Korean War–era flak jackets that Marines wore. They huddled behind a tree. The one with the camera was filming another Huey gunship firing rockets into the top of the hill. "Does that say NBC on that camera?"

"You better can that mouth, Marine!" Captain Nelson barked.

"Aye-aye, sir!" Sam answered quickly.

The thunderous echoes of heavy bombing farther up the road took my mind off the camera.

"Guns up!" I moved forward and stood beside the captain and Lieutenant Lampe. "We're moving across in squads! I want the gun team with the chief's squad!" Lieutenant Lampe held my arm as he spoke.

The lead tank began moving into the clearing.

"All right! Get ready!" Lieutenant Lampe shouted. "Chief's squad will go first, along with the gun team. When you reach the hill make sure you knock out their machine guns first." The second tank moved into the clearing about twenty-five yards from the first. Finally the one we stood behind started rumbling forward. The lead tank fired its big gun. The explosion ripped dirt and rocks into the air from the top of the hill. AK fire whined across the open clearing. Another Huey gunship dove at a target on the other side of the river. His rockets started a yellow fire in the top of a tree.

"Ready!" Lieutenant Lampe shouted. He raised his hand. "Go!"

"Go!" Swift Eagle shouted from my right. I ran by the last tank in the line of three tanks. The lead tank had stopped twenty-five meters from the tributary. Two whining ricochets bounced off the steel tank as I ran by. AKs opened up from my right. I could hear a machine gun chattering from the other side of the river. Green tracers streaked between the first and second tank. I looked left. Hundreds of muzzle flashes were firing at us from the jungle on the other side of the river.

"Corpsman!" a scream came from behind me. I didn't look back. A sharp explosion threw rocks and dirt into the air twenty feet to the left of the second tank, followed by another one five feet closer. Someone screamed in pain.

"Corpsman up!" Another scream from behind me. I started zigzagging as I ran. I passed the second tank. Bullets whistled overhead. Others twanged off the big metal hull as I ran by. The lead tank fired its big gun. Suddenly a mortar round hit between the lead tank and the tributary. Then another hit ten meters closer. The third hit right on the tank's turret. I dove into the dirt fifteen meters behind it. The tank rang from the explosion like a giant bell. I jumped to my feet and started running again. Another mortar blast hit behind me. Someone started screaming in agony. I didn't look back. Finally the tributary was within range. Small telltale dust puffs shot from the road as bullets hit the earth around me. I dove to the ground as another mortar blast hit behind me. I felt scared and confused. I pulled my face out of the dirt and looked back. I could see Swift Eagle running and pointing, then a mortar explosion hit beside him. He fell. He didn't move. Chan dove in beside me.

"Let's go!" Chan shouted. I hesitated. I wanted to help the chief. Then those last words kept shouting at me:

"Don't stop for the wounded!" I jumped to my feet and ran. I took a running jump into the tributary, holding the M60 over my head. The ice-cold water took my breath away. A swift current swept my feet from under me. Chan grabbed me by the back of the lapel and pulled me up. I coughed up a mouthful of water. The steep hill rose up at a forty-five-degree angle just on the other side of the tributary. I could see muzzle flashes firing down at us from the top. Bullets sucked through the air around me, hitting the water with terrifying force. I tried to move faster. The cold water lapped at my throat. I stumbled over a large round rock. My head went under. Chan grabbed my shoulder to steady me. I regained my balance. A mortar blast hit the base of the hill in front of me. I closed my eyes instinctively. Dirt and debris fell into the water. Mortar rounds exploded in the clearing behind us. A row of tiny, violent waterspouts erupted in front of me, splashing cold water into my face. I tried in vain to move faster. A stream of green tracers sprayed over our heads and hit the small embankment now almost within arm's reach.

"That's from the other side of the river!" Chan shouted from behind me. I reached for a clump of grass on the embankment in front of me. I tossed the gun up and onto the level ground, then pulled myself up with both hands. I threw my right leg over the embankment and rolled onto the hard level ground. I reached back for Chan. He held out the butt of his rifle. I grabbed it with both hands and pulled him up onto the solid ground.

"Wait!" Doyle struggled through the deep water toward us. His thick-lensed glasses looked too water-blurry to be of any use. "Give me a hand!"

Chan held out his rifle, stretching as far as he could reach. Doyle stretched out one arm, moving it back and forth like a blind man feeling for a wall. I grabbed the M60, stood to a crouch, and ran across the dirt road to the base of the hill. I flattened against the rock-strewn hill and looked back. The crew of the lead tank scrambled out of the turret one at a time. A mortar round hit in front of the second tank. Bullets thudded into the earth around me. I looked up. I could see a muzzle flash at the top of the hill. Then the flash ceased. I looked back for Chan. Chunky Doyle rolled onto the solid ground. They both jumped to their feet and ran across the road, then flattened against the hill beside me. Chan looked back to the clearing, still gasping for air from the mad dash.

"The chief got it!" I said.

"Captain Nelson went down before we reached the first tank!" Chan said.

"They abandoned that tank!" I said. I pointed to the lead tank. The three crewmen ran for cover behind the second tank. "Look! Two bodies to the left."

"My God, what are we supposed to do, take the hill by ourselves?" Doyle's voice cracked.

"Don't panic!" Chan shouted.

A .30 caliber opened up on us from across the river. His first tracers hit the dirt road fifteen meters in front of us, then slowly walked toward us.

"Spread out!" I shouted. Doyle moved left and Chan moved right. I started firing back. My first tracers skipped off the water. A sleek Cobra gunship dropped from the sky and swept across the river ten feet above the water. I stopped firing. He fired two rockets into the dense green jungle, then shot straight up into the pale blue sky, barely avoiding enemy fire and the glowing shrapnel and debris from his own rockets. The enemy gun was swallowed up in smoke. It ceased firing. Chan started shooting up the hill. I turned my back to the Cobra just as it made another dive on targets across the river. I looked to see what Chan was firing at. The limp body of a dead NVA rolled to a stop against a charred bush seventy feet up the hill. I opened up with the gun, spraying a hundred rounds at every lump of earth or bush that could hide a man in front of me. I stopped firing and looked for muzzle flashes. I couldn't see any.

"What are we going to do?" Doyle shouted over another barrage of enemy mortars hitting around the tanks. He flattened against the hill and looked at me. Shrapnel whistled through the air around us, some of it smacking into the side of the hill. Just one tiny piece, I thought.

"We can't just stay here!" I shouted back. I looked behind me. I could see muzzle flashes coming from the brush on the other side of the river. They were firing from the river bank. Bullets thudded into the hillside above us. I cringed with each whining ricochet. I'm not going to die just sitting here, I thought. This is insane. We have to move! I pushed myself away from the hill and started climbing. Chan did the same. Fifteen yards up the steep incline we flattened out again. I looked back down at Doyle. Finally he broke into a frenzied run, firing on full automatic as he stumbled and clawed forward. He flattened against the hill ten meters to my left. Thoughts of hand-to-hand combat slipped across my mind.

"Hey, look!" Chan shouted from my right. He pointed at two Marines waving and shouting at us from beside the crippled lead tank.

"That's Lieutenant Lampe!" I said to Chan. "I thought you said he got it?"

"No, I said the captain!"

"He's waving us back!" Doyle shouted. "He don't have to ask me twice, brother!" Doyle started sliding down the rocky hill on his rear end. Once near the bottom he broke into a run across the road and jumped into the tributary to the right of the blown wooden bridge. It looked like the water was only up to Doyle's waist.

"It looks shallower there!" I shouted.

"Okay! Same place! Ready!"

"Go!"

Before I finished "Go!" we both started sliding back down the hill until we could make a clean run for the tributary. Cracks of AK fire echoed from the top of the hill. One of the tanks opened fire with a .50-caliber machine gun. Chan jumped into the cold water just ahead of me, both of us holding our weapons overhead. I sank up to my neck. Now one of the tanks opened up with its big gun. Two bullets smacked into the water just in front of my chin and just behind Chan. I tried to move my feet faster. I'm taller than Doyle, I thought. How come it's up to my neck? It was no use. It would be one slow step at a time. Three successive mortar blasts hit between us and the crippled lead tank. Doyle pulled himself out of the water. He ran for the lieutenant, squishing water from the air holes of his boots as he went. Now I could see who the smallish Marine crouching behind the tank beside Lieutenant Lampe was. Staff Sergeant Morey's pale skin and droopy mustache stood out clearly. Doyle dove the last five feet, landing in front of Sergeant Morey. Chan struggled out of the water, then turned. He stuck out his hand. I grabbed it. He pulled me to him. We scrambled to our feet and ran for the tank. I kept waiting for that sharp pain of a bullet. How could they not hit us?

"Just keep running! Keep running!" Lieutenant Lampe shouted as the three of them started running back across the clearing before we reached them. I ran as fast as I could, but the water weight dragged on each stride like a suit of lead. I could hear bullets hitting the earth and ricocheting. I wondered how many times they'd miss before I felt the pain. Finally the trees were close. I could see faces of Marines shouting and waving us on while others fired at the hills behind us. The last tank pulled out of the clearing and into the shade of the big oak tree. Lieutenant Lampe and Sergeant Morey ran by the tank and collapsed against the dirt embankment on the left of the road. Then Doyle. Now I could see all three panting for air on their hands and knees and looking back at us to see if we'd make it. We were back. I could feel Marines slapping me on the flak jacket. I dropped the gun, grabbed my knees, and gasped for air, wondering if it all had really happened and why I was still alive. Someone was screaming. I looked up. Staff Sergeant Morey was on the ground shouting, writhing in pain, and holding his rear end with his right hand.

"I'm hit!" He forced the words through clenched teeth, then shook his head back and forth like he was trying to shake something off his face. Chan rushed over to him. Lieutenant Lampe knelt down beside Chan.

"Move your hand, let me see how bad it is!" Chan said as he forced Sergeant Morey's hand away. He shoved Morey onto his left side. The seat of his pants was soaked with blood, water, and mud. Chan pulled out his K-bar and ripped the trousers open. "Looks like you caught a ricochet. It's not too deep."

"No! Don't touch it!" Morey shouted. He pushed Chan's hand away.

"I might as well get it out," Chan said.

"No way! Nobody is taking away my Purple Heart."

Every Marine within hearing distance who knew Morey started laughing. Chan looked back at me and winked, then turned solemnly to Staff Sergeant Morey. "I really should take that out. The chance for infection is very high."

"I can't believe it, Staff," Lieutenant Lampe said with a regretful pat on the shoulder. "Tomorrow was your last day ever as a grunt."

"It took three wars, but I finally got a Heart." A giant smile lifted Morey's droopy brown mustache. The lines of age spread from the corners of his eyes like a road map of three wars. He looked so out of place in the sea of young faces around him, all of them congratulating him with a barb or friendly insult. I felt happy for him.

"Hey, Lieutenant," I said. "How's the chief?"

"He caught a bunch of shrapnel. We medevaced him out."

"Lieutenant!" Joe Elbon shouted from the other side of the road. "I got Phantoms coming in on Hill 52. We need to spot 'em!"

"Sam, go ask that tanker if he's got a spotter round. If so, tell him to put it on top of that hill."

"Aye-aye, Lieutenant," Sam answered in Marine Corps fashion.

"How bad was the chief?" I asked.

"I'm not sure, John. Go get yourself an A-gunner. We need Chan to take over the other gun."

"What?"

"Yeah. We lost a gunner."

"Who was on the other gun?" I asked.

"I don't know. Hurry up! Get movin'! We're going up that hill again!" He turned away.

"I've already been up it," I snapped. "Where was everybody else?" My terse remark stopped him from walking away. He turned around quickly.

"I called you back, but you didn't hear me. We lost seven men before you got halfway across. Now saddle up, Marine!"

The tank fired at the hill. The big steel creature rocked from the recoil. A moment later a popping explosion followed by a white mushroom cloud rose over the hill. I turned back to the lieutenant. He was gone.

"I heard." I turned to find Chan standing behind me. "I believe you have acquired Doyle again," he said.

"Who's your A-gunner?"

"I don't know. Probably the pig farmer." Chan turned, looked up, and followed the flight of two Phantoms roaring overhead. A moment later the top of the hill exploded into fire. Before the flames of the first napalm bomb dimmed, the second Phantom repeated the bombing. Soon dark black smoke hid the top of the hill from view.

"The gunny got it." Chan spoke without taking his eyes off the smoking hill.

"Gunny?"

"Yeah."

"How bad?"

"Shrapnel in the thigh. Doc said it looked like a million-dollar wound."

"All right, let's get saddled up!" Corporal James walked by us, shouting the order.

"Hey, James," I said.

"Yeah," he answered. He stopped and pulled out his canteen. He took a long swig.

"I need Doyle for an A-gunner again."

"Okay, I'll tell him. Get ready to go up that hill."

He put his canteen away and started shouting again. "Saddle up! Second Platoon, Alpha! Saddle up!"

"Johnnie," Chan said. "Look." He paused like he wasn't sure how to say what he wanted. "This looks bad. Make sure you ask Jesus to 'cut you a huss.' "

I wanted to hug him, but I didn't. "You too, buddy. Twenty-round bursts." I gave him the thumbs up. He returned it and walked away. "Hey, Chan." He looked back. "Though I walk through the valley of death?"

He smiled. " 'Cause I'm the meanest mother in the valley."

"Hope God's got a sense of humor," I said.

"He has to. He made you." Chan gave another thumbs up and walked away.

Someone behind me spoke. "I don't believe we gotta go back up that hill!"

I turned. Doyle stood behind me trying to clear his glasses.

"I don't think we should have . . ." A Huey gunship fired three rockets into another hill to the right of the clearing, three hundred meters to the right of Hill 52. "Green Berets, my rear end!" Doyle said, disgusted, then spit. "Don't you have an E-tool?"

"No," I answered.

"All those guys back there in Seventh Marines said they already had hand-to-hand. They're all sharpening up their E-tools!"

I wished for a small million-dollar piece of shrapnel. That's all it would take, I thought. "One more Heart."

"What?"

"One more Purple Heart and I'm on my way home," I said.

The lead tank started rumbling into the clearing.

"Form up over here! Guns up!" Lieutenant Lampe shouted over noisy diesels.

"Let's go, Doyle."

I threw the heavy machine gun over my shoulder. The hot sun was just beginning to dry my clothes, but my boots squished with each step toward the lieutenant.

"Same procedure!" Lieutenant Lampe shouted. "When the first tank gets halfway across, I want second squad to beat feet to the base of the hill. When second squad gets halfway across, third squad take off."

"What about Chief's squad?" Striker asked from behind me.

"What's left of Chief's squad split up into Corporal James's and Murph's squads." The lieutenant spoke quickly. He looked flustered by the question. Then I realized why. He was on his own. The chief was gone, and so were the gunny and Staff Sergeant Morey. He looked scared, but I couldn't help thinking it was fear of making a mistake more than fear of dying. "Elbon up!" he shouted. Joe ran forward. The shoulder straps of his huge radio had pulled his flak jacket apart in the front, revealing a small bulge under his shirt. A tiny wet black nose poked comfortably between two buttons.

"You stay on my butt, Corporal! Keep Sudsy informed on what you call in, got it?"

"Aye-aye, sir." Joe's answer sounded tight-lipped. His dark eyes seemed in a constant state of intense thought.

He didn't look like the kind of person who'd go to so much trouble for a little dog.

"Ready!" Lieutenant Lampe shouted as the first tank neared the halfway point, with the second twenty meters back. I took the gun off my shoulder and held it on my hip. "Second squad! Go!"

We ran, jogging at first. The smoke from the big diesels mixing with sulphurous gunpowder clogged in my lungs. Then the first AK cracked from the hills to our right. An old .30 caliber opened up from the far side of the wide river. We started sprinting. A Huey gunship strafed the hill to our front while a sleek Cobra ripped low along the edge of the river on the other side, firing machine guns, then rockets. The mortars, I thought. Where are the mortars? I zigzagged as I ran. I could tell the fire wasn't as heavy this time. Not nearly as many bullets whizzing by my ears. I could see Striker ahead of me taking long-distance strides by the lead tank, then by the crippled tank, and finally to the edge of the rushing water. He took one long running jump, landing halfway across the tributary and ten meters left of the blown wooden bridge. He sank in over his head at first, with only his M16 and his forearms staying above the surface. Then his head popped up. He struggled for the other side. Short, stocky Corporal James jumped in behind him. James sank from view. Even his rifle went under. He popped up, threw his rifle to the other side like a spear, and started dog-paddling for it. I held the M60 over my head as I reached the edge of the tributary and jumped as far as I could. Cold water rushed up my nose. I came up choking. A bullet splashed water into my eyes. Another Marine jumped in beside me.

"Corpsman up! Corpsman up!" someone started shouting behind me. Striker pulled James up and out of the water in front of me. James grabbed his rifle and held it out, butt first, for me to grab. He stretched as far as he could. Striker held on to his feet. I reached for it, but my hands were too wet to grasp the plastic butt. An automatic burst splashed water into my face, followed by a loud crack. James's rifle butt smacked into the water. He pulled it out and reached it toward me again. The butt end of the stock was splintered away. I grabbed what was left. He pulled me to the edge of the water. I handed him the M60 and rolled out onto dry land.

"Put some fire up that hill!" James shouted and stuck his rifle out for the next man.

"Doyle, feed me!" I shouted back. He struggled toward James's rifle. His thick glasses were so smudged with water that he groped for James's rifle with one hand, as if he were blind. I aimed at a muzzle flash at the top of the hill and started firing. Another stream of orange tracers zeroed in on the same flash until both streams of tracers converged. A piece of clothing or pack flew into the air. The flash ceased. I took a quick glance back across the tributary. Chan lay prone beside the crippled tank still firing at the hill. Suddenly both remaining tanks opened up with their big guns. Rocks, smoke, and dirt blew into the air with each shot, like small volcanoes erupting.

"Let's go! Move it!" I shouted back at Doyle as he rolled out of the water. I ran across the dirt road and flattened out against the hillside until Doyle caught up.

"Are you ready?"

"For what?" Doyle gasped for breath. He pulled off his Coke-bottle lenses and tried to blow off some of the water.

"We're going up the hill!"

Doyle looked left as two more Marines flattened nearby. He took a deep breath and sighed, "Yeah."

"Give us cover!" I yelled at the Marines on Doyle's left. "We're going up!" Fear and excitement shot through me with the rhythm of a jackhammer.

"Gung-ho, maniac!" I heard Doyle shout as I ran and

stumbled and crawled. Twenty meters up we took cover under a large sharp-edged rock.

"Give us cover! We're coming up!" a voice shouted from below.

I moved to the right of the rock and laid down a fifty-round burst across the top of the hill. There was no return fire. I fired again. Still no return fire. We leapfrogged up. Twenty meters up I could see a pile of fresh dirt ringing the charred, blunt hilltop. The burnt scent of napalm covered the ground. Everything smelled like burning hair.

For the first time in the assault I felt too scared to go on. I knew there was a trench on the other side of that fresh dirt. I wondered why they hadn't hit us with grenades. I can't just sit here, I thought.

"Doyle! How many frags you got?" I asked impatiently. He slapped his chest, then felt his cartridge belt.

"Four!"

"I have three, and I ain't going over that dirt till they're all gone."

"I'm with you."

"Let's make it up to that bomb crater before we throw 'em."

"Which one?" he asked.

I pointed to a small crater about ten yards away. It looked about three feet deep.

"It's better than nothing," I said apologetically.

Doyle went for it first as I laid down fire. Then he covered me as I dove beside him. We laid our weapons down. I pulled a grenade off my cartridge belt. Doyle did the same. We straightened the pins and pulled them.

"Maybe we better pop the spoon and hold them for a two count?" I said.

"You've seen too many John Wayne movies!"

"Yeah, sucker! If these frags come flying back in your face, you'll wish you'd seen a couple!"

"I'm throwing!" he said. Doyle brought the grenade

back behind his ear with his right hand and let fly. He threw the grenade straight up the hill and over the fresh dirt.

I let the spoon fly, brought the grenade back like a football and counted, "One-thousand-one, one—"

"Throw it!" Doyle shouted as he stuck his face in the dirt and covered his head with his hands. I threw. I aimed left of where Doyle threw his. Doyle's grenade exploded, showering us with dirt and tiny rocks. My grenade exploded immediately after, with the same effect. Still no return fire. We repeated the procedure minus me holding for a two count.

"I think they pulled out!" Striker shouted from the far right. I couldn't see him but I knew that voice.

"I'm throwing another frag!" I shouted toward Striker.

"Ready!" Doyle said, his grenade already pulled off his belt and finger in the safety-pin ring.

"Outgoing!" I shouted and ducked down. Doyle let fly. The explosions were the same. No screams, no return fire. "Let's go in!"

We moved up the hill cautiously. Finally we waited just below the fresh dirt mound until most of the platoon caught up. Striker stood to a crouch ten meters to my right and gave me a thumbs up. Everyone around me returned it. Someone screamed, "Go!" Ten of us rushed forward. My trigger felt slippery with sweat. I took a deep breath, jumped over the dirt mound, and down into a waist-deep trench that ringed the top of the hill. I landed with a crunch on the charred corpse of an NVA soldier and stumbled against the inner wall of the trench. An unburned body lay face down five feet away, his back covered with dried blood. I stomped the man's head, then kicked him in the groin. No groan. Felt stiff. The heavy firing had stopped. Except for an occasional sniper round or quick burst of M16 fire, the battle sounded over.

"Hey, napalm got this sucker!" someone shouted from my left.

"Got fried gook over here!" another Marine shouted from the right.

"Why didn't somebody bring a flag? We could raise the flag for the TV guys!" Striker sounded oddly enthusiastic.

A few minutes later Elbon climbed over the top with Lieutenant Lampe beside him, hanging on to the field phone attached to the radio on Elbon's back. I walked to the other side of the trench. There was another hill just in back of this one and to the right. It looked heavily wooded and covered with brush. I could see the helmets of Marines moving up a narrow twisting trail. The small blue tributary went by the wooded hill and hooked around the far side. Beyond stood more green hilltops stretching to the gray mountains four miles away. From here I could see the wide Vu Gia River bending sharply right and turning sapphire as it snaked off into the mountains with the dusty beige road tagging along beside it like a puny brother.

"That's where America's Green Berets are sitting on their rear ends and screaming for help," Corporal James said, measuring his pauses carefully. "The chief sure called it, didn't he?" He spoke to me, but his eyes glared at the gray mountains.

"Yeah," I answered, but we both knew those soldiers were good. Not Marines, but good.

"We're moving over there for the night." He nodded at the wooded hill with the Marine helmets crawling through breaks in the canopy of trees and brush. I wanted to ask why, but it didn't matter. One hill was as comfortable as another.

We piled the five dead gooks in a small stretch of the trench and pushed dirt over them. It was supposed to make the flies go away, but it didn't. An hour later we filed down the hill as a company of Seventh Marines marched up. They were lean, unsmiling, hard-Corps faces. We gave each other curious gazes as the columns passed. No one spoke. We marched down the hill and along the tributary until we reached our new hill. The column stopped at a small rocky clearing at the base of the wooded hill. Another column of Marines filed down the twisting clay path.

"Okay, saddle up!" Lieutenant Lampe shouted. His words came to him a bit awkwardly, as if he were waiting for the chief or Gunny or the staff to shout the men into movement. Doyle muttered something behind me. I turned.

"What?" I asked.

"We lost a lot of men." His voice was on the point of complete dejection.

"I don't think any of 'em were KIAs, though," I said, trying hard to find something positive to think about.

"Who says?" he asked.

"I asked the lieutenant about the gunny and Chief. The gunny's going to make it, and he thought the chief would."

I turned to look for Sudsy. He'd know the casualty status. I couldn't find his antenna or his freckled face. "Did you ask Sudsy who got hit?" I asked, still looking for him in the column.

"He was medevaced out. I think he's KIA."

"What?" My stomach rolled and sank, and for a moment I felt sick.

"He didn't make it to the first tank the second time across."

"Saddle up! I want the squad leaders to put your squads in three-man positions around the top of this hill and down the sides. The gooks still control the next hill, so don't go giving them any targets! Is that clear?" Then the lieutenant started again without waiting for an answer. "The CP is going to be right here where I'm standing."

We moved up the narrow path. The heat pressed heavily on the back of my neck. Empty C-ration boxes lay strewn about everywhere. The higher we climbed, the clearer the enemy hill became. It stood taller than the one we were on. The tributary took a sharp left below us. It separated us from them. Its cold water looked beautiful and inviting, splashing against huge round boulders jutting up from the water.

"Hey! Look!" A shout echoed from behind me to the head of the column. Suddenly I saw the reason for the commotion. One hundred meters below, leaning out over a large round boulder, was an NVA soldier filling his American-looking canteen. An AK47 lay beside him. Two more NVA stood behind him on the huge boulder, chatting nonchalantly, with rifles slung over their shoulders. Before anyone fired a shot the three of them casually disappeared back into the lush green canopy of trees and leafy jungle vines. I was shocked. For the NVA to be so brazen there must be a ton of 'em, I thought. The column stopped. Corporal James and Corporal Murphy started setting their squads up in three-man positions around the top of the hill and down the sides, splitting it down the center.

"I want your gun team over there," James said. I looked to the right of the path where he pointed. It looked good. There was even a small level area like a tiny shelf on the hillside where we could sleep without rolling to the bottom.

"It'll have to be just you and Doyle tonight."

"Great," I mumbled sarcastically. "I'm too tired to sleep tonight anyway."

An hour later the sun turned into a moon and the shadowy fears of the night held my eyes open, but just barely. I wondered where Chan was. I knew he was positioned at the bottom of the hill somewhere. My eyes felt heavy. The moon disappeared behind a layer of clouds. I wondered about our positioning. It seemed haphazard. I wasn't even sure where the other positions were, except for the one ten yards below us. I knew the chief had made mistakes. He wasn't perfect. Still, I wanted him back. I wanted the gunny back, too. God! I'm one of the only salts left! I gotta talk to God about this. Things are looking real grim.

"Wow!" Doyle whispered from the other side of the M60. "This is the big time!" The sky behind the enemy hill lit up in pink, red, and pastels, silhouetting the steep dark mountains of Thuong Duc four miles away. Bright white flashes sent booming shock waves of sound that shook the earth beneath me.

"Pssst!" Another whisper came from the darkness below us.

"You guys see that?" Another series of shock waves and flashes lit up the sky for miles around. It felt like God was waking everything up. "What is it?" the voice whispered from below.

"It's arc-light raids," I whispered.

"What's that?"

"B-52s, man," Doyle whispered impatiently. "Must be another boot."

The brutal light show was awesome. It went on and on until it seemed impossible for anyone to live through it, yet I knew some would, somehow. Maybe without eardrums, but still able to pull a trigger.

Suddenly a quick burst of AK fire opened up above us, followed immediately by five semi-automatic shots from an M16.

Something heavy rolled through the brush. Then silence. Doyle sat up. Something thudded into the bushes beside him. A ripping explosion shattered the silence. My night vision was gone. All I saw were bright spots. Doyle cried. I started firing the M60 into the brush in front of us until the gun went silent.

"I'm hit! I'm hit!" Doyle screamed.

"Corpsman!" a voice shouted from above us.

"Johnnie, I'm hit!"

"I know it. Don't talk. I can't see yet."

"I'm hurt!"

"Shut up! They're right on top of us!" I opened my eyes as wide as I could. My vision was coming back. I could see the outline of a tree silhouetted by the flashes of the arc-light raids. Finally I could see Doyle holding his knee and shaking his head back and forth. His teeth shined white from the moon's glare as he clenched them in pain. Someone was coming up the path fast, breathing hard and stumbling in the dark.

"Corpsman coming in! Don't fire!"

"Doc!" I called. "We got wounded over here!"

"Coming in!" He turned right, off the path, and stumbled over a thornbush. "Where?" He looked up from all fours. "Where are you?"

"Straight ahead! Ten meters!"

He crawled forward until he could see us, then stood to a crouch and walked over to us. "Who's hit?"

"Doyle," I said.

"Hurry up!" Doyle said angrily.

Doc moved closer to Doyle. "Can you walk if I help?"

"I think so."

"Let's go. I want to get you below, where I can work on you."

"Doc," I said. "Somebody else got hit up above us."

"Can you hold on for a few minutes while I go check it out?" Doc said.

"Yeah. But hurry, Doc," Doyle whispered.

Doc moved back toward the path. Five minutes later I heard him again. *"Pssst."*

"Over here," I said.

He stumbled over the same thornbush, hitting the ground harder this time. I held back a laugh. He crawled over to us.

"You ready?" he asked.

"Yeah," Doyle said. He struggled to his feet with Doc's help.

"What happened up there?" I asked.

"A gook crawled up to the top of the hill and opened up. Killed one guy. His buddy killed the gook. Better keep your eyes open. They might be probing for an all-outer."

"Tell 'em down at the CP I'm down to a one-man gun team."

"Right," Doc answered as he helped Doyle hobble toward the path.

"Hey, Doyle," I whispered. They stopped and Doyle looked over his shoulder. "Have a good trip home."

"I got your address, John. I'm going to be looking you up."

"Send me a hot sauce when you get back," I said. "And the little fishes—you know, sardines!"

"Semper fi, buddy." Doyle gave me a thumbs up. I returned it. They disappeared into the darkness. I sank into the lowest, loneliest, bluest funk I'd ever been in. I'd never make it home. No one will even remember that I died over here. Doyle's boot to me, and even he's going home. I should be happy for him. It's not his fault he's lucky. That turd. He's really a good person. That turd.

An hour later the war went silent again. Corporal James and Striker crawled in from the darkness and spent the night. Early the next morning the whirring blades of a medevac chopper greeted the sunrise. I walked over to the path to get a better look at Doyle's departure.

"Look out!" The stumbling feet of men carrying something heavy accompanied the shout. I turned in time to see two Marines carrying something wrapped in a drab green poncho. The poncho ripped in half. The stiff heavy body of a dead Marine with ash-blond hair rolled straight at me. I was too shocked to move. He rolled into my shins and stopped. He felt like a bag of cement. I didn't move. I stared down at him until the other two Marines started asking me something.

"Hey, you got a poncho we can use? We got to hurry and get him on that chopper!"

"Yeah, sure. Here, hold him and I'll get it." I ran back to the gun and got my poncho out of my pack. My hands were shaking. It made me mad. I gave the men the poncho and watched as they struggled down the steep hill with the heavy weight. I watched until the chopper was out of sight.

"Me and Striker are sitting with you until we get some replacements."

I turned to see Corporal James take a spoonful of beef and rocks then spit out a potato in disgust.

"I haven't had a decent bite of food since Bangkok!"

"R&R!"

"What?" he asked with a puzzled look on his face.

"That's what's wrong with me. I haven't had an R&R yet. Do you know that I've been here over nine months without an R&R?"

"I thought you and Chan went to Australia?" James turned his head and spit out another potato.

"That's when we got hit. Do you think Bangkok is better than Australia?"

"Well, I don't know. Australia has round-eyed women. I loved Bangkok, though. I bought a Corvette through the PX in Bangkok."

"You're kidding?"

"It's waiting on me right now in California. Emerald green." James drifted off just thinking about it.

"Clark!" I looked down the path. A black boot Marine still wearing stateside utilities and stateside boots with a glaring shine on them made his way up the path with a handful of mail.

"Up here!" I said. He looked up. Something was odd about him. No rifle! "Hey, boot! Where's your rifle?"

"I left it down there," he said indignantly, as if it were none of my business.

"Give me the mail."

He handed me four letters. "No. Give it all to me. I'll hand it out. Now, you go get your rifle, and don't make a move without it from now on." He looked defiant and cocky.

"And tie those dog tags into your boot laces and blacken 'em so they don't shine. If you get blown away the boots usually stay in one piece so you'll get identified." He started to say something, but I didn't give him time. "Don't forget your salt tabs, not even once." I could hear Red's words coming out of my mouth. Then I heard the chief. "And don't put the twenty-round maximum in your magazines. It weakens the spring and it'll jam on you and get you KIA'd." The cocky look on the black Marine's face melted into one of apprehension. "Now go get that rifle and keep it clean and maybe you won't make the trip home in a plastic bag."

He handed me the mail, turned, and went back down the hill without saying a word. I turned to Corporal James. He smiled.

"Feeling salty today?"

"I don't know. I just miss a lot of friends. I need an R&R." I looked at the mail and found a letter for James and two for Striker. I handed them to him and went up the hill. I found the position where the ash-blond guy got killed. His buddy sat alone against a tree with one hand over his eyes and the other on his M16. I didn't speak. A dead gook with no shirt and bullet holes scattered from his face to his navel lay spread-eagled in the weeds a few feet away. Flies by the thousands buzzed around the bloody body. I walked over to it and started to give it a shove with my boot to roll it down the hill toward the tributary.

"What are you doing?" The young, dirty, thin-faced Marine stared at me blankly.

"I was going to push this stiff down the hill so you wouldn't have to smell him."

"No." He spoke quickly, barely moving his lips, with no change of expression in his blank stare. "I want 'em

to come after his body so I can kill some more of 'em."
His voice was a monotone, like a talking robot's.

I walked away, then looked back. His stare hadn't changed, even though I wasn't there to stare at. I handed out the remaining mail, then went back to my position and opened mine. The first one was a birthday card from Polly.

"Hey! Today's my birthday!" I shouted.

"Happy birthday, Baby-san!" Corporal James surprised me with his friendliness. "How old?"

"Nineteen!"

"Columbus Day's your birthday?" Striker asked without looking up from oiling his rifle.

"Yep," I said.

"Nineteen! Were you seventeen when you joined the Crotch?"

"Yeah." A photo fell out of the birthday card.

"Hey, she sent a picture!"

Striker and James dropped what they were doing. A picture from home was like a quick trip back to civilization, proof that it still existed. It was a color photo of Polly at a party in her college dormitory in Missouri. "She says her girlfriends and her had a birthday party for me!" Polly stood with her arms around two girls who held a bottle of beer in each hand. They all wore miniskirts eight inches above the knees.

"Boy, looks like *they're* having a good time!" Striker said as he hung over my right shoulder.

"Look at that fag in the background! He's got hair longer than the chicks," Corporal James said angrily.

"You know . . ." Striker paused to consider the rest of his statement. "When I get home"—he paused again—"I'm gonna deck the first hippie I see, just for the guys in the Nam." I looked at Striker. He sounded like he meant it. Striker was big and strong and not particularly handsome with that big black mole between his eyes. I started to feel sorry for the first hippie he was going to meet. Then I reconsidered.

"I like that idea. I might do that too," I said. "If I ever get home."

"Six more weeks, bro." Striker fell back with his hands behind his head. "I'm so short the gooks probably can't see me."

"You ain't as short as me, brother," James said. "I could walk under doors!"

"How short are you?" I asked.

"Four weeks! November 12. I'll be on the freedom bird heading for my Vette."

"I don't know if I even remember how to drive," I said.

"Are you Corporal James?" a hesitant high-pitched voice asked from behind us. We all turned back to the path. Four boot Marines stood together. They all had stateside utilities on and stateside boots. They were clean-shaven and healthy-faced, with white-sidewall haircuts.

"Yeah, I'm James," he said gruffly.

"Lieutenant says we're in your squad for now." The high-pitched voice came from a boot with snow-white skin.

"Man," Striker said. "The sun is sure going to tear him up!"

Corporal James led the boots up the hill to position them. The rest of the day passed noisily by. We didn't move. We just watched as Phantoms and Cobras and Huey gunships strafed and bombed and bombed and strafed all around us. The lush green jungle on the other side of the river geysered up wildly until it was marred with ugly brown patches. The green hills on our side of the wide Vu Gia River became potted and cratered like a picture of the moon. Then came the napalm and fiery death. The night brought Puff the Magic Dragon and the massive roar of its quavering mini-guns. Sporadic green single tracers spit into the dark sky in defiance of the enormous wavering golden rod.

"The boots are getting their money's worth tonight," Striker mumbled.

"It's kind of nice having that FO with us," James mused.

"Is that who's calling in all the stuff?" Striker asked.

"His name's Elbon," I said. "Do you know that crazy guy's got a little tiny dog with him."

"You're kidding?" James said.

"No. He really does."

"Does Lieutenant Lampe know that?" James asked.

"I'm sure he doesn't."

"He will tomorrow!" James threatened. All at once I got this aggravating urge to hit James in the mouth. The Marine Corps wouldn't be so bad if it weren't for punk corporals. I was spared a court martial by a sudden burst of M16 fire at the bottom of the hill. A scary silence followed.

Twenty minutes later a voice came from the dark path behind us. "Comin' in!" A moment later the half-moon broke through a cloud long enough to light up Mike Flanagan's freckled Irish face. I had begun to feel that all my friends were gone. It filled me with joy to see good ol' Mike.

"Mike?"

"Johnnie?" he asked, straining to see me in the darkness.

"What in the world are you doing here? Daggone it's good to see you!" I said.

"I think they're trying to make me a grunt." He moved in closer beside me and handed me an M16. "Here's a bandolier."

"What are you doing?" I asked.

"Lieutenant Lampe wants me to take the gun out on an ambush."

"My gun?"

"Just for tonight."

"Got an A-gunner?"

"Allen," he said.

"The professor?"

"Yep."

"Well . . ." I hesitated. I didn't like parting with the gun. "Take care of her now." I gave the gun a friendly pat. "And, Mike, no more than twenty-round bursts, man. It makes a good target."

"I'll treat her like a baby," Mike said. He picked up the gun and four hundred rounds of ammo and headed back to the path. Then he stopped and turned back. "Did you hear that shooting?"

"What was it?" Striker asked.

"Some boot panicked, heard a noise in the bushes near him and opened up. They killed that FO that came out with us."

"Oh no! Joe?" I asked. I felt as though the wind had been kicked out of me.

"Did you know him?" Mike asked in a slow whisper.

Visions of Joe and his brother Harpo and the little dog forced me close to tears. I felt tired, sick, and angry. "Who shot him?" I blurted angrily and louder than I meant to.

"Keep it down!" James whispered quickly.

"I don't know. I don't think they were sure yet. I'm sorry, John. I'll let you know what I can find out."

"How 'bout his little dog?" I asked.

"I didn't hear anything about a dog. I'll let you know tomorrow." Mike disappeared into the darkness.

"Shake it off, John."

James's voice broke me out of a numb, prolonged stare toward the dark path. I turned around. James and Striker were both sitting up and looking at another arc-light raid of 1,000-pound bombs crashing into the mountains of Thuong Duc. Darting spurts of abrupt orange spread through the mountains, then reached into the sky, turning it crimson. It looked like the end of the world. A small *pop* followed by a bright light lifted my eyes up. Puff was dropping flares. The hills around us lit up from the reddish glare of twenty tiny suns swinging down under their midget parachutes. Now it was bright, as if daylight had shocked away the night. I looked down at my M16. Something hit the ground beside Striker. I ducked, covering my head. A violent explosion rolled me toward the path. Striker screamed piteously. I looked up. Ten meters ahead and slightly above on the slope of the hill an NVA sprang out of the bush firing full automatic from the hip. Corporal James screeched and fell backward on my right. I raised to my knees and fired full automatic. Suddenly I was lying on my face. My mouth was full of dirt. My thigh burned like no burn I'd ever felt. It ached like someone had knocked it off with a sledgehammer in one mighty blow. I raised my eyes with my chin still in the dirt and stared straight into the wide-open, dead black pupils of an Oriental lying stomach down ten inches away. Blood gushed from two small round holes in his forehead, one above each eye. Five or six straight black hairs stuck out from his upper lip in what looked like a futile attempt at a mustache. I could hear Striker screaming. Everything went gray, then black.

"Snap out of it!" Sam's pitted face was in front of me. "Don't go into shock, you moron!" He slapped me hard across the face. It stung. I felt anger and started to swing, but someone held my arm. "Are you ready? I'm taking you off the hill! You're all right! Don't panic!" he shouted into my face. His breath smelled like week-old cat food.

"My leg!" I heard myself shouting. "Is it on?"

"It's there! It's there! How many times do I have to tell you!"

Sam picked me up with a fireman's carry over one

shoulder and around his neck. The path was steep and treacherous. My leg ached and burned. I wondered if I was crippled.

"James and Striker!" I shouted as we reached the bottom.

"James is shot in the calf!" Sam gasped for air before finishing. "Striker looks bad." He gasped again. "But he's alive."

"How is he?" Doc yelled. "Bring him over here!" Sam carried me over to the Doc and Lieutenant Lampe. He laid me down gently onto my back.

"Here's a souvenir for ya." Sam laid an AK banana clip magazine on my chest. "Weak spring. It jammed. He put in too many rounds. That's why you're alive. Tell your kids." He turned and ran back toward the path. Puff hummed overhead. Another batch of flares popped open, renewing the dissipating light.

"Thanks, Sam!" I yelled too late for him to hear. The pain in my thigh felt worse. Doc tore the top off a small plastic container. He pulled out a tiny needle and stabbed it into my throbbing thigh.

"Morphine," Doc said. "You'll feel better in a minute."

"What's it look like, Doc?" Lieutenant Lampe asked. He held a field phone in his hand. I'd never seen him look so confused. His eyes darted up the hill, back to me, then back up the hill.

Doc cut my pants leg away with his K-bar and looked close at the inside of my thigh. "Can you roll over?" I rolled. "Went clean through. Made a big hole, Lieutenant. He's lost a lot of blood. We got to get him to Da Nang."

"Can it wait till morning?"

"No way!"

Memories of Jack Ellenwood crept through the pain. I lifted my head to look at my leg. A flickering flare cast a pulsating light into the gaping hole on the inside of my thigh. Dark red blood shot out of the hole between two pieces of torn muscle in steady spurts. I felt faint. I lay back down. Doc began wrapping the leg tightly. An M60 opened up somewhere. I closed my eyes. The war went silent.

"You got him?" a voice shouted. I tried to open my eyes. The steady cracking of AK fire resounded from every direction. A hard wind hit me in the face. A chopper! "Give 'em cover! Get out of here, quick!" Someone dragged me along a metal floor. I could hear the engine get louder. We were airborne. A bullet smacked through the thin walls of the chopper just above my head. Then another. The old helicopter shuddered and dropped. I felt my life ending. Just as suddenly as the drop, we pulled up. The door gunner blazed at flashes in the blackness below. I prayed. The door gunner stopped firing.

"Did they make it?" the door gunner shouted at the pilot.

"They went down!"

"Who?" I asked, but my voice trailed off. A stuffy, overpowering drowsiness grayed-out my mind. The choppy engine faded. I wondered if I was dying. Jesus save me . . . Jesus save me . . . Jesus . . . Black silence.

I felt cool. I moved my head. Soft? There was something soft under me. My leg ached all the way into my stomach. I groaned. My eyes felt heavy, almost sealed shut with old tears and dirt. "Guns up! Guns up!" I forced my eyes open. A bright white glow stung them shut again. I jerked my head to the side. Someone was laughing. A deep hearty laugh that made me wish I could laugh with him. Now I could hear others laughing. Their laughter echoed. I'm in a building, I thought. Pillow! I opened my eyes again. The room was white. Too white. "Guns up! Guns up!" a familiar voice called again. I lifted my head and felt for the gun like a blind man. My blurry vision began to clear. It was a small, round-looking ceiling. A Quonset hut. I grew up in a West Virginia Quonset hut, and I know a Quonset hut when I see one, I thought. Men were laughing. "I knew that would get your butt up!" the familiar voice shouted from my left. I raised onto my left elbow and looked down a row of metal hospital beds. Men in blue pajamas filled each bed. They all laughed. I tried to focus in on the nearest one. Then I saw him.

"Chief!"

The room erupted into laughter. Now all the faces were clear. Staff Sergeant Morey lay in the bed next to him. In the bed after that was a Marine who looked familiar, but no one I knew well. He was laughing too. In the bed next to him was Corporal James, and next to him, at the end of the row, was Striker. I looked to my right to see more beds and blue pajamas but no familiar faces. Then one of the men on my right shouted, as if admitting the obvious, "Yeah, we're Fifth Marines too!" Everyone started laughing.

"How long have I been here, Chief?"

"The better part of a day."

"Where are we?"

"Da Nang. But cheer up. The Doc said you're on your way to Japan with that wound."

"Japan? Really?" I looked at my right leg. I had thick bandages from the knee to the groin.

"Your war's over, John."

"Chan! Did anybody hear anything about Chan?"

Swift Eagle's face looked uncomfortable with the question, and my heart sank to the pit of my stomach. "I don't know, John. I heard they took some more casualties, but no one knows who."

I felt slightly relieved.

"Hey, Clark! We're on our way to Japan!" Corporal James shouted from his bed.

"How's Striker?" I asked.

"He's going to Japan too," James said.

"Striker got shrapnel bad," the chief said quietly. "It went up his rear end and tore up his insides."

"Is he going to make it?" I asked. A corpsman dressed all in white strode up to the front of my bed pushing a cart full of pills and needles.

"Yeah. I think so," Swift Eagle said, watching the corpsman in a state of nervous discomfort.

"How 'bout you, Chief?"

"I'm okay. Just some shrapnel," he said nervously, still staring wide-eyed at the Navy corpsman. "I want no shot!"

"Is this it? Are you going home? How many Hearts have you got?" I asked as the corpsman cleaned a spot on my arm with alcohol.

"Seven or eight, I think. They're sending me home." He winced and turned his head as the corpsman shoved in the needle.

"You're not comin' back again, are you?"

"I don't know." He looked away like the subject bothered him.

"Look, Chief, if we were going to try to win this war I might come back. I don't know what we're doing over here, but we sure aren't trying to win, and you know it."

"I know. I knew that on my first tour." The corpsman pushed his cart past the chief's bed. Swift Eagle took a deep sigh of relief.

"Then why do you keep coming back?" I asked.

He turned his eyes toward me and off the corpsman. "I don't have anyplace else to go."

"Go home!"

"I have no home. I was born on a reservation."

His remark sounded terse. I didn't like it.

"I wouldn't try to compare my life to yours, Chief. But I grew up poor too. We lived in garages and Quonset huts. My dad was blind and crippled, and we lived off seventy bucks a month, and our food came out of those green government cans for the poor that coal-mining towns are famous for, so you ain't talkin' to some spoiled brat. And you're not ever going to convince me that America's worse to go back to than this hole!"

Swift Eagle looked at me with a curious smile, and I wondered if I'd shot off my big mouth too much.

"You have the spirit of an Indian, John."

I wanted to put that compliment in bronze. I felt sad that no one else heard it.

"But," he continued after a pause, "you react like an Apache. I did not mean that America was at fault. I have no family. No reason to go back. No home or work. The Marine Corps is my home."

"Then stay in the Corps."

"I don't think I could stand the spit-and-polish crap. Stateside duty sucks. That's why I'm only a corporal. I get busted every time they send me home."

"You can't fight the war forever," I said.

"I know. I've been thinking about it." The chief put his hands behind his head, leaned back, and looked at the ceiling.

Two corpsmen wheeled in a double-layer cart stacked with trays of meals. A half hour later I shoved down the last bite just as a boot-looking second lieutenant walked through the swinging doors at the end of the room.

"Are any of you men from the Fifth Marines?" he asked somberly.

"Aye-aye, sir," Staff Sergeant Morey replied.

"We need a positive ID on a Corporal Joseph Arthur Elbon. Did anyone of you know him personally?"

My heart sank. "I did," I said hesitantly.

"Would you mind coming with me if your doctor says it's okay?"

"Aye-aye, sir," I answered.

A few minutes later the lieutenant and two corpsmen unhooked an IV from my arm and placed me gingerly into a wheelchair. The lieutenant wheeled me out of our

building and into the bright hot sun. Sweat popped out
of every pore almost immediately. He wheeled me past
two large gray Quonset huts and into a cold concrete
one-story building with two heavy white doors. We entered a small room with a desk and a group of large
Army-green file cabinets. He stopped in front of two
wooden swinging doors that had no windows.

"Have you ever been here before?" he asked.

"No, sir."

"It's not a very happy place. Get yourself prepared for
it. We'll get it over with as fast as possible. I just need you
to sign a couple of papers saying whether or not this is
Corporal Elbon."

He turned me around and pulled me through the
doors, then faced me toward what looked like a wall of
giant filing cabinets. I knew they were filled with bodies.
In front of the wall of cabinets lay ten large green plastic
bags with heavy metal zippers. An irritating hum filled
the cavernous room. I looked right to see the cause of the
noise. Two men in blood-splattered white coats were
busy embalming the naked, bloody corpse of a muscular
young man lying on a long concrete table with a drain at
one end. The noisy machine pumped fluids in while another machine sucked fluids out. The lieutenant wheeled
me in front of the last one in the line. He bent over and
pulled the zipper down the center until a pale, dead face
showed.

"Yeah, that's Joe."

An hour later two corpsmen hauled me out of bed
again. This time they dumped me onto a stretcher.

"You're going to love Japan!" Swift Eagle said. "I've
thought about it."

"And . . . ?" I said.

"I'm going home."

"I'll miss you, Chief. I think you're making the right
decision."

He gave me a thumbs up. Everyone shouted goodbyes, ranging from Semper fi to gung-ho to good luck, as the corpsmen carried me through the swinging doors. "Guns up, Clarkie!" Swift Eagle shouted. I knew I'd never hear that again. They carried me to a familiar-looking Army-green truck with a big red cross on a white background painted across the back doors. It made me think of Texas and redheads. A few minutes later two corpsmen loaded Corporal James in beside me. Then came Striker with IV bottles and blood bottles hanging over him on metal poles. They stuck an IV in my right arm and hung a bottle over me, too. The drive to the airstrip was quick. It seemed like only a few minutes had passed when two corpsmen carried me onto a big C-130 that had been converted into a hospital plane with metal bunk beds that folded out from the sides of the hull. They put me on a top bunk. Then they carried Corporal James in and laid him below me. They laid Striker across the aisle from us.

"You guys sure are lucky!" A black corpsman smiled down at Corporal James. "Only serious wounds get to go to Japan!"

I laughed. I thought of Chan and asked God to take care of him.

The tail section of the big converted cargo plane dropped open, and the icy air of Yokosuka startled me. I could see a wintry layer of trackless snow on both sides of the runway. It really is over, I thought.

"Get ready, men!" an Air Force medic shouted from the front of the plane. "You are about to experience a ninety-five-degree drop in temperature!"

Some of the wounded started cheering. A couple of minutes later two Navy corpsmen dressed in thick warm pea coats threw a blanket over me and wheeled me down the tail ramp. The overcast sky melted into a gray sleep that turned black and deep. The next thing I heard was a soft faraway voice. It was a woman talking.

"You have to be awake for this, Marine." My eyes wouldn't open. "Try to keep your eyes open, Marine. You might feel a little sting." Oh, no! Where had I heard that before?

"Yes. I agree," a male voice said. "The hole is too large for a local." The voices began fading farther and farther away until I no longer heard anyone.

When I opened my eyes, puffy white clouds drifted across a powder-blue sky through a large old wood-frame window. Right below the window was a hospital bed. The guy in the bed was all bandages except for eye, nose, and mouth holes. I rolled my head left to see a spacious old hospital ward with rows of beds all filled with young Americans. It reminded me of old Saint Petersburg High School. It was even the same color—drab green. Vintage 1930s, I guessed. Someone rubbed my right arm, and I turned to see who.

"How do you feel, PFC?" An American nurse with dark hair, blue eyes, and a fat face was rubbing my arm with cold cotton that reeked of alcohol. She picked up a needle from a pill cart beside her and stabbed me in the arm.

"I'm not sure," I grimaced. "My leg hurts."

"How's he doing, Nurse?" A familiar-looking man in his early forties was asking from the foot of my bed as he lifted a sheet away from my leg.

"He seems to be doing fine, Doctor. He says his leg hurts."

"I don't doubt it." The doctor dropped the sheet and picked up a clipboard attached to the foot of my bed. "The bleeding seems to have stopped. Watch the bandages. Keep him on antibiotics and check his vitals every hour." He paused and flipped through a couple of pages on the clipboard. "Your chart says you are PFC Johnnie Clark."

"Yes, sir."

"Why are you still a PFC with the record I'm looking at?" He looked up from the chart. "You get busted?"

"No, sir. They told me promotions were frozen in the Fifth Marines."

The doctor's face grew flush with anger. He wrote something on my chart, walked around the end of the bed, then slammed the clipboard down on the nurse's pill chart with a bang. "You've just been promoted to lance corporal, Marine." He turned and walked away briskly, talking to himself all the way to the end of the ward, where he turned and went down a staircase and out of sight.

"Congrats, man!" an unfamiliar voice said from the bed on my right.

I looked around the fat nurse as she pushed the pill cart away toward the next bed. A young guy with a flattop haircut that looked like it came out of the fifties was lying on his stomach. A sheet covered him from the waist down.

"That's the fastest promotion I've ever seen!" He laughed in a friendly way. "We need more officers like that."

"Yeah, I'll say. Who were you with?"

"Bravo, One-seven."

"We were working with the Seventh Marines when I got hit."

"Oh, yeah? I'm a corpsman."

"How bad are you hit?" I asked.

He pulled back the sheet. He was naked from the waist down, with a large bandage covering his rear end. He pulled it back, and I felt myself make a face. The entire right cheek of his rear end was gone. What was left looked like raw hamburger. "Got hit by a fifty cal'. I was behind a tree. It went through the tree and then did this. I won't be wearing tight jeans for a while." He flipped the sheet back over himself and laughed again. "Hey, you've had some buddy of yours in here a couple of times, but you were still out."

"Really! Wasn't Oriental by any chance?" I asked, not really expecting the answer to be yes.

"No. As a matter of fact it's that guy right there."

"It's about time you woke up." I turned to my left to see Corporal James hobbling up on a pair of crutches, wearing a blue bathrobe and a cast from the knee down on his left leg. He looked happy to see me. "How do you feel?" he asked as he sat on the edge of my bed, carefully avoiding my legs.

"Sore. It feels like I got hit by a one-five-five and two Ban-San Bombers."

"They've really had you drugged out, man!" the corporal said.

"How long have I been here?"

"Let's see," James mumbled to himself. "This is our fourth day in Japan."

"You're kidding!" I said, but my headache told me he wasn't. "Anybody else here we know?"

"Yeah. Striker's here."

"Where?"

"Downstairs. You'll never believe what he's been doing down there." James chuckled.

"No tellin'," I said.

"Every time I drop in on him, he's reading a Bible."

"Our Striker?"

"Yeah, really!" James laughed again.

"I love it. Sure wish Chan could see that!"

"When you're well enough to get out of bed, I'll take you down for a visit. He won't be there long. We got orders for the world! You'll probably be getting yours soon. I better get back before I miss chow. You only get one chance at it around here. Take it easy. I'll get back with you later."

"Okay, James."

James hobbled across the shiny waxed brown tile floor and then down the same staircase that my doctor had disappeared down. I never saw him again. He and Striker were sent home. The next four weeks went by faster than even one day had seemed in the bush.

Everything felt new and strange. Eating hot food with spoons, forks, and knives felt foreign. It was too quiet to sleep, so the nurse would feed me a sleeping pill each night. Sometimes it worked, sometimes it didn't. It didn't feel right with no one standing watch. Sometimes at night one of the wounded Marines would wake up screaming. It never bothered me, because I was usually already awake. Then one night I woke up screaming and covered with sweat. The buttless corpsman said I was screaming "Incoming!" He thought it was a riot, because two beds down some guy dove onto the floor. The doctor assured me that an occasional scream was normal. I wondered if I would ever be really normal.

The buttless corpsman became my alarm clock. He woke me each morning with a stereo setup that the fat-faced nurse had purchased with his money at the PX. Each day started with the Young Rascals singing "It's a Beautiful Morning." It sounded like every guy who could hobble or crawl to the PX, which was right next door, had bought a stereo, radio, tape deck, or anything that would play music. The doctors didn't mind. They seemed to think it was good therapy. One day the Beatles' new hit single became available. From then on "Hey, Jude" reverberated through the cavernous room constantly, usually from three different sources. Of course it was never coordinated, so I'd listen to the beginning, middle, and end at the same time. It somehow became my favorite song.

I kept waiting to feel good. I was supposed to be excited about being out of the bush, I thought. I should be jumping up and down and getting ready for Christmas or something. Anything! I kept waiting. I wrote home a lot to keep the folks from worrying. I lied about how great I felt, but the truth was that I felt more depressed each day and didn't know why. I got the fat-faced nurse to paste up a new photo of Nancy Diez in a black bikini. It helped a little.

I sent a steady stream of letters to Chan. They all said pretty much the same thing: "Write me soon and let me know how you are or I'm going to kick your butt all the way to China." The letters started returning, each one stamped with four or five different locations ranging from Alpha Company to Da Nang to An Hoa to Casualty Company Okinawa and back to me with ADDRESS UNKNOWN RETURN TO SENDER stamped over all the other stamps in dark red letters. I wanted to kick myself for not getting Chan's parents' address. It just had never occurred to me that I would need it.

Then one day the fat-faced nurse handed me a dirty, tattered envelope. It was another one of my letters being returned. I started to toss it into the wastepaper basket next to my bed when I noticed three little letters scribbled in pencil down in one corner: KIA. My stomach reacted like a heavy ball of ice-cold lead had dropped into it. Killed in action. I didn't cry. I don't know why. Maybe because I wasn't going to believe Chan was dead just because some office pogue in An Hoa felt like using his pencil. Maybe because it just didn't look official.

Frustration, confusion, and finally despair took control of my thoughts. After five weeks in Japan I was sent to Okinawa for rehabilitation. By December my leg was getting strong again. I still hadn't received any more information about Chan. A strange, illogical sense of guilt began taking hold of me. I had left him. I had to go back to Nam. I had to finish my tour or I'd never be able to live with myself.

I knew my leg wasn't ready yet, but I didn't care. Each

day I requested orders for the Fifth Marines and each day my request was refused. The doctor in charge of the rehabilitation program told me I was suffering from mild combat fatigue. They started feeding me Valium to calm me down and Darvon to stop the pain in my leg and something else to sleep. Nothing seemed to help. Then one day in early December some of my gear from An Hoa caught up to me. The first thing I found in my sea bag was a small green hospital bag containing the things I had on me when I was brought into Da Nang. I dumped it open and out fell my little Gideon with the shrapnel hole. I could almost hear Chan laughing at my depression. I cried for a long time. I figured I had about three months of tears built up. After that I started reading the Word and talking to the Man again. I even went to chapel on occasion.

Christmas came and went. Then New Year's. I was still on Okinawa. I felt better every day. I was ready to go home. In March they put me in Casual Company. That was a good sign. I knew I'd be going home soon. My third day in Casual Company I got a letter that had been forwarded from Yokosuka. The return address was Saint Albans Naval Hospital in New York. It was from someone named Dr. J. T. Adelman, Lieutenant, USN. At first I thought I had someone else's mail, but it was my name and serial number so I tore it open. The first line lifted me out of my bed and banged my head on the top bunk so hard I started bleeding, but I couldn't feel a thing.

Dear L/Cpl. Clark,

I'm writing in reference to L/Cpl. Richard Chan, who is a patient of mine here at Saint Albans Naval Hospital.

That was as far as I could read. I had to move. I had to jump. I had to run. So I ran up and down the barracks screaming and waking total strangers to tell them that Chan was alive. Then my leg reminded me that it wasn't quite ready for the hundred-yard dash. By the time I settled down enough to read the rest of the letter I realized I had lost it somewhere. I started to panic, then someone tapped me on the shoulder. I turned around to see one of the total strangers I had just shaken awake.

"Is this yours, Mac?" the bleary-eyed Marine asked as he handed me my letter.

"Yeah, it's mine! Thanks!" I grabbed it and started reading again.

I hope you won't be offended, but I have taken the liberty of opening L/Cpl. Chan's mail. He has undergone three operations up to this point in an effort to repair serious fragmentation wounds to his right arm. We believe the arm will eventually be functionable. Even more serious than his physical injuries though, is the state of psychological depression that he has fallen into. He refuses to open his mail or receive visitors, including family or clergy. If you feel that you could be of any assistance in this situation, please contact me at this address or call the number below between the hours of 8 a.m. and 4 p.m.

I was stunned. He was alive! I had to call, but how? I walked back over to the bleary-eyed Marine's bunk. He was already lying on his back with his eyes shut. "Say, do you know how I could call the States?"

He opened one eye and didn't look happy to see me. "Yeah. You know that little restaurant right outside the main gate?"

"The one that says something about American food on the window?"

"Yeah. They have a phone there. It's kind of like a Mars station."

"A what?" I asked.

"They patch you through a bunch of ham radio operators all the way home." He looked at his watch. "It's probably about zero-eight-hundred right now back home."

"Great!" I ran to my bunk to grab my hat. Lying under it was my little Bible with the shrapnel hole. I stared at it for a moment, and I couldn't help feeling that it was one of those little reminders from Jesus that most of the time I foolishly called coincidence. I picked the Bible up, shoved it in my shirt pocket, and headed for the main gate. It was only a couple of blocks away, but that gave me almost too much time to think. I wondered if Chan was crippled. If he wouldn't see his family, would he even talk to me? What had happened to him to make him turn off like this? What could I say to help him? It had always been the other way around.

Who cares! I thought. He's alive! I don't care how depressed he is! I started saying it aloud. "He's alive! I knew it! He's alive! That turd! Why didn't he write me?" I kept talking to myself right through the front gate and up to the door of the restaurant.

It was a strange little restaurant. They offered American steaks on the menu for fifteen bucks, which along with the phone made it the classiest place in Kim Village. The moment I sat down on a small wooden stool and pulled the varnished wood and glass door of the rather large phone booth shut, I was scared. Getting through took about five minutes, but finally I heard some lady answer, "Dr. Adelman's office."

A few moments later Dr. Adelman had expressed his thanks and had Chan brought to the phone.

"Hello," Chan said. His solemn tone told me right away this wasn't going to be easy.

"You little turd! Why didn't you write me? I thought you were dead! Did I wake you up?"

"It's good to hear you." He spoke with no emotion, cold and detached.

"Okay, what gives?" I said.

The silence that came through the phone was deafening. For a moment I thought he was going to hang up. Then he finally said something that sounded like Chan. "How are you? Are you all right?"

"Yeah. I limp a little, but I'm fine. Now talk to me, Chan. What's going on? How bad did you get hit?" There was another long pause.

"Well," his voice cracked. There was another pause, and I heard him clear his throat. Tears started tickling my chin as they dropped off, but I managed to swallow back any sound that would give me away. "Let's just say I won't be tying any surgical knots." He forced out a weak chuckle, and I felt a burning need to hug him and pound him on the back and tell him everything was great just because he was alive, but I knew it would be of no use. He needed more than the "Cheer up, everything's okay" routine. I pulled out my wounded Bible and asked God for help.

"Why won't you see your family?" I asked as I opened the Bible, praying for something to jump out at me. I wanted to kick myself for not going to the chaplain before I called.

"I don't want to see them. My folks got a divorce while I was gone. They didn't tell me. I found out when I called home."

"What about Valerie?"

"She came by. It's over between us. It was just too painful for her mother. It's better this way."

He sounded angry. I kept thumbing through the Bible, almost nervously. I could feel the tension, but I didn't know how to break it. "You'll love coming home, Johnnie," he snapped sarcastically. "These skinny little long-haired wimps, fellow Americans, greet the wounded Marines with protest signs calling us murderers. You'll love coming home." I'd never heard Chan sound this bitter. He sounded like a different person. I tried to think of something positive to say.

"You'll still be a doctor. Get your mind on that. You have a job—"

"Doctor," he cut in. "I was going to be an open-heart surgeon, remember? There aren't too many one-armed open-heart surgeons operating out there."

"Your doctor said you'd be able to use that arm."

"They don't know yet," he scoffed. "I'm going under the knife tomorrow. This will be the fourth time. There's no way I can be a doctor now. I'm glad you're okay, but I have to go now." Chan spoke quickly, as if he were mad at me and in a rush to end the conversation.

Suddenly it happened. Those words I needed jumped out at me. There they were, soiled with Vietnam mud but still legible in fading red ink, the words Chan had written in the front of my Bible.

"Hold it, mister!" I barked. "I've been listening to you all the way from Hue to Laos! You're going to listen to me this time!" I waited for a long moment, expecting a loud klick as he hung up. Nothing. Then a barely audible mumble told me he was still there.

"Yeah."

"A buddy of mine wrote this to me once." I pulled the phone away as a gush of emotion sealed up my throat and pushed out a couple of tears. I cleared my throat and started reading:

Who shall separate us from the love of Christ? Shall tribulation, or distress, or persecution, or famine, or nakedness, or peril, or sword?
    Just as it is written,

"FOR THY SAKE WE ARE BEING PUT TO DEATH ALL DAY LONG;
    WE WERE CONSIDERED AS SHEEP TO BE SLAUGH-TERED."

But in all these things we overwhelmingly conquer through Him who loved us.

For I am convinced that neither death, nor life, nor angels, nor principalities, nor things present, nor things to come, nor powers, nor height, nor depth, nor any other created thing, shall be able to separate us from the love of God, which is in Christ Jesus our Lord.

"Are you listening?" I asked. I heard him clear his throat, then he tried to say something but started crying.

"There's more," I said, trying to keep my voice from cracking.

And we know that God causes all things to work together for good to those who love God; to those who are called according to His purpose.

We didn't say any more for a while. I knew my voice would crack and I'd start crying like a jerk, so I didn't say anything. I could hear him sniff every little bit, and I knew he couldn't talk either. Finally he managed two words before he hung up.

"Guns up!"

EPILOGUE TO THE 2002 EDITION

I'm just a former lance corporal, now a writer, who had the privilege of serving with some extraordinary Marines in the Fifth Marine Regiment. We were young. We all made some mistakes, some bad decisions. We were not, and are not, perfect, but these Marines were consistently courageous and America should be proud of them. I barely touched on some of their stories. *Guns Up!* was written from an eighteen-year-old's point of view.

As a machine gunner, I was formally attached to Weapons Platoon, though I never actually served with Weapons Platoon. As a gunner, I was always with the First, Second, or Third Platoons of Alpha Company. Most of the time I was with the Second Platoon, but when another platoon needed a gunner and they pointed at me, I got shipped to the First or Third platoon. That meant a different lieutenant, different squad leaders, different corpsmen, different radioman, different Marines.

No one had a real name in Nam. We mostly used just nicknames. Over the years, I have discovered some of their real names, and I would like to honor some of those Marines by telling you what happened to them after Nam. I say that and yet I am not sure there will ever be an after-Nam for some of us.

It never, ever leaves you.

Compared to heroes like Cpl. Jesus Quintana and Sgt. Vince Rios and thousands of others who gave their legs

and arms and lives for our country in Vietnam, I hesitate
to mumble even the slightest complaint. But for the sake
of that Nam vet you may be acquainted with, a smell, a
sound, a blur, a helicopter flying overhead, rain, bright
sunlight, or a dark night, almost anything can turn a distant memory into a flashback as real as your next breath.
It is not always a bad memory, but when one of those
moments strikes, it is impossible to explain it to others.

The story of how I hooked up with some of these remarkable Marines so many years later is another book.
Like the first one, the Lord was in obvious control.

After I left Yokosuka Naval Hospital in Japan, I spent
quite a while in Okinawa. Part of my rehabilitation there
was training in martial arts. By February 1969, I was
healthy again. While I was in Okinawa, serving as an
MP, S.Sgt. James Monroe and L/Cpl. Charlie Goodson
came through on their way back to the States. I loosely
based the fictional character Goody in my novel *Semper
Fidelis*, on Goodson. He was the kind of man you
wanted beside you in a firefight. Typical of all Marines,
he would risk his life in some insane act of heroism and
then immediately curse the Marine Corps and everyone
associated with the Marine Corps. He was an absolute riot, and I loved him. Charlie Goodson had been
wounded in the neck, and his tour was over. He began to
fill me in on what had happened to most of the guys after
I left.

I felt ashamed sitting in Okinawa, fat and healthy,
while the guys were going through hell. I tried on more
than one occasion to go back to Vietnam, but they would
not let me return until I spent a year stateside. At that
time in my nineteen-year-old life, a year of stateside duty
sounded like prison. The Corps gave me an early out.
For the rest of my life I have deeply regretted not going
back. I came home with a planeload of wounded guys.

We landed in El Toro, California, and we saw our first
war protesters. They mooned us and threw tomatoes and

waved Baby Killer signs. After a day or so of classes telling us about the Veterans Administration and job opportunities, the Marine Corps gave those Marines that were able a three-day pass.

It took me just two hours to get arrested for decking a disloyal American in the L.A. Greyhound bus terminal. The cops who arrested me were old Marines. They handcuffed me, drove me down the street, and told me it was against the law to deck cowards in front of cops. They tried to warn me that America was not treating returning veterans very well. It was not the way I wanted to come home.

I continued training in martial arts, learning Tae Kwon Do, a Korean martial art. I eventually taught martial arts at the University of South Florida. It was a good way to release some of the anger. I married a beautiful woman named Nancy. I became a mailman but got injured delivering a crate of books and was down for about a year. That's when I started writing *Guns Up!* The book was born in anger; it was my way of fighting back against a steady stream of lies coming out of the media about our guys in Vietnam.

A couple of years ago, I got a package in the mail. It was from the *Cincinnati Enquirer*. The editors were searching for anyone who may have served with a U.S. Marine named PFC Richard Weaver. I'd never heard of Richard Weaver. The newspapers in the package had articles about Weaver. There was a photo of a handsome young Marine in his dress blues. We never looked like that in Nam, so he didn't look familiar. I started reading the articles. They were letters written by Weaver to a man named Hank Beucker.

The story was fascinating. Richard had been unofficially adopted by this old Marine named Beucker. Beucker had been wounded at Guadalcanal and served with Admiral Halsey. Hank Beucker taught Richard Weaver to hunt and fish and fight while the rest of us were still watching cartoons. Richard Weaver was a big, tough redhead who had been a bouncer in the toughest bar in town when he was fifteen. As I continued to read, a lump the size of a golf ball formed in my throat. The letters home to the old Marine from the young Marine read like excerpts from *Guns Up!* They threw me off balance for a few days. It was like opening a grave. Suddenly I was back in the bush and feeling guilty for the times that I failed. There were more memories than I wanted to deal with, and my family knew something was wrong.

I called the phone number with the newspapers. It belonged to another Marine, Bill James. Bill was one of the guys who organized information about the 5th Marine Regiment. Bill James had fought with A 1/5 in Hue City in 1968. He served as a radioman for Sgt. James Monroe. I wrote inaccurately about Sergeant Monroe in this book. I called him Staff Sergeant Morey. He was wounded at Thuong Duc in the last chapter. I served with some three-war Marines. I thought he was one of them. Writing the book ten years after the war led to more than one mistaken exaggeration. Sergeant Monroe was a small Marine with a big walrus mustache. He was humble, brave, and absolutely loved by his men. Another hero from the battle of Hue City, he was a father for eighteen-year-old kids like me. Sergeant Monroe went on to become a sergeant major and now lives in Japan. I told Bill James that the newspaper articles had to be by the same Marine I knew as Big Red. Bill told me that some of the guys in the platoon had already figured it had to be Red, but he wanted me to confirm it. He told me that high school buddies of Richard Weaver wanted to honor him. It seemed that about three decades later they were just discovering that Richard Weaver was a hero.

The battle for Truoi Bridge was Richard Weaver's story, not Johnnie Clark's. Richard "Big Red" Weaver helped hold off an estimated four hundred NVA regulars and sappers at Truoi Bridge. He was not the only hero at Truoi Bridge. There were many. Fifteen Marines died. Later, L/Cpl. Dennis Sliby was awarded the Navy Cross for saving the lives of fellow Marines. After having part of his leg blown off, he continued to pick up enemy grenades and throw them back at the NVA. The enemy left sixty-four dead, but the number of NVA killed was far higher than that. Taking that bridge was a major objective for the communists during the Tet Offensive. A small group of Marines said no. They held out against overwhelming odds. Maybe our newspapers should have been telling those stories.

Mr. Bill Wiederman and Mr. Lon Deckard asked me to come to Cincinnati and speak at the memorial dedication and the unveiling of a beautiful monument to honor Richard "Big Red" Weaver. Bill and Lon were high school buddies of Richard Weaver's; Lon is also a Vietnam veteran. They went above and beyond to see that Red's sacrifice was recognized. The monument was erected in front of Red's old high school, Indian Hills High. That was one hard journey for me. I had no idea how many wounds it would open. They treated me like I was something special because I wrote a book. It was very humbling, especially when I looked around me. Marines with more time in the bush than I had in the Corps watched as I spoke.

Jesus Quintana was there. I called him Sanchez or Paunchy Villa in the book. I wrote about the day he lost his legs. That one day could have been an entire novel. Words do not describe the awe-inspiring bravery of Marines like Cpl. Jesus Quintana, Gunnery Sergeant McDermott, and Navy corpsman Michael "Doc" Turley. Jesus Quintana was my gun team leader, a handsome, muscular Marine with more courage than most people could even bear watching. Chan and I were setting up our gun position in a break in a hedgerow when we were ordered to put our gun in another place. We picked up our gear and moved, passing Corporal Quintana on his way with his gun team to our spot between the hedges. One of the men in his gun team tripped a 155 mm booby-trapped artillery round. We found Quintana facedown on the ground. With help from the gunny, he sat up in a pile of blood and bones and looked at where his legs used to be. He did not go into shock. He looked around for his buddies, actually more concerned for them than himself. Doc Turley begged Quintana to let him help him, but he wouldn't let anyone help until the others were saved. Doc Turley, and likely another corpsman I cannot remember, did everything humanly possible. Doc also worked on a young Marine named L/Cpl. John L. Davis until the boy miraculously regained consciousness long enough to say, "I'm going to die." Then he died. Only after being convinced that the other four Marines were dead would Jesus Quintana allow Doc Turley and Chan to help.

Gunny McDermott was also seriously wounded but gave no thought to his own wounds while Quintana was seemingly dying. In Gunny McDermott's arms, Quintana pulled his little Gideon Bible out of his helmet, opened it, and read. Jesus Quintana looked up into the gunny's face and said, "I'm going to make it." We had to get Quintana out if there was any hope he'd survive. There were so many dead Marines on the chopper that it could not get off the ground, and there was incoming fire. Gunny McDermott refused to be medevaced. He jumped out to lighten the weight, allowing the chopper to lumber off the ground. Gunny stayed in the bush seriously wounded, but Quintana made it. Two days later, the gunny was medevaced, and I never saw him again.

Jesus Quintana kept right on being a hero, and he found an "A-gunner" for his new work. This wonderful, gutsy Christian and his equally brave and lovely wife have taken in more than sixty-five foster children. They also found time to raise two kids of their own. Jesus

Quintana is now a gunsmith in Indianapolis. He built a replica M60 and brought it to the memorial for Big Red. Five of us gunners who came home had a gunners' service at Red's grave: a helmet with GUNS UP! printed on it, some salty jungle boots at the foot of the grave, and the M60 in front of the marker. Richard Chan, Marty Lynch, Jimmy McGinnis, Jesus "Joe" Quintana, and me. I never knew any 0331s in the Fifth Marines who were not killed or wounded.

Jimmy McGinnis was Red's A-gunner. Jimmy was with Red when he died. Jimmy is a quiet, humble man from Tennessee, and those people who know him now probably have no idea what he has been through. Cpl. Marty Lynch taught a boot named Johnnie Clark how to fill sandbags and clean a machine gun. He was all-Marine in Nam and all-Marine now. John Carrow was there from Weapons Platoon, and he still looks like a Marine. Sergeant Hall played taps at our personal machine-gun ceremony for Red. I never mentioned Sergeant Hall by name in the book, but he was there.

M.Gy.Sgt. Stacy Watson was also at the service. He was a corporal in Nam with the Third Platoon. At one point I almost lost my foot to jungle rot and had to be medevaced out by riverboat down the Truoi River. It was Cpl. Stacy Watson and Gunny McDermott who took me out on that boat. I also wrote about a wonderful Marine named Jack Ellenwood. Jack Ellenwood's real name was Cpl. Frank Burris. He graduated from Dixie Hollins High in Saint Petersburg, Florida, the same school my wife and son graduated from. I wrote that he had the photo of his baby boy in his helmet. It was actually a baby girl with bright red hair. Frank Burris was Stacy Watson's best friend. They were squad leaders in Third Platoon.

At Bridge Two on Highway One going south from Phu Bai, Stacy ran into his buddy Frank showing off a photo of "the most beautiful baby anybody ever saw!" He and Stacy had served in H&I together. Stacy said that Frank wanted to get home to that baby and his wife more than anything. He wanted it so bad, he was going to refuse to go into the bush. He had to see his baby. Stacy talked to Frank, and eventually Frank decided to do his duty. Frank made Stacy promise to look his wife and baby up and tell them how much he loved them if he didn't make it back. Stacy still shows the pain when he speaks of that loss on August 9, 1968, when we could not get a medevac for Frank. Stacy Watson told me that the night Frank Burris got hit, he lay there saying that it was his million-dollar wound. He was going back to the World. Frank talked of looking up our old friends for us when he got home. Mostly, Frank was talking about his baby girl and clutching her photo. I hope that if she ever reads this she will know that her father's last thoughts on earth were of her. I was there. I want Mrs. Frank Burris to know that Frank wanted terribly to be with her. I want to tell Frank's daughter: "Your father was a brave Marine, and he clutched your baby photo to him as he died. He loved you and wanted to come home to you more than anything else in the world."

When the memorial service for Big Red was over, I came back to Florida. In so many ways, I was coming home from Nam again. Though I had trouble sleeping, it still felt like a chapter had finally been closed. I was wrong. The mail brought another surprise newspaper article. A Milton, Florida, man received his Purple Heart twenty-eight years after being wounded. That man was PFC Pat McCrary. Jesus Quintana sent me the article.

I called Quintana, and he told me that I had to know this guy because his story sounded like that of the night that Unerstute was killed in Dodge City. Quintana had been wounded and was not in the big graveyard battle I described in the chapter "Dodge City," but he had read about it in this book. After reading the article, I agreed with Quintana. The details were uncanny: Dodge City,

Arizona Territory, Second Platoon of Alpha 1/5, August 1968. I searched out a Pat McCrary in Milton, Florida, and gave him a call.

Our conversation was astounding. Not only was this guy in the same battle, but he was the Marine named Barnes: Pat McCrary was the one who was screaming for us to come help him with a wounded buddy that night in the Arizona Territory. Pat remembered me. He said that we actually joined the Corps together. I was doubtful because it seemed impossible to me that someone could remember a guy he stood in line with to join the Marine Corps almost thirty years ago. Then Pat told a detailed story that only someone who was there could possibly know. I was being given a 4-F discharge by Navy doctors in Jacksonville. I had a hernia, or so they said. They were not going to let me join the Marine Corps. I don't think I ever told anyone that story. I did not know anyone else on earth who would remember such a thing even if they witnessed it. Pat did.

"We thought you were the dumbest ——— on earth!" Pat said with his big country-boy laugh. "You started begging them doctors and doing back flips and push-ups until they finally brought you in some room. Then you came out and joined the Corps! We thought, This guy is nuts!"

I was absolutely blown away. I could not believe that anyone could possibly remember something like that. But it was true. Pat described me perfectly in all respects. It was like finding a lost brother. There was only a voice at the end of a phone, but it felt as warm as a big hug. Though Pat had joined the Corps with me in Jacksonville, we did not really know each other. When we reached Nam, Pat was put on Phu Bai security detail, so that afternoon and night in that graveyard was his first experience in combat. I thought he was a boot. In the chapter titled "Dodge City," I thought Pat was the Marine who got shot eleven times and was dragged away. In that story, I called the Marine yelling for help, Striker.

The man yelling for help was PFC Pat McCrary. The man who was hit at least nine times by three enemy .30-caliber machine guns (I wrote eleven times but have since been corrected by Richard "Medically Accurate" Chan) and dragged up in front of an enemy machine gun was actually a Marine named Sonny. We think Sonny was from New Jersey.

Though he was shot to pieces and nearly drowning in rising water, Sonny refused to call out when he heard us looking for him because he knew we would be killed. Pat McCrary lay out in that cemetery, yelling and kicking grenades away from himself and Sonny until he ran out of ammo. When he finally went looking for help in the pitch-black monsoon rain, we thought he was the NVA coming toward our lines. In the flash of an enemy mortar going off, I saw the silhouette of an American helmet an instant before we shot at him. I screamed, "Don't shoot!" and ended up nearly drowning him and myself when I pulled him in on top of me. Pat was not only brave, but he was also wounded that night.

In 1997, Pat McCrary, then a mailman in Milton, wanted a Purple Heart license tag. The State of Florida would not give him one because there was no record of his ever having been wounded in combat. Pat got mad. He raised a fuss and eventually discovered that our records had been destroyed during a 122 mm-rocket attack at the An Hoa combat base. There was a direct hit on the records shack that killed some Marines and blew up our records.

A couple of years ago, I was pursuing my usual impersonation of sleep when the phone rang. It was late. The voice at the other end of the phone sounded remotely familiar.

"It's Fred Huteson."

"Fred Huteson. Sorry, it doesn't ring a bell."

"Corporal Huteson, Johnnie. Alpha-one-five. Vietnam."

I was stunned for a few moments. Cpl. Fred Huteson

was the real name of one of the squad leaders I wrote about in *Guns Up!* He was one of those real heros our country ignored. We were wounded together, spent our last night in Nam together, and spent time in Yokosuka Naval Hospital in Japan together. I hadn't seen him since then.

"Johnnie. I've been trying to find you for twenty-eight years. For all these years I wanted to thank you for what you did that night in the graveyard in Dodge City, outside of An Hoa."

All I could do was cry. I had made a decision or two when I was eighteen that I'd give my life to correct. I was praying about some of those painful memories when Fred called. It was the most wonderful phone call I ever received in my life, and it was no coincidence that it came when it did. I admired Corporal Huteson a great deal. He was a salt. He had been wounded in the Battle of Hue City, and though only twenty, his cool courage under fire made him seem much older. He was a leader. Pat McCrary, Pvt. Buford Unerstute, and Sonny were part of his squad.

That night in that Vietnamese cemetery was the first time he had lost one of his men. He took care of his men even if it meant risking his own life, which he did more than once. After I almost drowned PFC Pat "Mac" McCrary, McCrary told Gunny McDermott that Sonny was still out there and badly wounded. Corporal Huteson volunteered to crawl back into that killing zone to search for two of his missing Marines. We could not find them: PFC Unerstute and the Marine named Sonny. Sonny had been dragged away by the NVA, and Unerstute was dead.

Buford Unerstute was very much as I described him. The guys called him Cowboy because he was from Oklahoma, not Idaho as I had thought. I won't give his real name because I do not want to hurt his family. If they already know that the Marine I wrote about was their son, I want them to know this. In my heart, I feel that

Cowboy was the bravest Marine I ever had the honor of serving with. I never met a Marine who was that terrified. He never should have made it through boot camp. Cpl. Bob Carroll, who was Sudsy in the book, recently told me a story about Pvt. Buford Unerstute. Bob said they were on a patrol one day in An Hoa Valley when they spotted three NVA troops standing on a hill a long way off. Bob said they were so far away that it would have been a long shot even for the M60. Lieutenant Pruit was thinking about calling in some 105s, artillery, just for the practice. Even at that distance, with an entire platoon of Marines around him, Unerstute began trembling in absolute terror. I relay this story for this reason. Try to imagine being in a jungle war like Nam. Then try to imagine being so torn apart inside with fear that you cannot control your body. Then try to imagine your lieutenant telling you the nightmare is over. You can go home. Then try to imagine what kind of courage it takes to say, "No." Cowboy may have died of fright, but he did not die for lack of bravery. I feel honored to have known him.

Corporal Huteson's phone call was from the Lord. It brought up a lot of tears but healed many wounds. Just having such a fine man think well of me for one of those times when I did something right seemed to ease much of the guilt I felt for those times when I dropped the ball.

In the chapter "Dodge City," I wrote that my A-gunner told me that Gunny was putting me up for the Silver Star. Corporal Huteson told me that he and a couple of the other guys were put up for medals that night and no one got them. Cpl. Fred Huteson's phone call made me feel better than any medal ever would, but Fred was curious about the records, too. I guess I had always wondered about that night. Wondered if my A-gunner was just exaggerating or if I had dreamed the whole thing up. But for twenty-eight years, I never pursued it. I knew that for each time I did well, I matched it with a moment of eighteen-year-old stupidity. In my foolish rationalization, I always thought a medal might balance those moments of disgrace or failure. I know the VA is full of men living with similar pain for a million different reasons. Sometimes you just can't forgive yourself. Thank God, He can and does.

Cpl. Bill James sent me a small roster of some of the guys from the old platoon. Up to that point, I never knew the gunny's name. I only knew him as the gunny with the shotgun. Not exactly a mailing address. Gy.Sgt. Mac McDermott, Yuma, Arizona. He was the most gung-ho Marine I ever knew. He was the kind of man those "hero" actors like to imitate, as long as they can put them in a WWII movie. He was happy to hear from me, and I was surprised that he even remembered me.

"Gunny, you remember that night in the graveyard? Dodge City? An Hoa?"

"Yep. And it wasn't that ——— Swift Eagle that led the men back into that graveyard, Clark."

"Oh?"

"That was me, Johnnie!"

"Sorry, Gunny. I couldn't remember every detail."

He laughed. "It's okay."

"What happened to you after we put you on that chopper, Gunny?"

His life sounded like a John Wayne movie. After the gunny was wounded with Corporal Quintana, he was medevaced out. I thought his time in Nam was over. I was eighteen and the gunny was in his thirties. I thought he was in his forties; he seemed like an old man to me— one very tough, very brave, very gung-ho, old Marine. He thought we were wasting Marine Corps money if we were not making contact with the enemy. He was the consummate Marine. He not only went back to Vietnam, in spite of objections, he got hit three more times while serving as an adviser. None of it impresses him. He is still the gunny.

Gunny remembers vividly the day Jesus Quintana was wounded. He speaks with reverence for God about that moment when Quintana took out his Bible as he lay in his own blood, with no legs below the waist. Gunny McDermott remembers clearly when Quintana looked up at him with a spiritual light in his eyes that went beyond reason and said, "I'm going to make it." That was one of the last times I remembered seeing the gunny.

Gunny McDermott made a lifelong impression upon me. I wrote a couple of other books loosely based on him and another warrior I admire greatly, a Korean War–era gunnery sergeant named Francis Killeen. Gunny McDermott is one of those special warriors the Marine Corps seems to breed when America is in trouble. The gunny went back to the States in September 1968. He immediately drove those around him insane until he was sent back to Vietnam. He got back in May 1969 and stayed until August 1970. He was assigned to the Army as an adviser with the Army of the Republic of Vietnam, 4th Battalion, 6th Regiment, 2d ARVN Division in Quang Nai Province. He said the Army called him "Mac the Magnet" because he managed to draw so much fire. I laughed. Those of us in Alpha Company understand. During his second tour, he managed to find the enemy with his usual regularity. He was wounded a total of six times but refused three of those Purple Hearts to keep from being sent home. Three Purple Hearts or two serious wounds, 48s, and you had to go back to the States.

Gunny McDermott was promoted to the rank of sergeant major in March 1977 and was transferred to Marine Corps Recruit Depot, San Diego. He was the Training NCO while stationed at Parris Island, South Carolina. Somehow, I always pictured the guy wearing a Smokey the Bear hat on Parris Island. Sgt. Maj. McDermott's personal decorations include the Silver Star, three Bronze Stars with Combat V, three Purple Hearts, the Meritorious Service Medal, two Army Commendation

Medals with Combat V, the Combat Action Ribbon, and two Vietnamese Crosses of Gallantry.

We spoke for a long time, then I decided to ask him a twenty-eight-year-old question. To tell you the truth, I did not know what to expect. It made me nervous to even broach the subject of a medal with a real hero. But after nearly three decades, I wanted to know if it was just my childish imagination or if he did tell my A-gunner he was putting me up for a Silver Star. I also now had a responsibility to the other guys who were put up for medals that night and never got them. One thing I could depend on with the gunny was that he would be blunt.

"Gunny, did you know our records got blown up by a 122?"

"Oh, sure. Killed a master sergeant, I think."

"Pat McCrary just got a Purple Heart after all these years because his records were blown up in that attack. Corporal Huteson and some of the guys were supposed to get medals for that night."

"I heard about that."

"Look, Gunny, I've wanted to ask you this question since I was eighteen. My A-gunner came to me that night and told me that the gunny was putting me up for the Silver Star."

"Yeah."

"Did you?"

"No."

Like I said, blunt. My heart sank a little. At least, and at last, I knew the truth. I felt embarrassed and a little bummed about it. "But why would my A-gunner tell me that?"

"It wasn't me. It was Gunny Poertner."

"Who is Gunny Poertner?"

"He was the company gunny. Remember Poertner at An Hoa, big red mustache?"

I did remember the guy. He had a really impressive

moustache, looked like a Viking. "I do remember that guy, Gunny! But he wasn't in the bush with us, was he?"

"Sure! On company-size operations. Remember when Lieutenant Molonolf of Third Platoon got killed in An Hoa?"

"Yeah." I remembered that Lieutenant Molonolf was an Australian. I called him Lieutenant Hawthorn in the chapter titled "Pay Back."

"That's when I took over the third herd. Gunny Poertner became company gunny with Captain Nelson."

I was flabbergasted. I never knew there were two gunnery sergeants in Alpha Company. Of course, at eighteen, there was a lot I never knew. Retired M.Sgt. Billy Poertner remembered every detail. He said that he did write me up. He would do it again. Our company commander, Capt. Scott Nelson, remembered some of that night and a few of the guys also remembered. Doc Turley remembered. He was everyone's favorite corpsman. Shortly after Gunny Poertner wrote me up for the Silver Star for the second time, he died. At least four other Marines, whose records were also destroyed, should have received medals for their selfless acts of bravery that night. Cpl. Fred Huteson, PFC Pat McCrary, PFC Richard Chan, and Chan's A-gunner, name unknown. And there may well be others and probably are. L/Cpl. Bruce Trebil may have been another Marine who risked his life to save others in the graveyard. Gunny McDermott, too. The Marines of Alpha 1/5 risked their lives for one another every day.

Some of these Marines had more time in combat than I had in the chow line. They showed up brave the way civilians show up for work. The Corps doesn't hand out medals easily, must be part of the budget problem, because it sure wasn't a lack of guts by 1/5 Marines. I pray and hope that the others will be honored. If it doesn't happen, it won't be due to a lack of effort by our officers. Our officers are still dedicated to their men. Total professionals. Lt. Col. Joe Griffis and Capt. Scott Nelson have always gone above and beyond for their men. They still do.

Capt. Scott Nelson left the Corps a highly decorated hero. He went on to become a big shot with the FBI. To all who watched him in Nam, that is no surprise. Leaders always rise to the top. He retired after becoming the head of the FBI in one part of the country and is now the head of security for Warner Brothers Studios.

I watch men like Scott in amazement and wonder how America finds these guys, for America found a lot of them in Vietnam. The media never seemed to notice them, but they were there, by the thousands, winning every major engagement in a decade of war, no matter the odds. It's like a football team winning every game when only it's defensive line is allowed to play. The U.S. Army did a great job over there, too. The Navy and Air Force didn't let anybody down either. The NVA lost three full divisions during the 1968 Tet Offensive. The Viet Cong were basically eliminated. The enemy could not mount another offensive for three years after their beating at Tet. We heard some scuttlebutt that retired general Douglas MacArthur said, "Give me the First Marine Division, and I'll be in Hanoi in a few weeks and end this war!" I think he was right. When President Nixon decided to force Hanoi to the peace table, it took only twelve days of B-52 strikes to bring them to their knees. Our combat forces left Nam in 1973. North Vietnamese troops marched into Saigon almost three years later. If anyone lost militarily, it sure was not my Marine Corps.

Michael "Doc" Turley was one of our Navy corpsmen. I'm not even sure how many corpsmen we had. Remember, as a machine gunner I was in Weapons Platoon. But if the Third Platoon lost a gunner, I might get attached to them for a while. It was the same for corpsmen. One of our corpsmen was sort of arrogant, and I wrote about him quite often. That corpsman was not Doc

Turley. By the way, that snob corpsman saved a lot of lives, too. Doc Turley was in the Navy from 1966 to 1970. He went to Nursing School at Wagner College. He was varsity quarterback on the football team from 1970 to 1972. Doc went to U.S. Public Health Hospital in Staten Island, N.Y., and graduated in 1973. He joined the Coast Guard the same year and served in the Reserves until 1999. In the Coast Guard, he became an ER physician assistant, level 1 and level 2 trauma cases. Doc worked in Jacksonville, where this hero continued to save lives. Doc is in a battle with Agent Orange right now, but he isn't whining, and he's proud to have served with the Corps in Vietnam.

When the story of the missing records first came out, it brought some sorrow and some joy. One of the joyful moments happened a couple of years ago as the mystery began to unfold. One day my doorbell rang. When you have teenagers, you never figure it is someone to see you, but I answered anyway. When I opened that door, all I could do was stare. A man who resembled a boy I once knew stood before me holding a gray shirt. The shirt had the picture of an M60 machine gun on it with words above and below: WHY WALTZ WHEN YOU CAN ROCK AND ROLL. I stood reading that shirt and remembering a hundred times when this man ran forward under fire to help wounded Marines. It was a wonderful reunion. Doc was one of the most respected and beloved men in Alpha Company. Hugging him was like holding on to all that was good and right about my time in Nam.

Doc Turley had just come back from touring Vietnam with one of our old radio men, J. B. MacCreight. He had gone back to Hill 55 and Truoi Bridge and Hue City and a few other places that still haunted him. He had lost his best friend on Truoi Bridge: Cpl. Walter Roslie. Doc was from Staten Island and Roslie was from Valley Stream, Long Island. Corporal Roslie was another remarkable hero from Hue. He had been awarded the Silver Star and

two Purple Hearts in the Battle of Hue City. He was offered a field promotion to second lieutenant but turned it
down. Truoi Bridge was his third and final Heart. Another hero, L/Cpl. Jim Tedesco, died trying to rescue
Roslie on that bridge. Doc and J. B. wanted to say a
prayer and throw some flowers off the bridge. A young
communist lieutenant would not allow them on the
bridge. There were machine-gun bunkers at each end as
if the war were still going on. The young lieutenant told
them he could be shot for allowing Americans on the
bridge. While visiting Hill 55, they decided to film a
monument that had been built to all the enemy soldiers
that the Marines had killed there. Mike looked up from
filming to discover that he, J. B., and their driver, a
former ARVN who had worked with the U.S. Marines,
were surrounded by little pith helmets carrying AK47s.
They told the Americans, "We can kill you, and your
government can do nothing about it." They took the
Vietnamese driver and grilled him for hours before letting them go. I'll not be visiting Nam with my tourist
dollars unless they let me bring along a few friends—the
First Marine Division and an M60.

In July 1998, my old executive officer, Fifth Marine
Regiment, Lt. Col. Joe Griffis, called me on the phone.
Aided by the tireless help of another retired Marine
named Bill Harley, the red tape involved in presenting a
medal thirty years late was worked out. It would happen
at the First Marine Division Reunion in Cincinnati,
Ohio, on August 8, 1998.

I drove up with my son, Shawn, and daughter, Bonnie
Kay. My wife met us there along with Richard Chan.
Chan is now the leading cardiovascular perfusion expert
in the world. We are still buddies and still argue. Chan
had a rough time when he came home. He had thirteen
surgical operations and battled like the rest of the guys
to fit in again. He finally met and married a great
lady named Doreen. She's a middle-school teacher. He

travels the world, teaching and lecturing on the subject of cardiovascular perfusion. He says that invariably at the end of a seminar, some person will approach him with a reluctant expression. He knows what's coming. "I know this will sound silly," the person will say, "but I read this war book called *Guns Up!* and it had a character named Richard Chan. Is it possible that you are the same Richard Chan?"

Chan was medevaced out only after two choppers were disabled. He still remembers the body bags on the medevac chopper. At 1st Med. Battalion doctors performed the first of thirteen operations on him. It took over a month for them to get Chan home. He had to be stabilized at each stop: Okinawa, Yokohama, Anchorage, California, Washington, D.C., and finally St. Albans Naval Hospital in Queens, N.Y. His weight went down to 130 pounds when he arrived at St. Albans. At 1st Med, they considered removing one of his arms because he'd spiked a fever. He begged one doctor, a family friend and commander of 1st Med, not to cut off the arm unless they were able to confirm a positive culture. The doctor said there was a terrible risk of gangrene spreading. He told the doctor that he was fully aware of the medical risks. Why does this sound so typical of Richard Chan?

Chan went into a coma for three weeks. He woke temporarily and has never forgotten the touching sight of a huge wounded Marine who had climbed out of the next bed. He was on his knees praying for Chan. "I was too dehydrated to shed many tears, but all that was left came out at that defining moment. It was then I was sure that God had spared me for better days. I wasn't sure if I would have normal neurological functions or even two arms, but I knew I would live and will live for His purpose."

Chan went through a postgraduate course that was two years long at Long Island Jewish Medical Center–Stony Brook University, one of the few universities in the country at that time to offer this advanced degree. Today, there are twenty-three, but only five that offer an advanced degree. One of them is NSUH-LIUCWP. Chan is the director of this school. He has helped to develop many devices used in cardioperfusion. He has also developed physiologic calculators with his name on them. (I would explain that, but I don't have a clue what it is.)

Chan and Doreen love my kids and spoil them rotten with their generosity. My son, Shawn McClellan Clark, is nineteen, a student at Saint Petersburg Junior College and heading for Florida State University, God willing. After that his father sees him as a second lieutenant in the First Marine Division, God willing. My daughter, Bonnie Kay Clark, is a sophomore at Keswick Christian School in Saint Petersburg, sixteen, beautiful, spiritual, and already more mature than her father, which is a little scary. They adore Chan and Doreen.

The day of the First Marine Division Reunion, there was a parade in downtown Cincinnati. The parade was to honor a Marine machine gunner killed in action thirty years earlier in Phu Loc, Thua Thien Province, Vietnam. He had been posthumously awarded the Bronze Star, thirty years late for helping a platoon of Marines hold off four hundred NVA at a place called Truoi Bridge. Of course, Red deserved more, as do many of the men who fought in Vietnam, but it still gave me goose bumps to watch his hometown finally say thanks.

Later that day, a smile walked through a group of Marines at the reunion. That smile made my heart stop. It was the same smile and same face I watched throughout my war: Sudsy. The real name of the radioman I wrote about is Cpl. Bob Carroll. Even as I write these words I feel ridiculous. I gave my limited view of a few incidents. I did not even touch on the depth of the men of Alpha 1/5. Bob "Sudsy" Carroll did not show up in Nam as a radioman. He was handed a radio during the Battle of Hue City, at the wall of the Citadel. He was one of the

3 percent of the First Battalion, Fifth Marine Regiment, 1/5, Marines who made it through Hue City. Bob, like so many of the Marines of the First Battalion, Fifth Marines, was wounded in Hue but never received a Purple Heart. The wounded were patched up and thrown back into the battle. The History Channel is currently doing a story about Hue City. When they asked the men for a good Marine to interview, a 1/5 Marine who saw it all, the answer was Bob Carroll. Bob "Sudsy" Carroll was involved in what could only be described as a suicide assault near the Citadel. That assault is considered to have been the turning point in the battle.

Sudsy was the Second Platoon radioman for most of my time in Nam. He eventually became a squad leader. At one point I thought Bob Carroll had been killed. He was seriously ill with malaria. When we were crossing the Thu Bon River on amtracks, he passed out from the fever and fell off. He was medevaced out for quite a while. He thinks that may be why I thought he got killed. I am thankful to be wrong. Everyone who served with Bob Carroll loved him. Bob's best friend was one of the Marines killed when Jesus Quintana lost his legs. His name was Ronald L. Powers. I believe this is the Marine that I called Private Simmons. He had a safe job in the rear but volunteered to change his MOS to join the grunts in the bush. Bob tried to talk him out of it, but he was a Marine. He lasted a month.

Cpl. Bob Carroll came home with combat fatigue as most of the guys did. It made his life and relationships tough. He escaped by becoming a park ranger and basically living in the woods for many years. He was a ranger at the Grand Canyon when he showed up in Cincinnati at the reunion. Bob worked with a friend who was constantly asking him why he chose to live the way he did. He got tired of ignoring this woman, so he finally gave her a copy of Guns Up! She read it over and over. When Bob mentioned that Johnnie and Chan would be

at the reunion, this woman talked him into coming. Here
is another one of those incidents where the guy who
wrote a book seems special, but the truth is that Johnnie
Clark was and is "boot" to Marines like Bob Carroll,
Corporal Huteson, Bruce Trebil, Big Red, Jesus Quintana,
Gunny McDermott, Lieutenant Pruit, Lance Corporal
Hensley, Cpl. Marty Lynch, John Carrow, James Mac-
Creight, Frenchie, Charlie Goodson, Lieutenant Mont-
gomery, Sgt. Stacy Watson, Sergeant Monroe, Sgt. Vince
Rios, Leonard Ramirez, First Lieutenant Lowder, Capt.
Scott Nelson, Lieutenant Colonel Griffis, and a thousand
others.

Sgt. Vince Rios, two Bronze Stars, three Purple Hearts,
is a Marine whose story is not in *Guns Up!* He was at the
reunion. PFC Pat McCrary and Cpl. Steve Britt idolize
the man. In the chapter "Happy Birthday, Baby-San,"
Steve was with me at Thuong Duc when the tanks were
blown up as we charged a hill beside the Vu Gia River—
the day Swift Eagle was wounded for the last time. They
told me that when Sergeant Rios was on his second tour,
he was the guardian that saved their lives a dozen times.
When he lost his legs and right arm, and his left hand was
mangled, they thought he was finished. He went home
and got two master's degrees and raised a new first lieutenant for the Marine Corps, his son. Where does America
find these Marines? There were a lot of them in Vietnam.

First Lieutenant Montgomery is another. Steve Britt's
squad was pinned down and in a hopeless position. Lieutenant Montgomery heard the mess on the radio. He ran
to the action and charged an enemy machine-gun position to save his men. He was wounded by .30-caliber
machine-gun fire. Another Marine hero with him was
killed. Montgomery was awarded the Navy Cross. He
became an FBI agent, and years later, he was on national
television for again being a hero for his country. Just another Nam vet.

Bill James and others have tried to find Cpl. Swift

Eagle. He seems to have dropped off the earth. The guys think he went back to some Indian reservation and is still there. One of my buddies, a Nam vet, recently visited an Indian reservation. He told me that quite a few of the men there were former Marines. He said that it was a revered custom for the veterans on the reservation to wear their medals on their shirts to show they had served. These warriors are respected by their people. I hope Swift Eagle is honored by his tribe.

I wrote about a character named "Sam the Blooper Man." Sam was actually based on two different men. The combat was as accurate as I could remember it, but part of his personality was based on a soldier who served in 1969. My blooper man risked his life for mine. If I ever had the choice, I wanted that Marine beside me in a fight.

There is more I'd like to say about the Marines of 1/5. There is more I'd like to tell you about this book. Like how a sixteen-year-old kid from Ireland came to America to join the Corps because he read a little book titled *Guns Up!* Stories of sergeant majors making every young Marine in their outfit read the book. Squad leaders in the Gulf War tearing the book into sections for every man in their squad to study. Nurses who hand it out in VA hospitals. Kids who have read it sixteen times. High schools and colleges making it required reading. Middle school and elementary teachers reading the book aloud to their students at the end of class each day.

This book has flaws, but God has used this book in ways I never dreamed. After four years of having *Guns Up!* rejected, I got nailed by a memory verse in a Bible study group: 1 Samuel 2:30, "but now the Lord declares . . . for those who honor me I will honor." I made a simple decision to remove all the curse words from the book, against the advice of professional writers. Within a month, nine publishers wanted *Guns Up!* I asked the editor who bought the book for Ballantine why she wanted it now, since she had rejected the exact same book six months earlier. Was it because I took the curse words out? She said not one reader or editor at Ballantine had noticed. She read and rejected the book six months earlier and could not explain it. I can.

My prayer is that this flawed effort will honor Jesus Christ first, His Marine Corps second, and everyone who served in Vietnam. To all of the valiant leathernecks I was privileged to serve with, be healed by forgiving.

Greater love has no one than this, that he lay down his life for his friends.

—John 15:13

Semper fi,
L/Cpl. Johnnie M. Clark

GLOSSARY

A 1/5   Alpha Company, First Battalion, Fifth Marine Regiment.

AK47   A Russian assault rifle.

ARVN   Abbreviation for Army of the Republic of Vietnam.

AWOL   Absent without leave.

B-40 rocket   A communist antitank rocket.

betel nut   A nut, widely chewed by the Vietnamese, that stains the teeth and gums a pomegranate red.

body bags   Plastic zipper-bags for corpses.

boot   Slang for a new recruit undergoing basic training.

bush   The outer field areas and jungle where infantry units operate.

Charlie   Slang for "the enemy."

ChiCom   Chinese communists. Slang for enemy grenade.

choppers   Helicopters.

claymores   Mines packed with plastique and rigged to spray hundreds of steel pellets.

Cobras   Helicopter gunships heavily armed with rocket launchers and machine guns.

concertina wire   Barbed wire that is rolled out along the ground to hinder the progress of enemy troops.

C-rats   C-rations or prepackaged military meals eaten in the field.

C-S   A caustic riot gas used in Vietnam.

C-4   Plastique explosive.

C-130   A cargo plane used to transport men and supplies.

C-141 Starlifter   A large jet transport.

deuce-and-a-half   A heavy transport truck used for carrying men and supplies.

dink   Slang for an Asian person, especially in reference to the enemy.

EM club   Enlisted men's club.

E.R.   Emergency room.

flak jacket   A vest worn to protect the chest area from shrapnel or bullets.

I Corps Tactical Zone   The northern five provinces of South Vietnam, called "Marineland" by some. I Corps stretched 225 miles from the Demilitarized Zone to the boundary with Binh Dinh province and II Corps Tactical Zone.

frags   Slang for fragmentation grenades.

Freedom Bird   Slang for the flight that took a soldier home after his tour.

friendlies   Friendly Vietnamese.

gook   Slang for an Asian person, especially in reference to the enemy.

grunt   Slang for any combat soldier fighting in Vietnam.

Hueys   Helicopters used extensively in Vietnam.

Ho Chi Minh Trail   The main supply route running south from North Vietnam through Laos and Cambodia.

hootch   Slang for any form of a dwelling place.

humping   Slang for marching with a heavy load through the bush.

K-bar   A Marine Corps survival knife.

KIA   Killed in action.

klick   One kilometer.

LAAW   Light antiarmor weapon.

LZ   Landing zone.

MACV   Military Assistance Command Vietnam.

medevac   A term for medically evacuating the wounded by chopper or plane.

M14   An automatic weapon used in Vietnam by American ground forces.

M16   Standard automatic weapon used by American ground forces.

M60   A machine gun used by American units.

M79   A 40 mm grenade launcher.

nouc mam   A strong-smelling Vietnamese fish sauce.

NVA   North Vietnamese Army.

pogue   A derogatory term for rear-area personnel.

punji sticks   Sharpened stakes used to impale men.

RPG   Rocket-propelled grenade.

R&R   Rest and relaxation.

sappers   Viet Cong infiltrators whose job it was to detonate explosive charges within American positions.

satchel charges   Explosive packs carried by VC sappers.

SDS   Students for a Democratic Society.

search and destroy   American ground sweeps to locate and destroy the enemy and his supplies.

short-timer   Someone whose tour in Vietnam is almost completed.

smoke grenade   A grenade that releases colored smoke used for signaling.

Tet   The Chinese New Year.

III Corps   The military region around Saigon.

Tiger beer/33 beer   Vietnamese beers.

tracer   A bullet with a phosphorous coating designed to burn and provide a visual indication of a bullet's trajectory.

VC   Viet Cong.

Viet Cong   The local communist militias fighting in South Vietnam.

web gear   Canvas suspenders and belt used to carry the infantryman's gear.

WIA   Wounded in action.

willie-peter   White phosphorous round.

INDEX

Look for Gary Linderer's two books on LRRPs, LRPs and Rangers in gut-chilling, extreme combat far behind enemy lines. When every mission may well have been their last, these brave men went willingly into harm's way with only their skills, sense of duty, personal weapons, and each other between themselves and death.

Phantom Warriors Book I and Book II: LRRPs, LRPs, and Rangers in Vietnam

by Gary A. Linderer

Published by Ballantine Books.
Available at a bookstore near you.

Experience the pain, the pride, and the triumph of the United States Marine Corps.

_____

Not Going Home Alone: A Marine's Story

_____

by James J. Kirschke

All the members of 1st Lt. James J. Kirschke's mortar platoon and then rifle platoon knew what was expected of them: the Marines are America's military elite, required to train harder, fight longer, sacrifice more. Kirschke led by example in the hotly contested zone just south of the DMZ and in the dangerous An Hoa region southwest of DaNang. Sparing no one, he has written a powerful chronicle of the deadly war his Marines fought with valor.

Published by Ballantine Books.
Available at a bookstore near you.

Forged in blood and courage, sacrifice and survival, in a jungle war none of the soldiers who experienced it will ever forget, this is a true story you won't want to miss.

Rites of Passage: Odyssey of a Grunt

---

by Robert Peterson

Robert Peterson arrived in Vietnam in the fall of 1966, a young American ready to serve his country and seize his destiny. What happened in that jungle war would change his life forever. Peterson vividly relives the tense patrols in the Viet Cong-infested Central Highlands, the fierce ambushes and enemy charges. From this deadly hell he reveals the special brotherhood formed between these brave young men.

Published by Ballantine Books.
Available at a bookstore near you.

Delivering death from a distance—one Marine's account of precision marksmanship in Vietnam.

Dead Center: A Marine Sniper's Two-Year Odyssey in the Vietnam War

by Ed Kugler

As a new sniper with the 4th Marines, Kugler picked up bush skills while attached to 3d Force Recon Company, and then joined the grunts. To take advantage of that experience, he formed the Rogues, a five-sniper team that hunted in the Co Bi-Than Tan Valley for VC and NVA. The result is the amazing true story of long, tense waits and sudden deadly action: the dangerous life of a Marine scout-sniper at war.

Published by Ballantine Books.
Available at a bookstore near you.